Teach Yourself VISUALLY™

Microsoft®
Office 2007

Visual®

by Sherry Willard Kinkoph

BICENTENNIAL
1807
WILEY
2007
BICENTENNIAL

Wiley Publishing, Inc.

Teach Yourself VISUALLY™ Microsoft® Office 2007

Published by
Wiley Publishing, Inc.
111 River Street
Hoboken, NJ 07030-5774

Published simultaneously in Canada

Library of Congress Control Number: 2006936753

ISBN: 978-0-470-04590-9

Manufactured in the United States of America

10 9 8 7 6 5 4 3 2

Trademark Acknowledgments

Contact Us

For general information on our other products and services please contact our Customer Care Department within the U.S. at 800-762-2974, outside the U.S. at 317-572-3993, or fax 317-572-4002.

For technical support please visit www.wiley.com/techsupport.

In order to get this information to you in a timely manner, this book was based on a pre-release version of Microsoft Office 2007. There may be some minor changes between the screenshots in this book and what you see on your desktop. As always, Microsoft has the final word on how programs look and function; if you have any questions or see any discrepancies, consult the online help for further information about the software.

WILEY

Wiley Publishing, Inc.

Sales

Contact Wiley
at (800) 762-2974 or
fax (317) 572-4002.

Praise for Visual Books

"Like a lot of other people, I understand things best when I see them visually. Your books really make learning easy and life more fun."

John T. Frey (Cadillac, MI)

"I have quite a few of your Visual books and have been very pleased with all of them. I love the way the lessons are presented!"

Mary Jane Newman (Yorba Linda, CA)

"I just purchased my third Visual book (my first two are dog-eared now!), and, once again, your product has surpassed my expectations."

Tracey Moore (Memphis, TN)

"I am an avid fan of your Visual books. If I need to learn anything, I just buy one of your books and learn the topic in no time. Wonders! I have even trained my friends to give me Visual books as gifts."

Illona Bergstrom (Aventura, FL)

"Thank you for making it so clear. I appreciate it. I will buy many more Visual books."

J.P. Sangdong (North York, Ontario, Canada)

"I have several books from the Visual series and have always found them to be valuable resources."

Stephen P. Miller (Ballston Spa, NY)

"Thank you for the wonderful books you produce. It wasn't until I was an adult that I discovered how I learn – visually. Nothing compares to Visual books. I love the simple layout. I can just grab a book and use it at my computer, lesson by lesson. And I understand the material! You really know the way I think and learn. Thanks so much!"

Stacey Han (Avondale, AZ)

"I absolutely admire your company's work. Your books are terrific. The format is perfect, especially for visual learners like me. Keep them coming!"

Frederick A. Taylor, Jr. (New Port Richey, FL)

"I have several of your Visual books and they are the best I have ever used."

Stanley Clark (Crawfordville, FL)

"I bought my first Teach Yourself VISUALLY book last month. Wow. Now I want to learn everything in this easy format!"

Tom Vial (New York, NY)

"Thank you, thank you, thank you...for making it so easy for me to break into this high-tech world. I now own four of your books. I recommend them to anyone who is a beginner like myself."

Gay O'Donnell (Calgary, Alberta, Canada)

"I write to extend my thanks and appreciation for your books. They are clear, easy to follow, and straight to the point. Keep up the good work! I bought several of your books and they are just right! No regrets! I will always buy your books because they are the best."

Seward Kollie (Dakar, Senegal)

"Compliments to the chef!! Your books are extraordinary! Or, simply put, extra-ordinary, meaning way above the rest! THANK YOU THANK YOU THANK YOU! I buy them for friends, family, and colleagues."

Christine J. Manfrin (Castle Rock, CO)

"What fantastic teaching books you have produced! Congratulations to you and your staff. You deserve the Nobel Prize in Education in the Software category. Thanks for helping me understand computers."

Bruno Tonon (Melbourne, Australia)

"Over time, I have bought a number of your 'Read Less - Learn More' books. For me, they are THE way to learn anything easily. I learn easiest using your method of teaching."

José A. Mazón (Cuba, NY)

"I am an avid purchaser and reader of the Visual series, and they are the greatest computer books I've seen. The Visual books are perfect for people like myself who enjoy the computer, but want to know how to use it more efficiently. Your books have definitely given me a greater understanding of my computer, and have taught me to use it more effectively. Thank you very much for the hard work, effort, and dedication that you put into this series."

Alex Diaz (Las Vegas, NV)

Credits

About the Author

Sherry Willard Kinkoph has written and edited oodles of books over the past 10 years covering a variety of computer topics, including Microsoft Office programs. Her recent titles include *Teach Yourself VISUALLY Photoshop Elements 3.0* and *Office 2003 Simplified*. Sherry's ongoing quest is to help users of all levels master ever-changing computer technologies. No matter how many times they — the software manufacturers and hardware conglomerates — throw out a new version or upgrade, Sherry vows to be there to make sense of it all and help computer users get the most out of their machines.

Author's Acknowledgments

Special thanks go out to publisher Barry Pruett and to acquisitions editor Jody Lefevere for allowing me the opportunity to tackle this exciting project; to project editor Sarah Hellert for her dedication and patience in guiding this project from start to finish; to copy editor Marylouise Wiack, for ensuring that all the i's were dotted and t's were crossed; to technical editor Jim Kelly for skillfully checking each step and offering valuable input along the way; and finally to the production team at Wiley for their able efforts in creating such a visual masterpiece. Extra special thanks go to my new Gunter boys, Matty, Matt, and Jeramiah — thanks for being so patient with me while I worked on this endeavor!

Table of Contents

chapter 1   Office Basics

chapter 2   Working with Files

chapter 3   Office Internet and Graphics Tools

WORD

chapter 4 Adding Text

Table of Contents

chapter 5 Formatting Text

chapter 6 Working with Tables

chapter 7 — Adding Extra Touches

chapter 8 — Reviewing and Printing Documents

Table of Contents

chapter 9   Building Spreadsheets

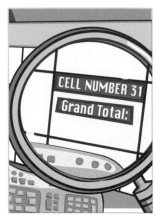

chapter 10   Worksheet Basics

chapter 11 Working with Formulas and Functions

chapter 12 Formatting Worksheets

Table of Contents

POWERPOINT

chapter 16   Assembling a Slide Show

chapter 17   Presenting a Slide Show

Table of Contents

chapter 18 — Database Basics

chapter 19 — Adding Data Using Tables

chapter 20 — Adding Data Using Forms

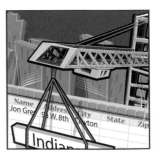

chapter 21 Finding and Querying Data

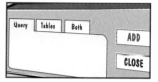

OUTLOOK

chapter 22 Organizing with Outlook

Table of Contents

chapter 25

Fine-Tune a Publication

PART

I

Part I: Office Features

The Office applications share a common look and feel. You can find many of the same features in each program, such as the new Ribbon feature, Quick Access toolbar, program window controls, and the new File menu. Many of the tasks you perform, such as creating and working with files, share the same processes and features throughout the Office suite. In this part, you learn how to navigate your way around the common Office features and basic tasks.

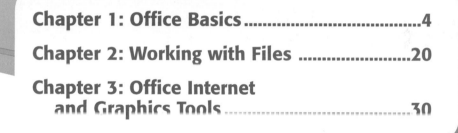

Start and Exit Office Applications

Before you begin working with any of the Microsoft Office programs, you must first open a program. When you finish your work, you can close the program. If applicable, you can save your work before exiting a program completely.

Start and Exit Office Applications

START AN OFFICE APPLICATION

1 Click **Start**.

2 Click **All Programs**.

3 Click **Microsoft Office**.

4 Click the name of the program that you want to open.

Note: *Depending on which programs you installed, not all of the Office programs may be listed in the menu.*

● The program that you selected opens in a new window.

Note: *See the next task to learn how to identify different areas of the program window.*

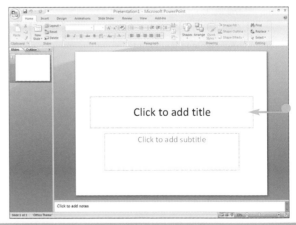

EXIT AN OFFICE APPLICATION

1 Click the **Close** button (☒).

● You can also click the **Office** button and then click **Exit**.

If you have not yet saved your work, the program prompts you to do so before exiting.

Note: *Outlook does not prompt you to save anything before closing, unless you have unsaved e-mail messages that you were composing.*

2 Click **Yes** to save.

The program window closes.

● If you click **No**, the program closes without saving your data.

● If you click **Cancel**, the program window remains open.

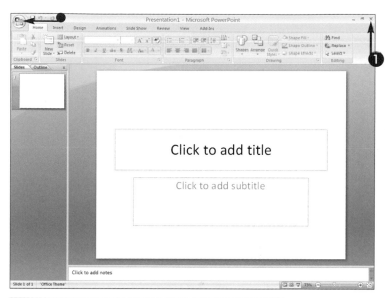

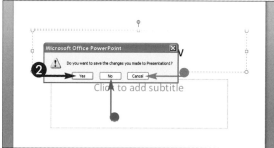

Can I create a shortcut icon for an Office application?

Yes. You can create a shortcut icon that appears on the Windows desktop. Whenever you want to open the program, you can simply double-click the shortcut icon. Follow these steps to create a shortcut icon:

1 Right-click over a blank area of the desktop and click **New**.

2 Click **Shortcut**.

The Create Shortcut dialog box appears.

3 Click **Browse**, navigate to the Office program, and double-click the filename.

4 Click **Next**.

5 Type a name for the shortcut.

6 Click **Finish**.

The new shortcut icon appears on the desktop.

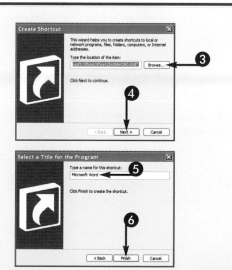

All of the Office programs share a common appearance and many of the same features, such as menu bars, toolbars, and scroll bars. When you learn your way around one program, you can easily use the same skills to navigate the other Office programs. If you are new to Office, you should take a moment and familiarize yourself with the types of on-screen elements that you can expect to encounter.

Title Bar
Displays the name of the open file and the Office program.

Office Button Menu
Click to display a menu of file commands, such as New and Open.

Quick Access Toolbar
Displays quick access buttons to the Save, Undo, and Redo commands.

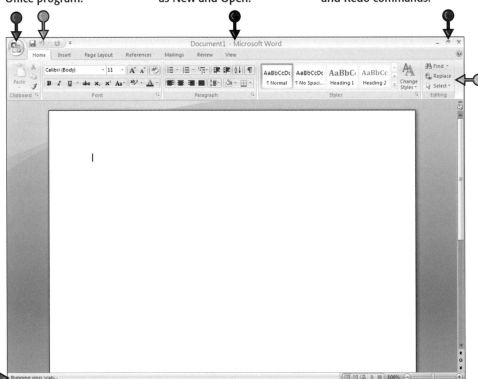

Ribbon
Displays groups of related commands in tabs. Each tab offers shortcut buttons to common tasks.

Status Bar
Displays information about the current worksheet or file.

Program Window Controls
Use these buttons to minimize the program window, restore the window to full size, or close the window.

Formula Bar

This appears only in Excel. Use this bar to type and edit formulas and perform calculations on your worksheet data.

Work Area

The area where you add, and work with, data in a program. Depending on the Office program, the work area may be a document, a worksheet, or a slide.

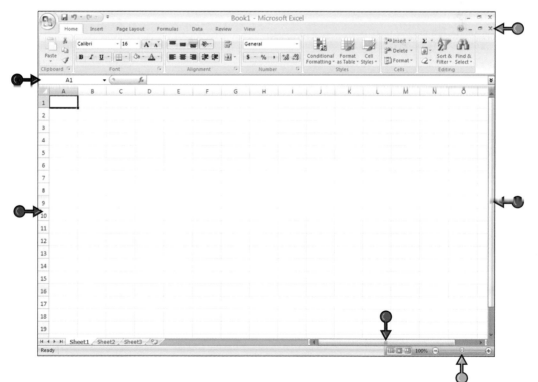

Document Window Controls

Use these buttons to minimize or restore the current document.

Zoom Controls

Use this feature to zoom your view of a document.

Scroll Bars

Use the vertical and horizontal scroll bars to scroll through the item displayed in the work area, such as a document or worksheet.

Work with the Ribbon

New to Office 2007, menus and toolbars in Word, Excel, PowerPoint, and Access are replaced by the new Ribbon feature. The Ribbon offers an intuitive way to locate commands that accomplish various program tasks. The Ribbon is grouped into tabs, and each tab holds a set of related commands. In addition, some tabs appear only when needed, such as when you are working with a particular object in a document.

Publisher and Outlook still use the familiar menu and toolbar features from previous versions of Office. However, some of the Outlook features, such as the Appointment window, use the new Ribbon features.

Work with the Ribbon

USE THE RIBBON

① Click a tab.

The tab organizes related tasks and commands into logical groups.

② Click a button to activate a command or feature.

● Buttons with arrows display additional commands.

● With some groups of commands, you can click the corner group button to display a dialog box of additional settings.

When you move the mouse pointer over Live Preview options on the Ribbon, you see the results in the document before applying the command.

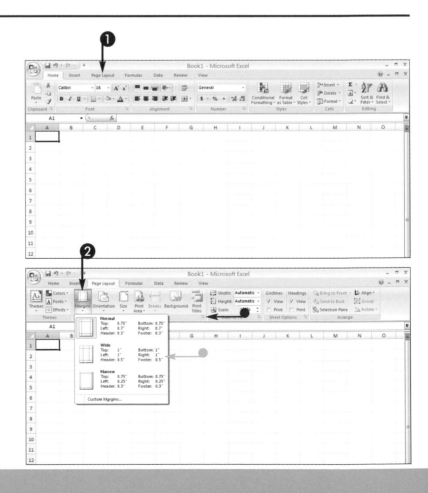

MINIMIZE THE RIBBON

① Double-click a tab name.

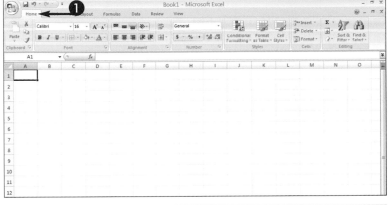

The Ribbon is minimized.

② Click the tab name again to maximize the Ribbon.

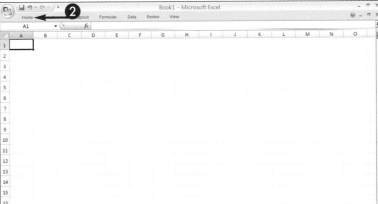

TIP

Is there a way I can keep the Ribbon minimized?

Yes. You can keep the Ribbon minimized and click a tab when you need to use a command. Follow these steps:

① Click the **Customize Quick Access Toolbar** button at the end of the Quick Access Toolbar.

② Click **Minimize the Ribbon**.

The program's Ribbon is minimized at the top of the screen.

To use a Ribbon while it is minimized, you can simply click the tab containing the tools that you want to access.

Customize the Quick Access Toolbar

The Quick Access toolbar appears in the top-left corner of the program window. You can use the toolbar to quickly activate the Save, Undo, and Redo commands. You can customize the toolbar to include other commands that you need to keep in view at all times. For example, you might add the Quick Print command or another common command you use. You can also choose to display the toolbar above or below the Ribbon.

Customize the Quick Access Toolbar

1 Click the **Customize Quick Access Toolbar** button.

Note: The Quick Access toolbar is not available in Publisher or Outlook.

2 Click **More Commands**.

● You can click any of the common commands to add them to the toolbar.

● You can click **Show Below the Ribbon** if you want to display the toolbar below the Ribbon.

The Options dialog box opens to the Customization tab.

3 Click the **Choose commands from** 🔽.

4 Click a command group.

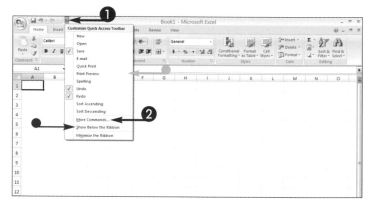

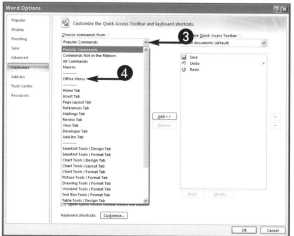

5 Click the command that you want to add to the toolbar.

6 Click the **Add** button.

● Office adds the command.

You can repeat Steps **5** and **6** to add additional buttons to the toolbar.

7 Click **OK**.

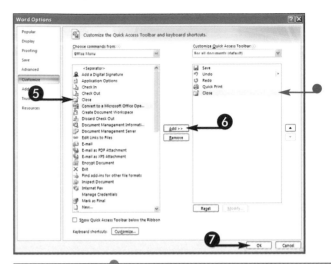

● The new command appears on the Quick Access toolbar.

TIPS

How do I remove a button from the Quick Access toolbar?

To remove a command, reopen the program's Options dialog box by following the steps in this task, click the command name in the list box on the right, and then click the **Remove** button. Click **OK**. The button no longer appears on the toolbar.

Are there other ways to customize the Quick Access toolbar?

Yes. You can add commands directly from the Ribbon and place them on the toolbar. Simply click the tab containing the command that you want to add, right-click the command, and then click **Add to Quick Access Toolbar**. The command is immediately added as a button on the toolbar.

Find Customizing Options

In previous versions of Office, you could customize the program window to suit the way you worked. You can do the same in Office 2007 using the Options dialog box. The dialog box features groups of settings that you can change to control how the program works, looks, and interacts with you.

Find Customizing Options

① Click the **Office** button.

② Click the program's **Options** button.

This example uses the Word Options button.

The program's Options dialog box appears.

③ Click the tab that you want to view.

Each tab displays sets of related controls that you can set for the program.

④ Make the changes that you want to the settings.

⑤ Click **OK** to apply your changes.

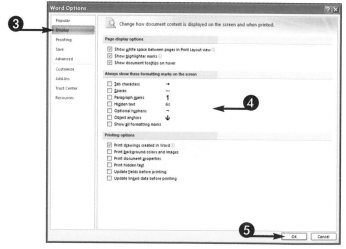

Turn Off Live Preview

Live Preview allows you to preview the effects of a feature before committing to a particular selection. Many of the Ribbon's tools offer Live Previews. For example, when you move the mouse pointer over a gallery item on the Ribbon, the style is immediately reflected in the document. You can turn the feature off if you find it too distracting.

Turn Off Live Preview

① Click the **Office** button.

② Click the program's **Options** button.

This example uses the Excel Options button.

The program's Options dialog box appears.

③ Click the **Popular** tab.

④ Click the **Enable Live Preview** check box to deselect the feature (☑ changes to ☐).

⑤ Click **OK**.

The program turns off Live Preview.

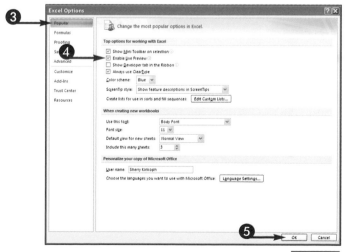

Find Help with Office

You can use the Office Help tools to assist you when you run into a problem or need more information about a particular task. With an Internet connection, you can use Microsoft's online Help files to quickly access information about an Office feature. The Help window offers tools that enable you to search for topics that you want to learn more about.

You must log on to your Internet connection in order to use the online Help files.

Find Help with Office

① Click the **Help** button.

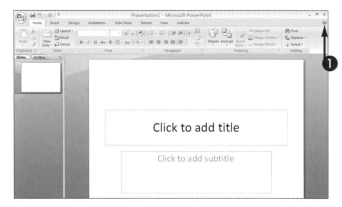

The Help window opens.

② Type a word or phrase that you want to learn more about.

③ Click the **Search** button.

You can also press **Enter** to start the search.

● You can click links to view other topics.

Note: You must log on to the Internet to access Microsoft's online Help files.

● The Search Results window displays a list of possible matches.

④ Click a link to learn more about a topic.

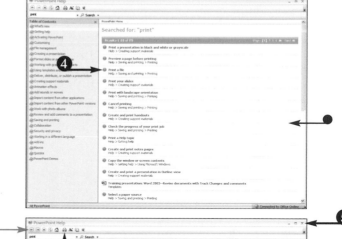

● The Help window displays the article, and you can read more about the topic.

● You can use the **Back** and **Forward** buttons (and) to move back and forth between help topics.

● You can click the **Print** button ( ) to print the information.

⑤ Click to close the window.

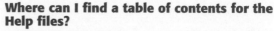

TIPS

Can I use the Help feature if I am offline?

Yes. You can still access the Help files that are installed with the program. However, the online resources offer you more help topics, as well as links to demos and other help tools.

Where can I find a table of contents for the Help files?

You can click the **Home** button ( ) on the Help window's toolbar to quickly display the table of contents for the Office program that you are using. You can click a help category to display subtopics of help information. You can click an article to view more about a topic. Many articles include links to related articles.

Add and Remove Office Components

You can add and remove Office components using the Office setup program. For example, you may choose to install two or three programs that you work with the most, and then add another component later. You might also decide to remove a program that you do not use.

Before you begin, you need the Office CD. Also, be sure to close any open programs.

Add and Remove Office Components

① Insert the Office CD.

Note: *Depending on your computer's setup, the Office window may open automatically. If not, see the tip in this task.*

The Microsoft Office window appears.

② Click the **Microsoft Office Professional Plus 2007** option (◯ changes to ◉).

③ Click **Continue**.

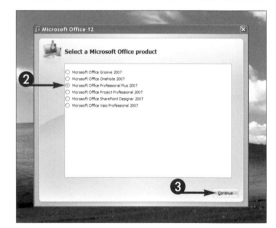

④ Click the **Add or Remove Features** option (◯ changes to ◉).

⑤ Click **Continue**.

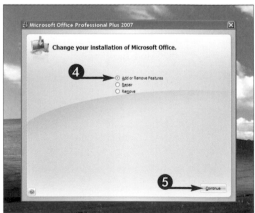

6 Click the 🔽 next to the program that you want to add or remove.

7 Click an option.

You can repeat Steps **6** and **7** to select additional programs.

8 Click **Continue**.

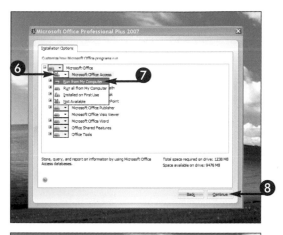

Office installs or uninstalls the selected programs.

9 When the procedure is complete, click **Close**.

 TIPS

What do the various installation options do?

If you select the Run from My Computer option, Office installs the program directly onto your computer. If you choose the Run all from My Computer option, all of the add-ins and extra features are also installed. If you select the Installed on First Use option, Office prompts you to install the program the first time you attempt to use it. If you select the Not Available option, the program is uninstalled from your computer.

If my Office window does not open automatically, how do I open the setup program?

You can open the My Computer window and navigate to the CD drive to view the contents of the Office CD. When you open the drive, Windows displays all of the files located on the CD, and you can double-click the **SETUP.EXE** file to start the setup program.

Diagnose Office Programs

You can use the Office Diagnostics tool to diagnose and repair problems that you are having with any Office program. For example, a program may not work properly if an important program file is corrupted or accidentally deleted. You can run the diagnosis to check the problem and attempt to make any repairs. Microsoft Word's diagnostic tool is shown in this example.

Diagnose Office Programs

① Click the **Office** button.

② Click the program's **Options** button.

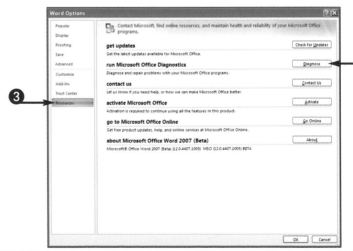

The program's Options dialog box appears.

③ Click the **Resources** tab.

④ Click **Diagnose**.

The Microsoft Office Diagnostics dialog box appears.

5 Click **Continue**.

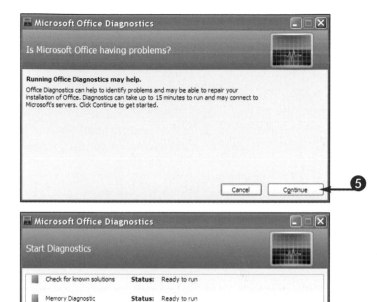

6 Click **Start Diagnostics**.

The Office Diagnostics program runs. The procedure may take awhile.

If the program finds any problems, you can follow the prompts to fix them.

What if I am still having trouble with my Office programs?

You can also run the repair program with the Microsoft Setup feature. To do so, insert your Office CD and click the **Repair** option when prompted. Setup runs the repair tool, which may take a long time, depending on your computer's resources.

How do I update my Office program?

You can use the Resources tab in the Options dialog box to check for program updates. Open the dialog box as shown in this task, and click the **Resources** tab. Next, click the **Check for Updates** button. You must log onto your Internet connection in order to check for program updates.

Start a New File

With the exception of Outlook, you can create new files whenever you want to add new data to an Office program. Depending on the program you are working with, you can create different types of new files. When you create a new file in Word, it is called a *document*. In Excel, a new file is called a *workbook*. In Access, it is called a *database*. In PowerPoint, it is called a *presentation*, while in Publisher it is called a *publication*.

In Word, Excel, and PowerPoint, you use the New dialog box to start a new file. In Publisher and Access, you use the Getting Started screen to start new files. Whenever you start a new file in Office 2007, you can choose to create a blank document, or base the file on a template.

Start a New File

START A NEW FILE IN WORD, EXCEL, OR POWERPOINT

① Click the **Office** button.

② Click the **New** button.

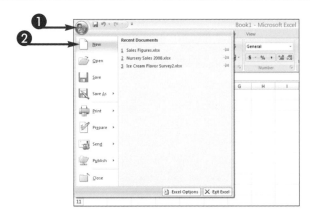

The New dialog box appears.

Depending on which Office program you are using, the New dialog box has different names. For example, in Word, it is called the New Document dialog box.

③ Click the type of file that you want to start.

④ Click **Create**.

The new file opens, and you can start adding your own data.

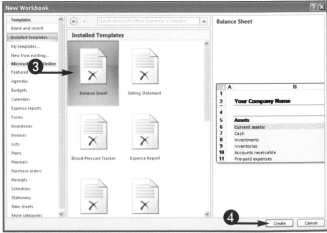

START A NEW FILE IN PUBLISHER OR ACCESS

① Click the **Office** button.

② Click the **New** button.

*Note: In Publisher, you can click the **File** menu and then click New.*

The Welcome screen appears, displaying the Getting Started window.

③ Click the type of file that you want to start.

● In Access, you can name the new file here.

④ Click **Create**.

The new file opens, and you can start adding your own data.

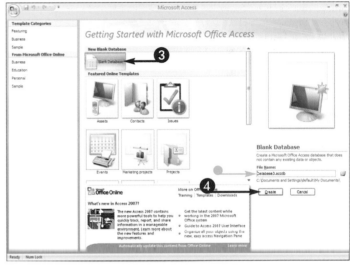
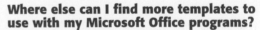

TIPS

How do I create a new file based on a template?

Many Office programs allow you to create a new file from a template. For example, in Word, you can choose from letters, faxes, memos, reports, and more. Templates are simply preformatted layouts that you can use to create files, substituting your own text for the placeholder text in the template. You can choose from a library of templates that install with Office. Simply click the template that you want to apply in the New dialog box or on the Welcome screen. You can also turn an existing file into a template by saving it in the program's template format.

Where else can I find more templates to use with my Microsoft Office programs?

Using your Internet connection, you can find more Office templates on the Microsoft Web site. Click the **Templates** link in the New dialog box or on the Welcome screen to access the site, and download any templates that you like. By default, Office is set up to store your downloaded templates in a default folder so that you can easily access them again using the New dialog box or the Welcome screen.

Save a File

You can save your data to reuse it or share it with others. You should also frequently save any file that you are working on in case of a power failure or computer crash. When you save a file, you can give it a unique filename, and store it in a particular folder or drive.

Each Office program saves to a default file type. For example, an Excel workbook uses the XLSX file format. If you want to save the file in a format compatible with previous versions of Office, you must save it in the appropriate format, such as Excel 97-2003 Workbook (*.xls) for previous versions of Excel.

Save a File

① Click the **Office** button.

② Click the **Save** or **Save As** button.

● For subsequent saves, you can click the **Save** button (🔲) on the Quick Access toolbar to quickly save the file.

*Note: In Publisher, you can click the **File** menu and then click **Save** or **Save As**.*

● If you click the arrow on the Save As button, you can view several save options that you can apply.

The Save As dialog box appears.

③ Click the **Save in** ⯆ to navigate to the folder or drive to which you want to save the file.

④ Click the **File name** ⯆ and type a name for the file.

● To save the file in another format, click the **Save as type** ⯆ and choose a format.

⑤ Click **Save**.

The Office program saves the file and the new filename appears on the program window's title bar.

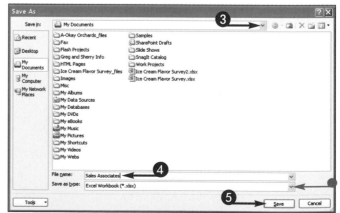

Open an Existing File

You can open a file that you previously worked on to continue adding or editing data. Regardless of whether you store a file in a folder on your computer's hard drive, on a floppy disk, or on a CD, you can easily access files using the Open dialog box.

With the exception of Outlook, each Office program automatically lists your most recent files to the right of the File menu or in the Getting Started screen.

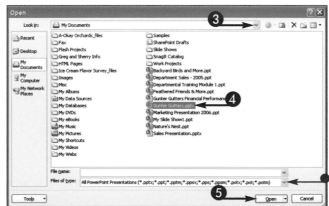

Open an Existing File

① Click the **Office** button.

② Click the **Open** button.

● You can also open a recent file by clicking a filename listed in the Recent Documents list on the Office menu.

The Open dialog box appears.

③ Click the **Look in** ☑ to navigate to the folder or drive where you stored the file.

● You can look for a specific file type using the **Files of type** ☑.

④ Click the name of the file that you want to open.

⑤ Click **Open**.

The file opens in the program window.

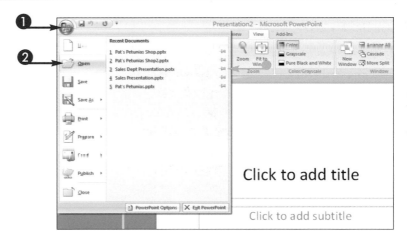

You can close a file that you are
no longer using without closing
the entire program window.
When you close unnecessary files,
you free up processing power on
your computer.

Close a File

① Click the **Office** button.

② Click the **Close** button.

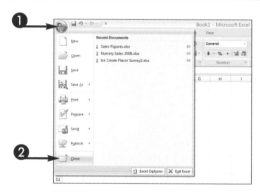

The file closes.

● In this example, the Excel program
window remains open.

Note: To learn how to close the program entirely, see
Chapter 1.

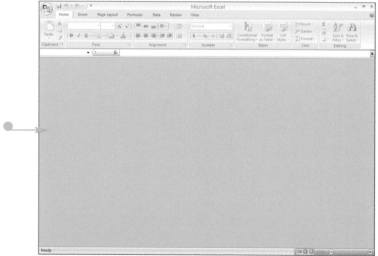

If you have a printer connected to your computer, you can print your Microsoft Office files. You can send a file directly to the printer using the default printer settings, or you can open the Print dialog box and make changes to the printer settings. These settings may vary slightly among Office programs.

Print a File

① Click the **Office** button.

② Click the **Print** button.

● You can click the arrow on the Print button to display several print options. You can click the **Print** command to open the Print dialog box.

If your Quick Access toolbar displays the Quick Print button, you can click it to print a file without adjusting any printer settings.

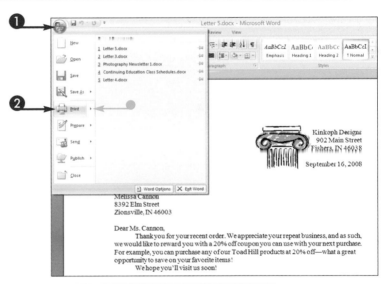

The Print dialog box appears.

● You can choose a printer from the Name drop-down list.

● You can print a selection from the file, or specific pages using the available settings.

● You can specify a number of copies to print.

● You can click here for more printer options.

③ Click **OK**.

The Office program sends the file to the printer for printing.

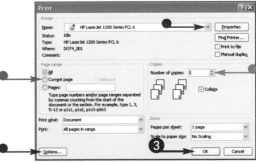

Cut, Copy, and Paste Data

You can use the Cut, Copy, and Paste commands to copy data within a program, or move and share data among Office programs. For example, you might copy a graphic from Word and place it in a PowerPoint slide, or copy data from Excel to display in a Publisher publication. You can also drag and drop data to move and copy it within a file.

The Copy command makes a duplicate of the selected data, while the Cut command removes the data from the original file entirely. When you copy or paste data, the Windows Clipboard stores it until you are ready to paste it into place.

Cut, Copy, and Paste Data

CUT AND COPY DATA

1 Select the data that you want to cut or copy.

2 Click the **Home** tab.

3 Click the **Cut** button (✂) to move data, or the **Copy** button (📋) to copy data.

Note: You can also use keyboard shortcuts to cut and copy. Press `Ctrl` + `X` *to cut or* `Ctrl` + `C` *to copy.*

The data is stored in the Windows Clipboard.

4 Click the point where you want to insert the cut or copied data.

You can also open another file to which you can copy the data.

5 On the Home tab, click the **Paste** button.

Note: You can also press `Ctrl` + `V` *to paste data.*

● The data appears in the new location.

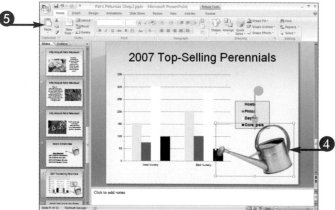

DRAG AND DROP DATA

1 Select the data that you want to cut or copy.

2 Click and drag the data to a new location.

The ⌖ changes to ⌖.

To copy the data as you drag it, you can press and hold the `Ctrl` key.

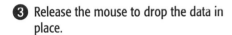

3 Release the mouse to drop the data in place.

The data appears in the new location.

When I cut or copy data, an icon appears. What is it?

The Paste Options smart tag (🖺) may appear when you perform any cut or copy task. Click the smart tag to view a drop-down list of related options for the task. Click an option from the list to activate the option. If you ignore the tag, it disappears. To turn the feature off, click the **Office** button, and then click the **Options** button for the program, such as Word Options if you are using Word. Click the **Advanced** tab, and then click the **Show Paste Options Buttons** check box (☑ changes to ☐) under the Cut, Copy, and Paste settings. Click **OK** to save the new settings and exit the dialog box.

Can I cut or copy multiple pieces of data?

Yes. You can cut or copy multiple pieces of data, and open the Office Clipboard task pane to paste the data. The Office Clipboard holds up to 24 items. You can paste them in whatever order you choose, or you can opt to paste them all at the same time. To display the task pane, click the **Clipboard** button in the Clipboard tools group on the Ribbon's Home tab. The Office Clipboard is just one of many task panes that are available in the Office programs.

View Multiple Files

You can use the Office View tools to display different views of your documents. You can view multiple files in your Office programs to compare data or formatting between files. For example, you might want to view two open Word documents side by side to check notes, or view two Excel workbooks to compare similar data. You can choose to view files horizontally or vertically.

When working with a particularly long document, you can choose to view different portions of the same document by splitting it into two scrollable panes.

View Multiple Files

① Open two or more files.

② Click the **View** tab.

③ Click **Arrange All**.

Note: In Excel, the Arrange Windows dialog box opens, and you can select how you want to display multiple files.

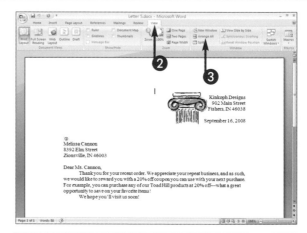

● The files appear stacked.

● You can click the **Close** button (⊠) to close a file.

● You can click the **View Side by Side** button on the View menu to view the two open files vertically.

● You can click here to scroll both documents at the same time.

● You can click the **Split** button to split a single document into two scrollable panes.

Note: To return the page to a full document again, click the **Remove Split** button.

What does the Switch Windows button do?

If you open two or more documents, you can click the **Switch Windows** button on the View tab, and then click the document that you want to view. The Switch Windows button displays a menu that lists every open Word document. You can use this feature to quickly display the document that you want to edit. In previous versions of Word, the list of open files appeared in the Window menu.

How do I redisplay full windows again?

If you use the Arrange All command to display several open documents at once, you can click the **Maximize** button (▢)in the upper-right corner of a document pane to open the document to its full window size again. Each open document has a set of window controls — Minimize (▬), Maximize (▢), and Close (✕) — to control the individual document window.

Create an HTML File

You can turn your Microsoft Office files into HTML documents that you can post on the Web. When you activate the Save As Web page command, you create a Web page file that contains all of the necessary HTML coding for it to be read by Web browsers.

Create an HTML File

① Click the **Office** button.

② Click **Save As**.

*Note: In Publisher, you can click **File** and then click the **Convert to Web Publication** command to convert a publication to an HTML page.*

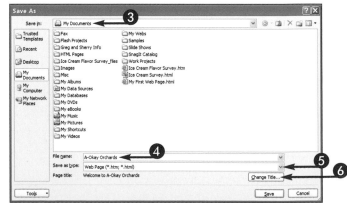

The Save As dialog box appears.

③ Navigate to the folder where you want to save the file.

④ Type a name for the file.

⑤ Click the **Save as type** and click **Web Page (*.htm; *.html)**.

⑥ Click **Change Title**.

Note: The Save As dialog box only displays the Web page options when you activate the Save as Web Page command.

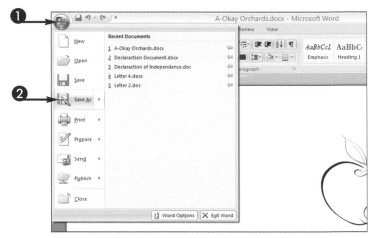

● The Set Page Title dialog box appears.

7 Type a title.

8 Click **OK**.

9 Click **Save**.

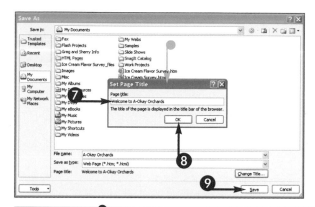

● The file is saved as a Web page.

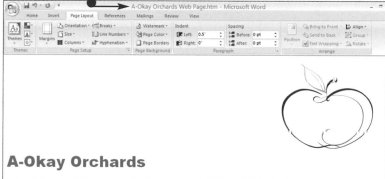

A-Okay Orchards

TIPS

What does the Publish button do?

If you are turning an Excel worksheet or PowerPoint slide into a Web page, and you are ready to publish the Web page to a server, you can click **Publish** in the Save As dialog box to open the Publish as Web Page dialog box. You can then use the Publish as Web Page dialog box to add spreadsheet functionality to the page and designate a server path and filename. When you activate the **Publish** command, Office publishes the page and opens it in your default browser to display the information.

Can I assign a password to a workbook?

Yes. You can assign a password from the Save As dialog box. Simply click the **Tools** button and click **General Options**. This opens the General Options dialog box. Type a password for the file and click **OK**. Then retype the same password again to verify it. When you save the file, the password is saved along with the workbook. You can also use the General Options dialog box to add a password that allows other users who know the password the opportunity to change the file.

Add a Hyperlink

You can insert hyperlinks into your files that open a Web page when a user clicks them. When linking to a Web page, you must designate a Uniform Resource Locator, or URL. This is the unique address that identifies the Web page.

You can also use hyperlinks to link to other files on your computer. You must designate the address or path of the page that you want to link to when you add links to a file.

Add a Hyperlink

① Select the text or image that you want to use as a hyperlink.

② Click the **Insert** tab on the Ribbon.

③ Click **Hyperlink**.

Note: In Word, click the **Links** button and then click **Hyperlink**.

Note: In Publisher, click the **Insert Hyperlink** button (🔗) on the Standard toolbar.

The Insert Hyperlink dialog box appears.

④ Click the type of document to which you want to link.

⑤ Select the page or type the address, or URL, of the page to which you want to link.

● To browse the Internet to look for the page, you can click the **Web Search** button (🔍) and open your default browser window.

⑥ Click **OK**.

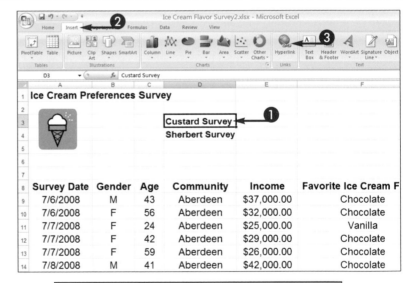

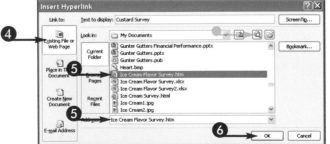

The hyperlink is created.

7 To test the link, press and hold the mouse button on the link for a moment and then release.

The ⬚ changes to 🖑 on the link.

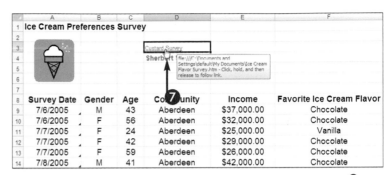

The default Web browser opens and displays the designated page.

● You can click ⊠ to close the browser window.

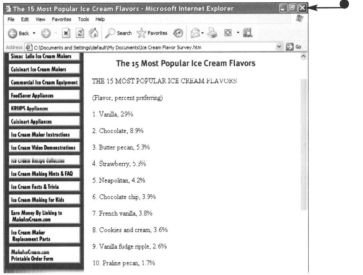

How do I edit a link?
To change a link, such as editing the Web page URL, you can open the Edit Hyperlink dialog box and make any necessary changes. Right-click the link and click **Edit Hyperlink** from the shortcut menu. The Edit Hyperlink dialog box appears. You can use the dialog box to change the hyperlink text and address, or the type of page that you want to use in the link.

How do I remove a hyperlink?
You can right-click a link and click **Remove Hyperlink** from the shortcut menu. The associated link is removed and the original text or image remains. To remove a hyperlink from the Edit Hyperlink dialog box, you can click **Remove Link**.

You can use AutoShapes to draw your own shapes and graphics for your documents, worksheets, slides, and publications. You can choose from a large library of predrawn shapes in the AutoShapes palette. Once you draw a shape, the Format tab displays the Drawing tools that you can use to format the shape, including tools for controlling the color and line thickness.

AutoShapes is just one of several features that you can find on the Insert tab on the Ribbon in Word, Excel, and PowerPoint. You can also use AutoShapes in Publisher. Graphics tools are not available in Outlook or Access.

Draw AutoShapes

① Click the **Insert** tab on the Ribbon.

② In the Illustrations group, click **Shapes**.

*Note: In Publisher, you can click the **AutoShapes** tool (⬚) on the Objects toolbar to draw shapes.*

The full Shapes palette displays.

③ Click the shape that you want to draw.

The ⬚ changes to +.

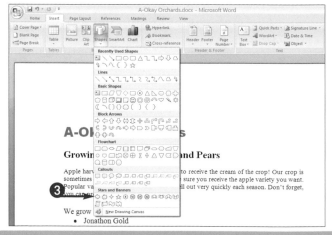

④ Click and drag in the work area to draw the desired shape.

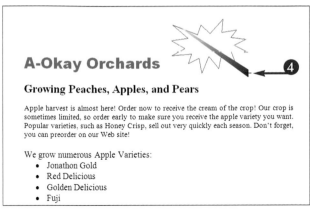

● When you release the mouse, the program completes the shape.

Note: You can move and resize the object or edit it with the Drawing toolbar buttons. See the "Move and Resize an Object" task to learn more.

● You can use these Shape Styles controls to define the fill color, line thickness, and color of the shape.

*Note: You can right-click a shape and click **Format AutoShape** to open the Format AutoShape dialog box.*

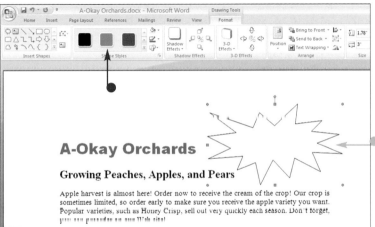

TIPS

How do I add text to an AutoShape?
To add text to a shape, you can click the **Edit Text** button on the Format tab that appears on the Ribbon when you select the shape. After you type your text, you can format it with the formatting tools found on the Home tab of the Ribbon. When you activate the Edit Text tool, the AutoShape converts to a text box object.

How do I remove an AutoShape?
You can easily delete any AutoShape object that you add to a document. Simply click the shape to select it, and then press Delete. You can also delete objects using the **Cut** command, found on the Home tab of the Ribbon.

Insert
Clip Art

You can add interest to your Office files by inserting clip art images. Clip art is simply predrawn artwork. Word, Excel, PowerPoint, and Publisher install with the Office clip art collection. In addition, you can look for more clip art on the Web using the Clip Art task pane.

Insert Clip Art

① Click where you want to add clip art.

You can also move the clip art to a different location after you insert the art.

② Click the **Insert** tab.

③ In the Illustrations group, click **Clip Art**.

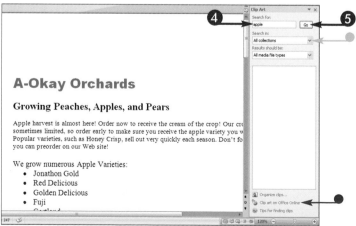

The Clip Art task pane opens.

④ To search for a particular category of clip art, type a keyword or phrase here.

● To search in a particular collection, you can click the **Search in** ⊡ and click a collection.

● You can also search for clip art on the Office Web site by clicking this link.

⑤ Click **Go**.

The Clip Art task pane displays any matches for the keyword or phrase that you typed.

● You can use the scroll bar to move through the list of matches.

● To view information about a clip art image, you can move ⌖ over the image.

6 To add a clip art image, click the image.

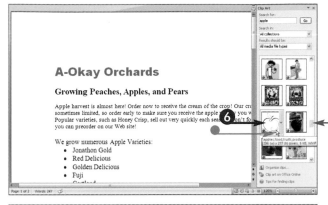

● The clip art is inserted.

● The Picture tools appear on the Format tab.

You can resize or move the clip art.

Note: See the "Move and Resize an Object" task, later in this chapter, to learn more.

To deselect the clip art, you can click anywhere else in the work area.

● You can click ⊠ to close the pane.

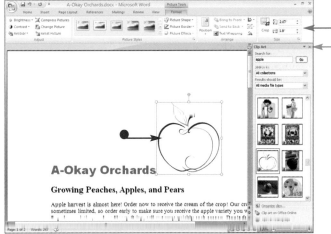

 TIPS

How do I search for a particular type of clip art, such as a photo or sound file?

To search for a particular type of media, click the **Results should be** ⊡. The drop-down menu displays a list of different media types. You can select or deselect which types to include in your search. If you leave the **All media types** check box selected (☑), you can search for a match among all of the available media formats.

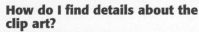

How do I find details about the clip art?

To find out more about the clip art's properties in the Clip Art task pane, move the ⌖ over the image, click the ⊡, and then click **Preview/Properties**. This opens the Preview/ Properties dialog box, where you can learn more about the file size, filename, file type, its creation date, and more.

View Clip Art with the Clip Organizer

You can use the Microsoft Clip Organizer to view clip art collections on your computer. You can also insert clip art from the Organizer window and place it in your Office file. The Clip Organizer does exactly as its name implies — it organizes clip art images and entire clip art collections to suit the way you work. For example, you might place all of the clip art related to your company newsletter in one collection.

View Clip Art with the Clip Organizer

① Display the Clip Art task pane.

Note: See the previous task to learn how to open this pane.

② Click **Organize clips**.

The Microsoft Clip Organizer window opens.

③ Click the **Collection List** button if the list is not already displayed.

④ Click a collection ⊞ to expand the collection list.

⑤ Click a category.

If some categories include subcategories, you can click a category ⊞ to expand the list.

● The Clip Organizer displays thumbnails of available clip art.

● You can use these buttons to change how clip art displays in the window: **Thumbnails** (▣), **List** (▥) or **Details** (▤).

● To view information about a clip art image, you can move ⌖ over the image.

  To add a clip art image to the current document, you can drag the clip art to your work area.

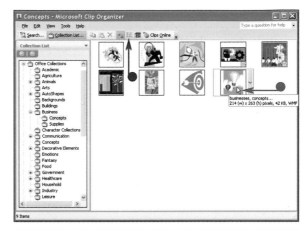

● You can click the **Search** button to display settings for conducting a search for clip art on your computer.

❻ When you finish viewing the clip art, click ⊠.

  The Microsoft Clip Organizer window closes.

 TIPS

How do I download clip art from the Web?

You can click the **Clip art on Office Online** link at the bottom of the Clip Art task pane to open your default Web browser to the Office Web site. From there, you can click a clip art category and locate the art that you want to download. Simply select the images that you want to download, click the **Download** link, and follow the instructions.

Can I copy clip art from one collection to another?

Yes. You can copy clip art from one collection and paste it into another collection using the Microsoft Clip Organizer. Simply click the clip art that you want to copy, and then use the **Copy** (▣) and **Paste** (▣) buttons on the Microsoft Clip Organizer's toolbar to copy and paste the clip art.

Insert a Picture

You can illustrate your Office files with images that you store on your computer. For example, if you have a photo or graphic file from another program that relates to your Excel data, you can insert it onto the worksheet. If you have a company logo, then you can insert it onto a Word document.

Image or picture files, also called _objects_ in Office, come in a variety of file formats, such as GIF, JPEG or JPG, and PNG. After you insert an image, you can resize and reposition it, as well as perform other types of edits on the image.

Insert a Picture

1 Click the area where you want to add a picture.

You can also move the image to a different location after inserting it onto the page.

2 Click the **Insert** tab.

3 In the Illustrations group, click **Picture**.

Note: In Publisher, click the **Picture Frame** button (🖾) on the Objects toolbar.

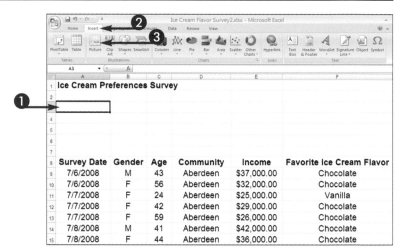

The Insert Picture dialog box appears.

4 Navigate to the folder or drive containing the image file that you want to use.

● To browse for a particular file type, you can click the **Files of type** ☑ and choose a file format.

⑤ Click the filename.

⑥ Click **Insert**.

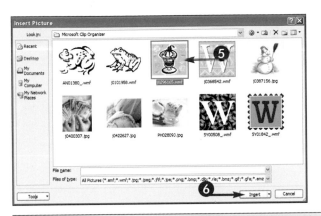

● The picture is added to the file.

● The Picture tools appear on the Format tab.

You may need to resize or reposition the picture to fit the space.

Note: See the "Move and Resize an Object" task to learn more.

To remove a picture that you no longer want, you can click the picture and press Delete .

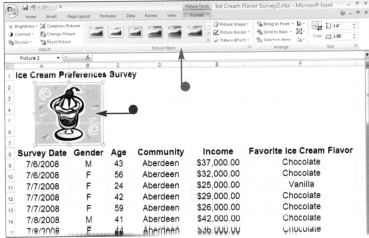

If I am sharing my file with others, can I compress the pictures to save space?

Yes. You can take advantage of the new compression features available in Office 2007 to compress image files that you add to any document. Simply select the picture and display the **Format** tab on the Ribbon. In the Picture Tools group of commands, click the **Compress Pictures** button. This opens the Compress Pictures dialog box. Click the **Options** button to open the Compression Settings dialog box, and fine-tune any settings that you want to apply. Click **OK**, and then click **OK** again to compress the pictures.

I made changes to my picture, and now I do not like the effect. How do I return the picture to the original settings?

You can click the **Reset Picture** button, located in the Picture Tools group on the Format tab, to restore a picture to its original state. This command removes any edits that you applied to the image. Activating this command does not restore the original size of the image.

Add a
Picture Border

You can quickly add a border to any picture or clip art image using the Picture tools. You can choose a border color from among the many theme and standard color selections. You can also assign a line weight to the border to make thin or thick borders.

Add a Picture Border

① Double-click the picture that you want to edit.

The Format tab appears on the Ribbon with the Picture tools displayed.

② In the Picture Styles group, click the **Picture Border** button.

③ Click a border color.

● To set a line thickness for the border, click **Weight** and click a thickness.

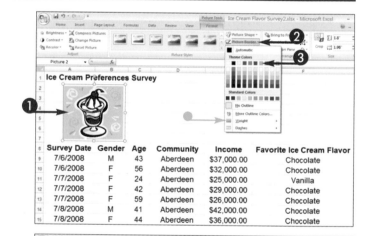

● The new border is assigned to the picture.

● To use a preset border, you can choose from among the Picture styles.

Note: *To set a border in Publisher, click the* ***Line/Border Style*** *button (▤) on the Picture toolbar.*

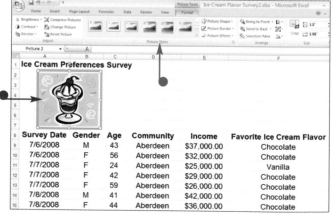

Add a Picture Effect

You can use the new Picture Effect tool to assign unique and interesting special effects to your pictures and clip art graphics. For example, you can make the edges of an image seem to glow, or create a mirrored reflection effect.

Keep in mind that the Picture Effects tool is not available in Publisher.

Add a Picture Effect

① Double-click the picture that you want to edit.

The Format tab appears on the Ribbon with the Picture tools displayed.

② In the Picture Styles group, click the **Picture Effects** button.

③ Click an effect category.

④ Click an effect style.

As you drag over each effect in the menu, the picture displays what the effect looks like when you apply it.

● The new effect is assigned to the picture.

Note: To cancel any picture effect, display the Picture Effect menu again and the style that you applied, and then select the **No** option at the top of the category palette to undo the effect.

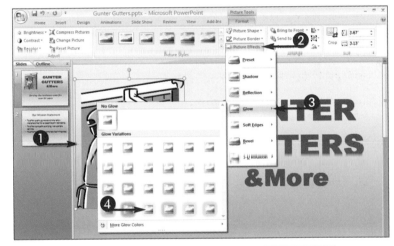

Insert a WordArt Object

You can use the WordArt feature to turn text into interesting graphic objects to use in your Office files. For example, you can create arched text to appear over a range of data in Excel, or vertical text to appear next to a paragraph in Word. You can create text graphics that bend and twist, or display a subtle shading of color.

In Word, the WordArt feature works the same as in previous versions of Office. In PowerPoint and Excel, the feature works a bit differently, as shown in this task.

Insert a WordArt Object

① Click the area where you want to add a WordArt object.

You can also move the WordArt object to a different location after inserting it onto the page.

② Click the **Insert** tab.

③ In the Text group, click **WordArt**.

④ Click a Quick Style.

Note: In Word, the WordArt Gallery menu appears, and you can choose a style in the same way as in previous versions of Office.

Note: In Publisher, click the **Insert WordArt** button ( ) on the Objects toolbar.

● The WordArt text box appears.

⑤ Select the text and replace it with your own text.

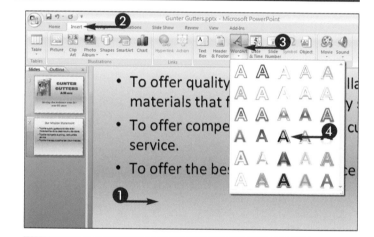

6 Click the **Text Effects** button.

7 Click **Transform**.

8 Click a transform style.

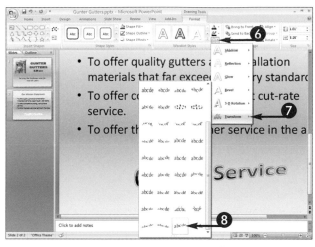

● The WordArt object is transformed.

You can resize or move the image.

● You can click here to change the text style.

● You can click these options to change the fill color and text color.

Note: See the next task, "Move and Resize an Object," to learn more.

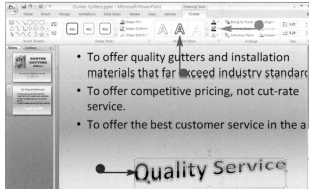

 TIPS

How do I edit my WordArt text?
To edit the WordArt text, simply click the WordArt text box and select the text that you want to change. When you type your changes, the object immediately reflects the new text. To edit the appearance of the WordArt object, use the WordArt Styles tools, located on the Format menu on the Ribbon.

How do I remove a WordArt object?
To remove the object entirely, click the WordArt text box, and then press Delete. In Excel and PowerPoint, you can also remove the WordArt style, and still keep the text. To do so, click the WordArt text box, click **Quick Styles** on the Format tab, and then click **Clear WordArt**.

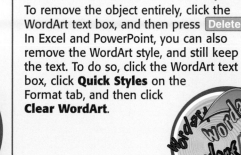

Move and
Resize an Object

You can move and resize any clip art, image, or shape that you place in a file. Clip art, images, and shapes are also called *objects* in Office. When you select an object, it is surrounded by handles that you can use to resize it.

Move and Resize an Object

MOVE AN OBJECT

① Click the object that you want to move.

The ⤧ changes to ✛.

② Drag the object to a new location on the worksheet.

● As soon as you release the mouse, the object moves to the new location.

Note: *When moving the object to fit with text, you may need to adjust the object's text wrapping settings. See the "Control Text Wrapping" task to learn more.*

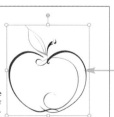

RESIZE AN OBJECT

① Click the object that you want to resize.

The ⌖ changes to +.

② Drag a selection handle to resize the object.

● As soon as you release the mouse, the object is resized.

TIPS

Can I also use the Cut, Copy, and Paste commands to move or copy an object?

Yes. You can easily cut, copy, and paste objects around your Office files. Simply select an object and then apply the commands. You can find the commands on the Home tab on the Ribbon in Word, Excel, and PowerPoint. In Publisher, you can click ✂, 📋, or 📋 on the Standard toolbar, or you can click the **Edit** menu to apply the commands.

Can I resize an object and keep the scaling proportional?

Yes. To maintain an object's height-to-width ratio when resizing, press and hold Shift while dragging a resizing corner handle. To resize from the center of the object in two dimensions at the same time, press and hold Ctrl while dragging a corner handle.

Rotate and Flip Objects

You can rotate and flip objects that you place on your documents, worksheets, slides, or publications to change the appearance of the objects. For example, you might flip a clip art image to face another direction, or rotate an arrow object to point elsewhere on the page.

Rotate and Flip Objects

ROTATE AN OBJECT

❶ Click the object that you want to rotate.

● A rotation handle appears on the selected object.

❷ Click and drag the handle to rotate the object.

The ▷ changes to ⟲.

● When you release the mouse, the object rotates.

Note: *You can also use the **Rotate** button on the Format tab on the Ribbon to rotate an object 90 degrees left or right.*

FLIP AN OBJECT

1 Click the object that you want to flip.

2 Click the **Rotate** button on the Format tab.

3 Click **Flip Vertical** or **Flip Horizontal**.

Note: In Publisher, you can click the **Arrange** menu to find the Rotate and Flip commands.

● The object flips.

TIPS

How do I rotate text?

The easiest way to rotate text is to create a WordArt object to rotate. You can learn how to create a WordArt object in the "Insert a WordArt Object" task, earlier in this chapter. After you create the WordArt, you can rotate it using the steps shown in this task. You can also choose from several preset vertical text styles among the WordArt styles.

Is there a way to constrain how much rotation occurs when I drag the rotation handle?

Yes. To constrain the rotation to 15-degree angles, press and hold **Shift** while rotating the object using the rotation handle. You can also choose to rotate the object in 90-degree increments by clicking the **Rotate** button on the Format tab, and then choosing the **Rotate Right 90°** or **Rotate Left 90°** command.

Crop a Picture

You can crop a picture that you add to any Office file to create a better fit or to focus on an important area of the image. The Crop tool, located on the Format tab, can help you crop out parts of the image that you do not need. You can also crop clip art pictures.

Crop a Picture

1 Double-click the image that you want to edit.

The Format tab opens and displays the Picture tools.

2 Click the **Crop** button.

Note: *In Publisher, click the **Crop** button (![crop icon]) on the Picture toolbar to crop a picture.*

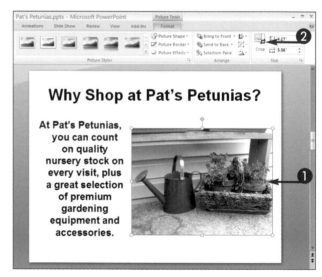

● Crop handles surround the image.

3 Move the mouse over a crop handle.

The ⌖ changes to ✛.

④ Click and drag a crop handle to crop out an area of the image.

● When you release the mouse button, the image is cropped.

⑤ You can continue cropping other edges of the image.

Note: *See the "Move and Resize an Object" task, earlier in this chapter, to learn how to resize an image.*

How can I reduce the overall file size of an image that I use in an Office file?

Image files are notorious for consuming large amounts of file space, and when you insert a large image into a document or worksheet, it adds to the size of the file. You can use the Compress Pictures tool on the Ribbon's Format tab to reduce the resolution of an image or to discard extra information from cropping the image. Click the **Compress Pictures** button to open the Compress Pictures dialog box, and then click the **Options** button to open the Compression settings dialog box, which offers several options to help you to control the overall file size of an image.

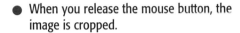

How can I return the image to its original state before cropping?

You can click the **Reset Picture** button in the Format Picture dialog box to reset the image to the size it appeared when you first inserted it onto your worksheet. Any cropping or other edits that you made to the image are discarded. Click the **Size** button, which is located in the bottom right corner of the Size command group on the Ribbon. The Size dialog box appears. Click the **Reset** button on the Size tab to resize the image.

Add Shadow and 3-D Effects

You can add shadow and 3-D effects to your AutoShapes, lines, arrows, and any other shapes that you create. You can also add shadow and 3-D effects to clip art and picture objects that you insert into a document. Adding shadow and 3-D effects can give an object the illusion of depth on the page.

Add Shadow and 3-D Effects

ADD A SHADOW

① Select the object to which you want to add shadow effects.

② Click the **Shape Effects** button on the Format tab.

Note: In Word, you can click the **Shadow Effects** tool to display a palette of preset shadow styles.

③ Click **Shadow**.

④ Click a shadow style.

Note: In Publisher, click the **Shadow Style** button (▣) on the Formatting toolbar to apply a shadow effect.

The shadow is applied to the object.

● This example applies a perspective shadow.

ADD A 3-D EFFECT

1 Select the object to which you want to add a 3-D effect.

2 Click the **Shape Effects** button on the Format tab.

Note: In Word, you can click the 3-D Effects tool to display a palette of preset 3-D styles.

3 Click **3-D Rotation**.

4 Click a 3-D style.

Note: In Publisher, you can click the 3-D Style button ( ) on the Formatting toolbar to apply a 3-D effect.

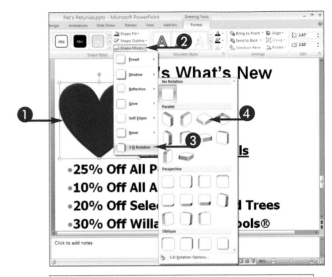

● The 3-D effect is applied to the object.

Note: You can also find preset 3-D bevel effects listed in the Preset category on the Shape Effects palette.

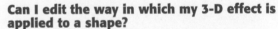

Here's What's New

February Specials
- 25% Off All Perennials
- 10% Off All Annuals
- 20% Off Select Shrubs and Trees
- 30% Off Willard Garden Tools®

TIPS

Is there a way to fine-tune a shadow effect?

Yes. You can click the **More Shadows** link, at the bottom of the Shadow palette in the Shape Effects or Picture Effects menu, to access the Format dialog box. Click the Shadow category in the dialog box to find options to adjust the shadow effect. These options include several settings for changing the angle and distance of the shadow effect. The dialog box also includes a button for changing the color of the shadow effect. You can experiment with the options to create just the right shadow for your object.

Can I edit the way in which my 3-D effect is applied to a shape?

Just like the shadow effect, you can fine-tune the 3-D effect using the 3-D Format category in the Format dialog box. Click the **Shape Effects** or **Picture Effects** button on the Format tab, click **3-D Rotation**, and then click **More 3-D Settings**. The dialog box includes a category for adjusting the rotation settings and the 3-D format.

Arrange Objects

You can control the placement of objects, such as AutoShapes, in your document to create different kinds of effects. For example, you might layer two shapes on top of each other to create a logo, or you might group several shapes together in order to move them around the document more easily.

Arrange Objects

CHANGE OBJECT ORDER

1 Double-click the object that you want to adjust.

● Handles appear around the selected object.

2 Depending on how you want to arrange the objects, click the **Bring to Front** or **Send to Back** button on the Format tab.

3 Click a placement.

The object moves forward or backward in the layer order.

● In this example, the heart shape now appears behind the banner.

GROUP OBJECTS

1 Click the first object that you want to include in a group.

● Handles appear around the selected object.

2 Press and hold **Shift** and click the next object that you want to include in the group.

You can continue clicking other objects to add to the group.

3 Click the **Group** button on the Format tab.

4 Click **Group**.

● The objects are grouped as one unit.

● A single set of handles replaces the multiple selection handles around the entire group.

TIPS

How do I align shapes?
You can use the Align controls in the Format tab of the Ribbon to align and distribute shapes evenly on the page. For example, you might want to line up three shapes on the left side of a document. To do so, select the first shape, and then press and hold **Shift** while selecting the additional shapes that you want to align. Next, click the **Align** button on the Format tab and click an alignment. The shapes align immediately.

Is there another way to select and group multiple objects?
Yes. If you have several objects scattered around a page, you can drag a selection handle around them to create a group. Simply click and drag across the page to include each object in the selection rectangle. When you release the mouse button after dragging across the objects, the objects are automatically grouped for you.

Control
Text Wrapping

You can control the way in which your document's text wraps around any object that you place on a page. For example, you might want the text to wrap tightly around a clip art graphic, or to make the text appear to overlap a shape.

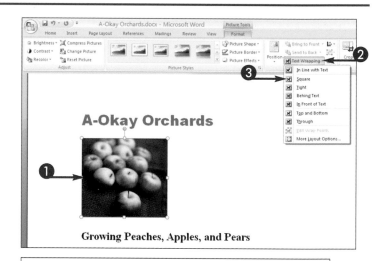

Control Text Wrapping

1 Click the object that you want to wrap.

2 Click the **Text Wrapping** button on the Format tab.

3 Click a wrap style.

The wrap style is applied.

● This example wraps the text squarely around the clip art object.

Note: Text wrapping is not available in PowerPoint.

Recolor
a Picture

You can use the Recolor command to quickly recolor a clip art object or a picture. For example, you might want to choose a color that matches the other elements in your document. You can choose from several preset color modes, in light and dark variations.

Recolor a Picture

① Double-click the clip art or picture that you want to edit.

② Click the **Recolor** button on the Format tab.

③ Click a color style.

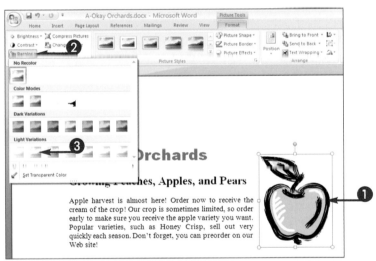

● The new color setting is applied.

Add SmartArt

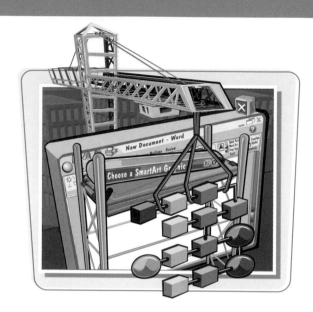

You can use the SmartArt feature to create all kinds of diagrams to illustrate concepts and processes. For example, you might insert an organizational diagram in a document to show the hierarchy in your company, or you might use a cycle diagram to show workflow in your department.

Add SmartArt

① Click the **Insert** tab.

② Click the **SmartArt** button.

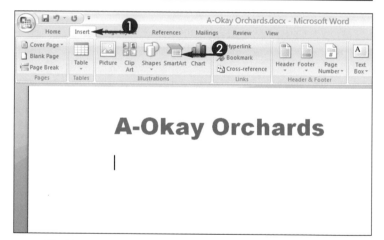

The Choose a SmartArt Graphic dialog box appears.

③ Click a category.

④ Click a chart style.

⑤ Click **OK**.

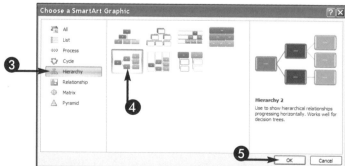

The diagram and placeholder text boxes appear, along with the Text pane.

6 Click in a text box, or click in the Text pane, and type the text for the item.

● You can change the layout here.

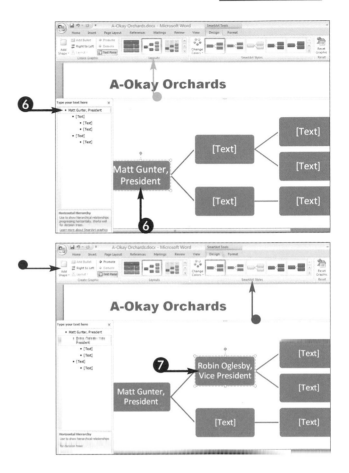

7 Continue typing text in each diagram text box.

● To add another text box and element to the diagram, click the **Add Shape** button.

● To change the shape style, click another shape from the SmartArt Styles group.

TIPS

Can I resize my diagram?

Yes. The diagram is an object that you can move and resize just like other objects in the Microsoft Office programs. To move or resize a diagram, see the "Move and Resize an Object" task. You can also use the control on the Diagram toolbar to change the sizing of the diagram layout, such as fitting the diagram to the contents or expanding the chart. Click **Layout** on the Diagram toolbar to view your options.

Can I change a shape's position or shape in the diagram?

Yes. To change the position, click the shape element in the diagram, and then click the **Promote** or **Demote** button in the Create Graphic group on the Design tab. To change the shape to a new shape, first click the shape to select it, then click the **Format** tab and click the **Change Shape** button in the Shape Styles group.

PART

Part II: Word

You can use Word to tackle any project involving text, such as correspondence, reports, and more. Word's versatile formatting features allow you to enhance your text documents with ease, and add additional elements such as tables or headers and footers. Word offers a variety of editing tools to help you make your document look its best. In this part, you learn how to build and format Word documents and tap into Word's many tools to preview, proofread, and print your documents.

Change Word's Views

As you work with Word, you can choose several ways to view your documents. For example, you can use the Zoom tool to control the magnification of your document. You can also choose from five different layout views: Print Layout, Outline, Web Layout, Full Screen Reading Layout, and Draft.

Print Layout view shows margins, headers, and footers. Outline view shows the outline levels in a document. Web Layout view displays a Web page preview of your document. Full Screen Reading Layout view optimizes your document for easier reading. Draft view shows a draft version of your document.

Change Word's Views

USE THE ZOOM TOOL

1 Drag the **Zoom** button on the Zoom bar.

● You can also click a magnification button to zoom in or out.

● Word applies the magnification to the document.

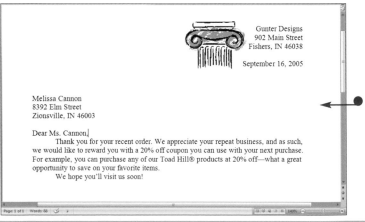

SWITCH LAYOUT VIEWS

1️⃣ Click the **View** tab on the Ribbon.

2️⃣ Click a layout view button.

Word immediately displays the new view.

● You can also switch views using the View buttons at the bottom of the program window.

● In this example, Print Layout view displays all of the positioning of text, graphics, and other elements on the page.

3️⃣ Click another layout view icon.

● In this example, Draft view displays the text without graphics or other elements.

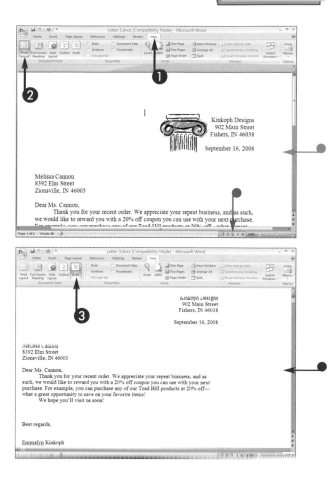

TIPS

How do I move through a Word document?

You can use the scroll bars to move up and down a document page, or you can use the keyboard keys. For example, you can press the arrow keys to move up, down, left, and right in the document, or you can press the Page Up and Page Down keys to move up and down in the document.

What can I do in the Outline view?

If you create documents built on a structure such as headings, subheadings, and body text, you can use the Outline view to see and make changes to the document structure. When you activate the Outline view, the Outlining toolbar appears. You can use the buttons on the toolbar to change heading styles and levels to modify your document's structure.

Type and Edit Text

When you launch Microsoft Word, a blank document appears, ready for you to start typing text. Whether you want to write a letter, a memo, or a report, you can use Word to quickly type and edit text for your project.

Type and Edit Text

TYPE TEXT

① Start typing your text.

● Word automatically wraps the text to the next line for you.

● The insertion point, or cursor, marks the current location where text appears when you start typing.

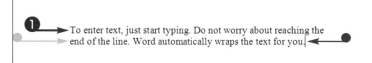

① To enter text, just start typing. Do not worry about reaching the end of the line. Word automatically wraps the text for you.

② Press **Enter** to start a new paragraph.

● You can press **Enter** twice to add an extra space between paragraphs.

● You can press **Tab** to quickly create an indent for a line of text.

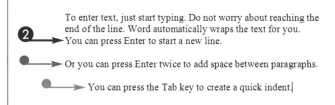

To enter text, just start typing. Do not worry about reaching the end of the line. Word automatically wraps the text for you.

② You can press Enter to start a new line.

● Or you can press Enter twice to add space between paragraphs.

● You can press the Tab key to create a quick indent.

EDIT TEXT

① Click in the document where you want to fix a mistake.

② Press `Backspace` to delete characters to the left of the cursor.

To enter text, just start typing. Do not worry about reaching the end of the line. Word automatically wraps the text for you. You can press Enter to start a new line.

Or you can press Enter twice to add space between paragraphs.

You can press the Tab key to create a quick indent.

③ Press `Delete` to delete characters to the right of the cursor.

You can also delete selected text.

Note: See the next task to learn how to select characters, words, and paragraphs in Word.

Note: If you make a spelling mistake, Word's AutoCorrect feature either corrects the mistake or underlines it in red.

To enter text, just start typing. Do not worry about reaching the end of the line. Word automatically wraps the text for you. You can press Enter to start a new line.

Or you can press Enter twice to add space between paragraphs.

You can press the Tab k to create a quick indent.

TIPS

How do I add lines to my Word documents?

If you type three or more special characters and press `Enter`, Word replaces the characters with a line style. For example, if you type three asterisks and press `Enter`, Word displays a dotted line. Use this table for more line styles that you can add:

Character	Line Style
*	Dotted line
=	Double line
~	Wavy line
#	Thick decorative line
_	Thick single line

What is the difference between Insert and Overtype mode?

By default, Word is set to Insert mode, which means that anywhere you insert the cursor and start typing, the existing text moves over for any new text that you type. If you switch to Overtype mode, any existing text is overwritten with the new text. To use the Insert key to toggle between modes, you must set the option in the Word Options dialog box. Click the **Office** button, and then click the **Word Options** button. Click the **Advanced** tab and view the Editing options. Click the **Use the Insert key to control Overtype mode** check box (☐ changes to ☑). Click **OK**. You can now press `Insert` to toggle between Insert and Overtype mode.

Insert
Overtype

You can select text in your document to perform different tasks, such as editing and formatting. For example, you can select a word and make it italicized, or select a paragraph to remove it from the document. Word offers several different selection techniques that you can apply to select a single character, a word, a sentence, a paragraph, or the entire document.

Select Text

CLICK AND DRAG TO SELECT TEXT

① Click to one side of the word or character that you want to select.

①

You can |select text in your document to perform different types of tasks, such as editing or formatting text.

② Drag the cursor across the text that you want to select.

Word selects any characters that you drag across.

You can use this technique to select characters, words, sentences, and paragraphs.

To deselect selected text, simply click anywhere outside the text or press any keyboard arrow key.

②

You can select text in your document to perform different types of tasks, such as editing or formatting text.

SELECT TEXT WITH A MOUSE CLICK

1 Double-click anywhere inside a word that you want to select.

Word selects the text.

You can also triple-click anywhere inside a paragraph to select a paragraph.

You can select text in your document to perform different types of tasks, such as editing or formatting text.

SELECT TEXT USING THE MARGIN

1 Click inside the left margin.

Word selects the entire line of text.

You can double-click inside the left margin to select a paragraph.

You can triple-click inside the left margin to select all of the text in the document.

You can select text in your document to perform different types of tasks, such as editing or formatting text.

TIP

Can I also use my keyboard to select text?

Yes. You can use keyboard shortcuts to select text in your document. You can use `↓`, `←`, `→`, and `↑` to move around the document. To select text, use one of these shortcuts:

To select a single word, press `Ctrl` + `Shift` + `←` or `Ctrl` + `Shift` + `→`.

To select a paragraph, press `Ctrl` + `Shift` + `↓` or `Ctrl` + `Shift` + `↑`.

To select all of the text from the cursor onward, press `Ctrl` + `Shift` + `End`.

To select all of the text above the current cursor location, press `Ctrl` + `Shift` + `Home`.

To select the entire document, press `Ctrl` + `A`.

Move and Copy Text

You can move text from one location to another in your document. You can also duplicate text and paste a copy in another spot on the page. You can use the Cut, Copy, and Paste commands to move or copy a single character, a word, or an entire paragraph.

Move and Copy Text

DRAG AND DROP TEXT

1 Select the text that you want to move or copy.

Note: See the previous task to learn how to select text.

2 Drag the text to a new location in the document.

To copy the text, press **Ctrl** while dragging.

3 Release the mouse button.

Word moves or copies the text.

---

1 Need to rearrange your text? Do you want to copy a word or sentence? You can move text from one location to another in your document. You can also duplicate text and paste a copy in another spot on the page. **2**

---

3 Need to rearrange your text? You can move text from one location to another in your document. Do you want to copy a word or sentence? You can also duplicate text and paste a copy in another spot on the page.

MOVE OR COPY TEXT WITH BUTTONS

1 Select the text that you want to move or copy.

2 Click the **Cut** button (✂) to move the text, or click the **Copy** button (📋) to copy the text.

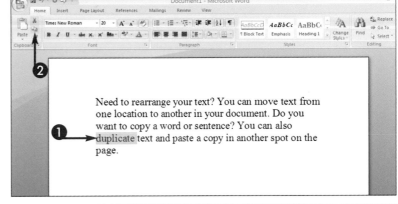

3 Click where you want to insert the cut or copied text.

4 Click the **Paste** button.

Word pastes the text in place.

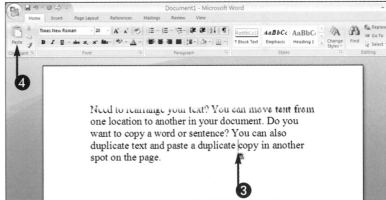

How do I use the smart tag to paste text?

As soon as you finish pasting text into place, Word displays a smart tag icon (📋) next to the pasted data. You can click the icon to display a menu of related moving or copying options for the text, such as copying formatting along with the text. You can click the smart tag to reveal the list of options. If you ignore the smart tag, it goes away when you continue working in the document.

What does the Paste button do?

You can click the **Paste** button on the Ribbon to reveal the three Paste commands: Paste, Paste Special, and Paste as Hyperlink. The Paste command simply pastes the data, while the Paste Special command opens the Paste Special dialog box, where you can specify a format for the pasted data. The Paste as Hyperlink command allows you to turn the pasted data into a link to the original data.

Insert Quick Parts

You can speed up your text entry tasks by using the new Quick Parts tool. For example, if you repeatedly type the same company name in your documents, then you can add the name to the list of Quick Parts entries. The next time you begin to type the name, you can reuse the entry from the Quick Parts Gallery.

Quick Parts are a part of Word's Building Blocks — preformatted content that you can add to your documents. Word installs with a wide variety of preset phrases that you can use, or you can create your own.

Insert Quick Parts

ADD A QUICK PARTS ENTRY

① Select the text that you want to add to the Quick Parts Gallery.

Note: *See the "Select Text" task, earlier in this chapter, to learn how to select text.*

② Click the **Insert** tab on the Ribbon.

③ Click the **Quick Parts** button.

④ Click **Save Selection to Quick Part Gallery**.

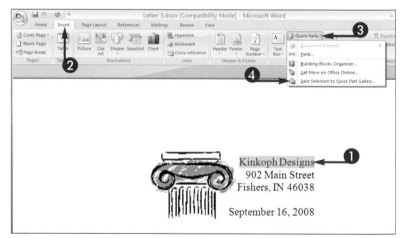

The Create New Building Block dialog box appears.

⑤ Type a name for the entry, or use the default name.

● You can also assign a gallery, a category, and a description for the entry.

⑥ Click **OK**.

INSERT A QUICK PART ENTRY

1. Click in the text where you want to insert a Quick Part.

2. Click the **Insert** tab on the Ribbon.

3. Click the **Quick Parts** button.

4. Click the entry that you want to insert.

Melissa Cannon
8392 Elm Street
Zionsville, IN 46003

Dear Ms. Cannon,

Thank you for your recent order. We appreciate your repeat business, and as such, we would like to reward you with a 20% off coupon you can use with your next purchase. For example, you can purchase any of our Toad Hill products at 20% off—what a great opportunity to save on your favorite items. As a favored guest at

We hope you'll visit us soon!

● Word inserts the entry into the document.

Melissa Cannon
8392 Elm Street
Zionsville, IN 46003

Dear Ms. Cannon,

Thank you for your recent order. We appreciate your repeat business, and as such, we would like to reward you with a 20% off coupon you can use with your next purchase. For example, you can purchase any of our Toad Hill products at 20% off—what a great opportunity to save on your favorite items. As a favored guest at Kinkoph Designs

We hope you'll visit us soon!

Best regards,

TIPS

Where can I find Word's preset building blocks?

You can insert building blocks from the Building Blocks Organizer. The dialog box keeps a full list of entries, including watermarks, pull quotes, and more. Building Blocks and Quick Parts are organized into galleries and categories. To display the dialog box, click the **Quick Parts** button on the Insert tab, and then click **Building Blocks Organizer**. To insert an entry, simply click it and click the **Insert** button.

How do I remove a Quick Parts entry?

You can remove a Quick Parts entry that you no longer need. Click the **Insert** tab, click **Quick Parts**, and then click **Building Blocks Organizer** to open the Building Blocks Organizer dialog box. Next, scroll through the list and select the entry that you want to remove. Click **Delete** to remove the entry, and then click **OK** to close the dialog box.

Apply a Template

You can use Word templates to speed up your document creation. Templates are ready-made documents that you can use to quickly assemble memos, letters, faxes, and more. Templates contain preformatted placeholder text. All you need to do is replace the placeholder text with your own.

Word installs with a variety of templates that are stored in the Templates folder, a subfolder found in the Microsoft Office folder on your computer. You can also download additional templates from the Microsoft Office Web site.

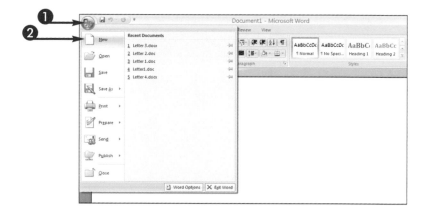

Apply a Template

1 Click the **Office** button.

2 Click **New**.

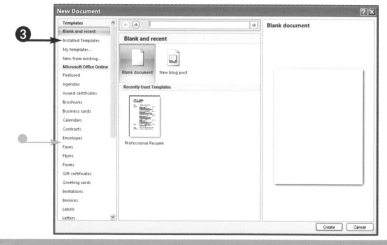

The New Document dialog box appears.

3 Click **Installed Templates**.

● If you are connected to the Internet, you can choose an online Office template from among these categories.

④ Click the template that you want to use.

● The Preview area shows a sample of the template.

⑤ Click **Create**.

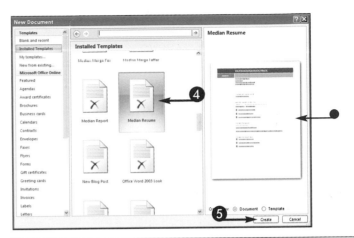

Word applies the template to a new document.

● You can click the placeholder text and start typing to add your own text to the document.

When you finish filling in the template, you can save the file just like any other Word document.

Can I create a custom template in Word?

Yes. You can turn any template into a customized template by saving the document as a template file type, which uses the .dot file extension. For example, you might want to save a memo with your department name and contact information as a template and reuse it for future memos. The easiest way to create a custom template is to base it on an existing template. In the New Document dialog box, click a template, and then click the **Template** option (○ changes to ◉) in the bottom corner of the dialog box before opening the document in Word. This creates a copy of the existing template. Add your own text and then save the file. The next time you want to use the document, you can find it listed among the available templates.

Insert
Symbols

From time to time, you might need to insert a special symbol or character into your Word document, such as a trademark symbol or an em-dash character. The Symbol palette displays several common symbols and recently used symbols that you can quickly reinsert. You can also use the Symbol dialog box to access a wide range of special characters and symbols, including mathematical and Greek symbols, architectural symbols, and more.

INSERT A SYMBOL

1 Click where you want to insert a symbol.

2 Click the **Insert** tab.

3 Click **Symbol**.

4 Click the symbol that you want to insert.

● Word inserts the symbol.

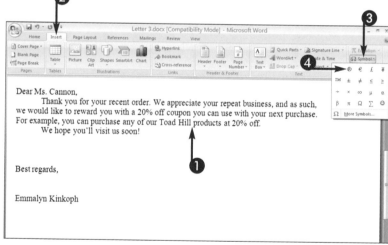

INSERT A SPECIAL CHARACTER

1 Click where you want to insert a character.

2 Click the **Insert** tab.

3 Click **Symbol**.

4 Click **More Symbols**.

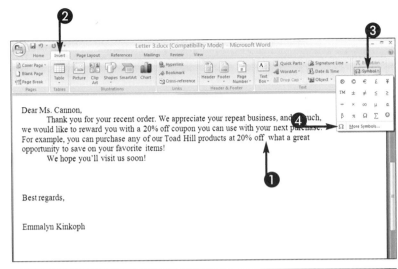

The Symbol dialog box appears.

5 To add a special character, click the **Special Characters** tab.

6 Click the character that you want to insert.

7 Click **Insert**.

● Word adds the character to the current cursor location in the document.

The dialog box remains open so that you can add more characters to your text.

8 When finished, click **Close**.

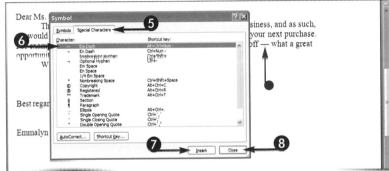

 TIPS

How do I change the display of listed symbols in the Symbols tab in the Symbol dialog box?

In the Symbol dialog box, you can click the **Font** ⬛ and click another font to change the list of symbols shown in the Symbols tab. For example, the Wingdings font includes a library of character icons, such as clocks and smiley faces, while the Symbols font lists basic symbols.

When I type some special characters on the keyboard, Word inserts a symbol for me. Why does this happen?

Word's AutoCorrect feature automatically inserts common symbols for certain keyboard combinations. For example, if you type (c), AutoCorrect immediately changes it to the copyright symbol, ©. To undo the occurrence, simply click the **Undo** button (🔄) immediately to return to (c). To learn more about AutoCorrect, see Chapter 8.

Create a Blog Post

You can use Word to help you create a document to post on your online blog. When you create a blog document, Word changes the Ribbon to display only the tools that are associated with creating a blog post document. You can take advantage of Word's many proofing and formatting tools to help you create your HTML page.

Create a Blog Post

① Click the **Office** button.

② Click **New**.

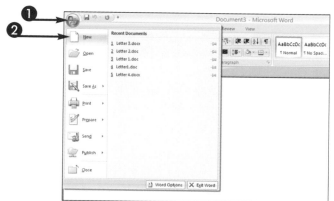

The New Document dialog box appears.

③ Click **New blog post**.

④ Click **Create**.

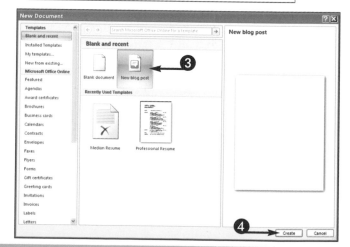

The first time that you use the blog feature, Word prompts you to register a blog account.

⑤ Click **Register Later** to create a blog account at another time.

● If you already have a blog account, click **Register Now** and follow the directions for registering the account.

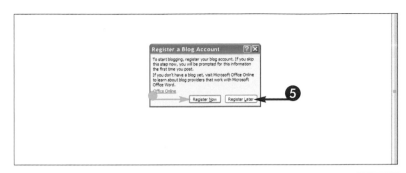

● Word opens the blog post document and you can start filling in your text.

● When you are ready to post your blog, click the **Publish** button.

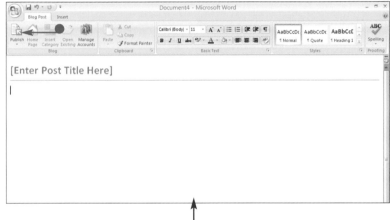

[Enter Post Title Here]

How do I edit my blog accounts?
You can click the **Manage Accounts** button on the Blog Post tab when viewing a blog page in Word. This opens the Blog Accounts dialog box where you can edit an existing account, add a new account, or delete an account that you no longer use.

Can I turn an existing Word document into a blog post?
Yes. If you create a text document first and then decide to use it as your blog post document, you can easily turn it into a blog page for publishing on the Web. To do so, click the **Office** button, click **Publish**, and then click **Blog**. Word immediately turns it into a blog file, and you can publish it to your online blog account.

Add Basic Formatting

You can use Word's basic formatting commands — Bold, Italic, and Underline — to quickly add formatting to your text. These three formatting styles are the most common ways to change the appearance of text in a document.

My Document

You can use Word's basic formatting commands – **bold**, *italic*, and underline – to quickly add formatting to your text. These three formatting styles are the most common ways to change the appearance of the text.

Add Basic Formatting

① Select the text that you want to format.

Note: See Chapter 4 to learn how to select text.

② Click the **Home** tab on the Ribbon.

③ Click a formatting button.

You can click **Bold** (B) to make text bold.

You can click **Italic** (I) to italicize text.

You can click **Underline** (U) to add an underline to text.

Word applies the formatting to the text.

● This example applies bold formatting to the text.

● To undo basic formatting, simply click the appropriate button again to toggle the formatting off, or click the **Undo** button (↺) on the Quick Access toolbar.

You can use keyboard shortcuts to quickly apply formatting. Press Ctrl + B to apply bold formatting, press Ctrl + I to apply italics, or press Ctrl + U to apply underlining.

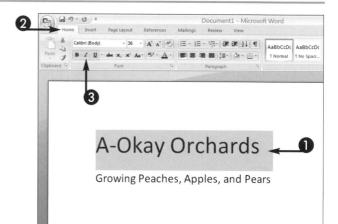

A-Okay Orchards

Growing Peaches, Apples, and Pears

A-Okay Orchards

Growing Peaches, Apples, and Pears

Word's new mini toolbar feature gives you quick access to common formatting commands. The mini toolbar appears faintly when you select text in a document. If you want to use the toolbar, you can activate its tools. If you prefer not to use the toolbar, you can continue working, and the toolbar disappears.

Use the Mini Toolbar

1 Select the text that you want to format.

Note: See Chapter 1 to learn how to select text.

● The mini toolbar appears faintly.

You can also right-click over the selected text to display the toolbar.

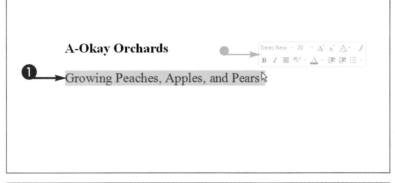

2 Move the mouse pointer over the toolbar and click the tool that you want to activate.

● Word immediately applies the formatting.

Change the Font

You can change the font to alter the appearance of text in a document. For example, you might change the font of the title of your document. By default, Word 2007 applies Calibri to every new document that you create. You can change the font by using the Font tool.

Change the Font

QUICKLY CHANGE THE FONT

1 Select the text that you want to format.

Note: See Chapter 4 to learn how to select text.

2 Click the **Home** tab on the Ribbon.

3 Click the **Font** ▾.

4 Click a font.

Note: With Word's Live Preview feature on, you can immediately preview any font in the list by moving over it.

● Word applies the font to the text.

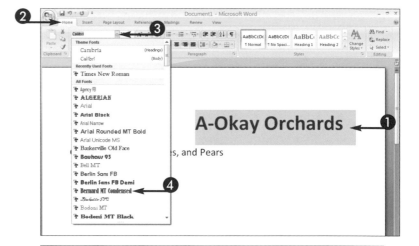

USE THE FONT DIALOG BOX

① Select the text that you want to format.

Note: See Chapter 4 to learn how to select text.

② Click the **Home** tab on the Ribbon.

③ Click the **Font Dialog** button (⬚).

The Font dialog box appears.

④ Click the font that you want to apply.

You can also use this dialog box to change the font style and size, and to apply other text effects.

⑤ Click **OK**.

● Word applies the font change.

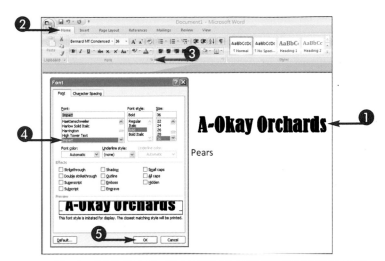

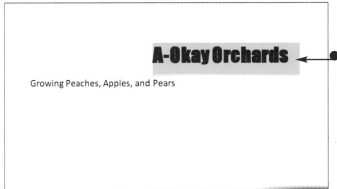

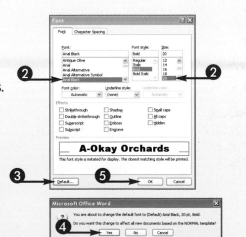

TIP

Can I change the default font and size that Word always applies to new documents?

Yes. To change the default font and size, follow these steps:

① Display the Font dialog box as shown in this task.

② Click the font and font size that you want to set as defaults.

③ Click **Default**.

A confirmation prompt appears.

④ Click **Yes**.

⑤ Click **OK**.

The next time that you create a new document, Word applies the default font and size that you specified.

Change the Font Size

You can change the font size to alter the appearance of text in a document. For example, you can increase the title text to appear larger than the other text in your document. Font sizes are measured in points. By default, Word applies a 11-point font size to every new document that you create. You can change the font size to suit your document needs.

Change the Font Size

QUICKLY CHANGE THE FONT SIZE

1. Select the text that you want to format.

Note: *See Chapter 4 to learn how to select text.*

2. Click the **Home** tab on the Ribbon.

3. Click the **Font Size** □.

4. Click a size.

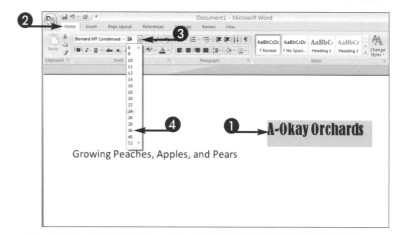

Word applies the font size to the text.

● This example applies a 36-point font size to the text.

USE THE FONT DIALOG BOX

① Select the text that you want to format.

Note: *See Chapter 4 to learn how to select text.*

② Click the **Home** tab on the Ribbon.

③ Click the **Font Dialog** button (⬚).

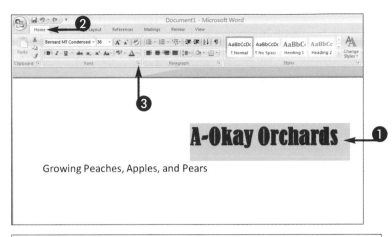

The Font dialog box appears.

④ Click the font size that you want to apply.

● You can use the scroll arrows to view the various sizes.

You can also type a size directly into the Size text box.

● You can also use this dialog box to change the font style and size, and to apply other text effects.

⑤ Click **OK**.

● Word applies the font size.

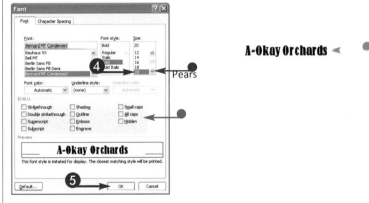

How do I apply superscript or subscript text?

You can apply superscript and subscript text for reference numbers or scientific coding. Superscript text appears smaller and slightly above the baseline, while subscript text appears smaller and slightly below the baseline. To apply superscript or subscript text, simply click the **Superscript** or **Subscript** buttons (⬚ and ⬚) on the **Home** tab of the Ribbon.

Is there another way to change my font sizes?

Yes. You can click the **Grow Font** and **Shrink Font** buttons (A̅ and A̅) on the **Home** tab to quickly change the font size. Word increases or decreases the font size with each click of the button. You can also find these buttons on the mini toolbar when you move the mouse pointer over selected text or right-click the text.

Add Color to Text

You can add color to your Word text to enhance the appearance of a document or to add emphasis to your text. When selecting text colors, you should avoid choosing colors that make your text difficult to read.

Add Color to Text

1 Select the text that you want to format.

Note: See Chapter 4 to learn how to select text.

2 Click the **Home** tab on the Ribbon.

3 Click the **Font Color** [▾].

4 Click a color.

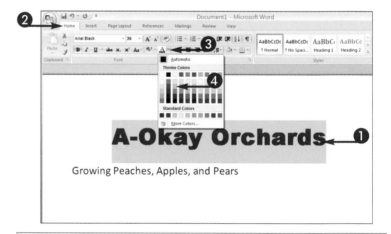

Word applies the color to the text.

● This example applies brown to the text.

Align Text

You can use Word's alignment commands to change how text is positioned horizontally on a page. By default, Word assigns the Left Align command. You can also choose to center your text on a page, align it to the right side of the page, or justify it so that it lines up at both the left and right margins of the page.

Align Text

① Select the text that you want to format.

② Click the **Home** tab on the Ribbon.

③ Click an alignment button.

Click the **Align Left** button (≡) to left-align text.

Click the **Center** button (≡) to center text.

Click the **Align Right** button (≡) to right-align text.

Click the **Justify** button (≡) to justify text between the left and right margins.

Word applies the alignment to the text.

● This example centers the text on the document page.

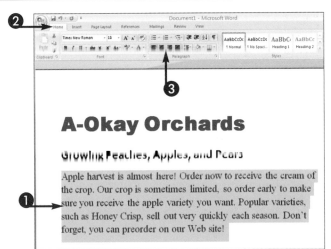

Set Line Spacing

You can adjust the amount of spacing that appears between lines of text in your paragraphs. For example, you may need to set double-spacing to allow for handwritten edits in your printed document, or set 1.5 spacing to make the paragraphs easier to read. By default, Word assigns single spacing for all new documents that you create.

Set Line Spacing

1 Select the text that you want to format.

2 Click the **Home** tab on the Ribbon.

3 Click the **Line Spacing** button (⬚).

4 Click a line spacing option.

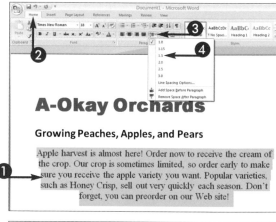

Word immediately applies the new spacing.

● This example applies 1.5 line spacing.

● To control the spacing that surrounds a paragraph, you can use the **Before** and **After** options in the Paragraph dialog box. Click the **Paragraph Dialog** button (⬚) to display the dialog box.

You can control the spacing that occurs between characters in your text. For example, you may want the title text of your document to appear stretched out across the top of the page, or you may need to condense the spacing to make the title text fit on one line.

Set Character Spacing

① Select the text that you want to format.

Note: See Chapter 4 to learn how to select text.

② Click the **Home** tab on the Ribbon.

③ Click the **Font Dialog** button (▣).

The Font dialog box appears.

④ Click the **Character Spacing** tab.

⑤ Click the **Spacing** ▾.

⑥ Click a spacing option.

● To decrease or increase the spacing, you can click ▴▾.

● You can see a preview of the spacing here.

⑦ Click **OK**.

Word applies the formatting to your text.

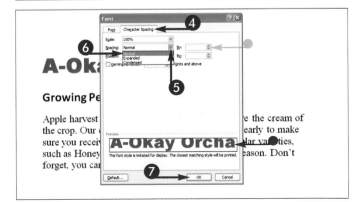

Apply
Color Shading

You can add color shading behind text to create emphasis or to set the text apart from the rest of the document. Word's Shading feature allows you to choose from a palette of complimentary theme colors for your document, or you can choose from standard colors.

Apply Color Shading

1 Select the text that you want to format.

2 Click the **Home** tab on the Ribbon.

3 Click the **Shading** button (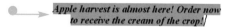).

4 Click a color.

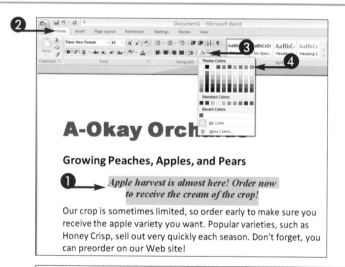

● Word immediately applies the shading behind the selected text.

You can use Word's Highlight tool to add highlighting to text in a document. For example, if you share a document with others, you can highlight a sentence or paragraph that you add to the page to draw attention to the new addition. You might also highlight text that you want a colleague to check. When you apply highlighting, you can specify a highlight color.

Highlight Text

① Click the **Home** tab on the Ribbon.

② Click the **Text Highlight Color** button ().

③ Click a color.

④ Click and drag over the text that you want to highlight.

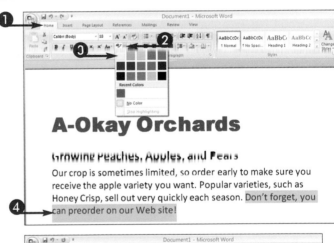

● Word applies the color highlighting to the text.

● To undo highlighting, you can select the text, click the **Text Highlight Color** button (), and then click **No Color** for the highlight color.

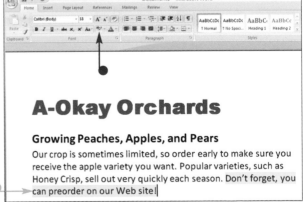

Copy Formatting

You can use the Format Painter feature to copy formatting to other text in your document. For example, you may have applied a variety of formatting to a paragraph to create a certain look. When you want to re-create the same look elsewhere in the document, you do not have to repeat the same steps that you applied to assign the original formatting. Instead, you can "paint" the formatting to the other text in one swift action.

Copy Formatting

① Select the text that contains the formatting that you want to copy.

Note: See Chapter 4 to learn how to select text.

② Click the **Home** tab on the Ribbon.

③ Click the **Format Painter** button (✅).

④ Click and drag over the text to which you want to apply the same formatting.

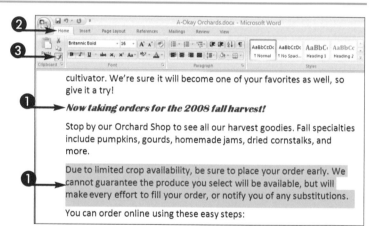

● Word immediately copies the formatting to the new text.

● To copy the same formatting multiple times, you can double-click ✅.

You can press Esc to cancel the Format Painter feature at any time.

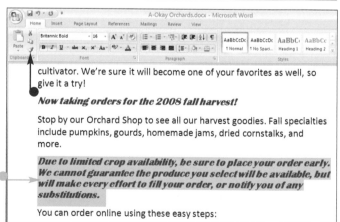

Clear Formatting

You can use Word's Clear Formatting command to remove any formatting that is applied to the document text. When you apply the Clear Formatting command, Word removes any formatting that is applied to the text, and restores the default settings.

Clear Formatting

① Select the text containing the formatting that you want to remove.

Note: See Chapter 4 to learn how to select text.

② Click the **Home** tab on the Ribbon.

③ Click the **Clear Formatting** button (🖺).

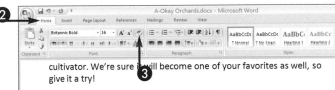

● Word immediately removes the formatting and restores the default settings.

Indent Text

You can use indents as another way to control the horizontal positioning of text in a document. Indents are simply margins that affect individual lines of text or paragraphs. You can use indents to distinguish paragraphs on a page.

Indent Text

SET QUICK INDENTS

1 Click anywhere in the text line or paragraph where you want to indent.

2 Click the **Home** tab on the Ribbon.

3 Click an indent button.

You can click the **Decrease Indent** button (🔲) to decrease the indentation.

You can click the **Increase Indent** button (🔲) to increase the indentation.

● Word applies the indent change.

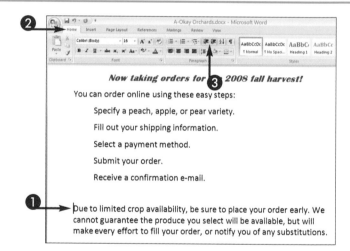

SET PRECISE INDENTS

① Click anywhere in the text line or paragraph where you want to indent.

② Click the **Home** tab on the Ribbon.

③ Click the **Paragraph Dialog** button (🔲).

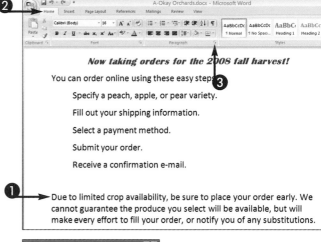

The Paragraph dialog box appears.

④ Type a specific indentation in the **Left** or **Right** indent text boxes.

● You can also click 🔼 to set an indent measurement.

● To set a specific kind of indent, you can click the **Special** 🔽 and then click an indent.

● The Preview area shows a sample of the indent.

⑤ Click **OK**.

Word applies the indent to the text.

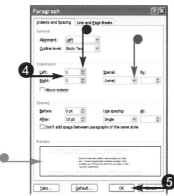

TIPS

What is the difference between an indent and a tab?

You can use tabs to create columnar text across a page, while indents control where a paragraph or line of text starts in relation to the margins. However, you can press Tab to quickly create an indent for a line of text or for the first line of a paragraph. By default, pressing Tab indents the text by 0.5 inches.

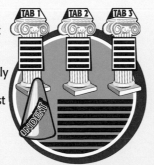

Can I set indents using the Word ruler?

Yes. You can drag the indent marker (📑) on the ruler bar to quickly set an indent. If the ruler is not displayed, move ⌖ over the top of the work area and pause. The ruler opens and displays markers for changing the left indent, right indent, first-line indent, and hanging indent. You can move ⌖ over the marker to identify the correct marker.

Set Tabs

You can use tabs to create vertically aligned columns of text in your Word document. By default, Word creates tab stops every 0.5 inches across the page, and aligns the text to the left of each tab column. You can set your own tab stops using the ruler or the Tabs dialog box. You can also change the tab alignment and specify an exact measurement between tab stops.

You can use tab stop alignments to control how text aligns. For example, you can align tab text to the right or center of the tab column, use a decimal tab to line up decimal points, or use a bar tab to set a vertical bar between columns.

Set Tabs

SET QUICK TABS

❶ Move ⌖ over the top edge of the work area, and pause to display the ruler.

● You can also click the **View** tab and click **Ruler** to turn on the ruler.

❷ Click the **Tab marker** area on the ruler to cycle through to the type of tab marker that you want to set.

  ▫ sets a left tab.

  ▫ sets a center tab.

  ▫ sets a right tab.

  ▫ sets a decimal tab.

  ▫ sets a bar tab.

❸ Click in the ruler where you want to insert the tab.

❹ Click the beginning of the text that you want to tab.

❺ Press Tab .

  Word applies the tab to the text.

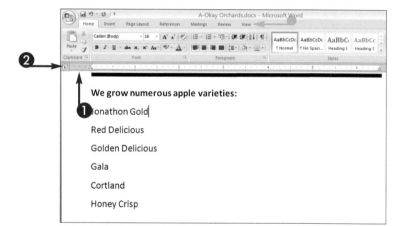

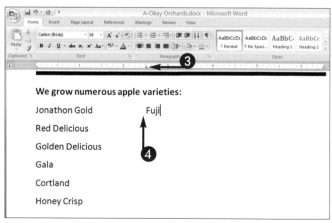

SET PRECISE TABS

1 Click the **Home** tab on the Ribbon.

2 Click the **Paragraph Dialog** button (⬚).

   The Paragraph dialog box appears.

3 Click **Tabs** on the Indents and Spacing tab.

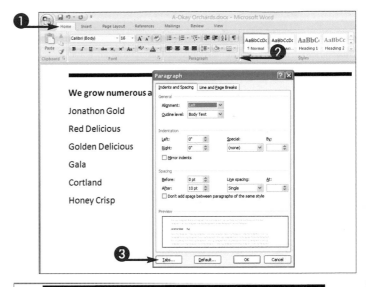

   The Tabs dialog box appears.

4 Click in the **Tab stop position** text box and type a new tab stop measurement.

5 Click a tab alignment (○ changes to ⦿).

● You can also select a tab leader character here (○ changes to ⦿).

6 Click **Set**.

   Word saves the new tab stop.

7 Click **OK**.

   Word exits the dialog box, and you can use the new tab stops.

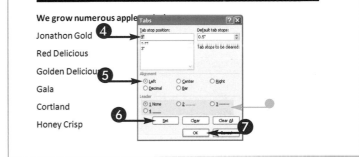

TIPS

How do I remove tab stops that I no longer need?

To remove a tab stop from the ruler, simply drag the tab stop off of the ruler. To remove a tab stop in the Tabs dialog box, you can select it, and then click **Clear**. To clear every tab stop that you saved in the Tabs dialog box, click **Clear All**.

What are leader tabs?

You can use leader tabs to separate tab columns with dots, dashes, or lines. Leader tabs can help readers follow the information across tab columns. You can set leader tabs using the Tabs dialog box, as shown in this task.

Create Bulleted or Numbered Lists

You can set off lists of information in your documents by using bullets or numbers. A bulleted list adds bullet dots in front of each list item, while a numbered list adds numbers in front of each list item. Bulleted and numbered lists can help you keep your information better organized.

Create Bulleted or Numbered Lists

SET QUICK LISTS

① Select the text that you want to format.

② Click the **Home** tab on the Ribbon.

③ Click a list button.

You can click the **Bullets** button (▤) to create a bulleted list.

You can click the **Numbering** button (▤) to create a numbered list.

You can click the **Multilevel** button (▤) to create a multi-level list.

Word applies the formatting to the list.

● This example shows a bulleted list.

To add more text to the list, you can click at the end of the line and press Enter; Word immediately starts a new line in the list with a bullet or number.

● To turn off a bulleted or numbered list, you can press Enter twice after the last item in the list, or click the **Bullets** (▤) or **Numbering** (▤) button.

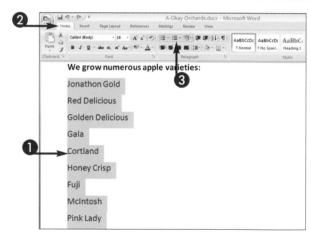

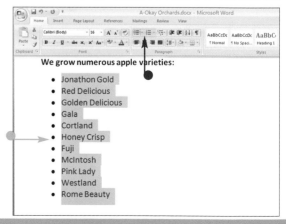

CHANGE BULLET OR NUMBER STYLES

1. Select the text that you want to format.

2. Click the **Home** tab on the Ribbon.

3. Click either the **Bullets** or **Numbering** 🔽.

4. Click a style.

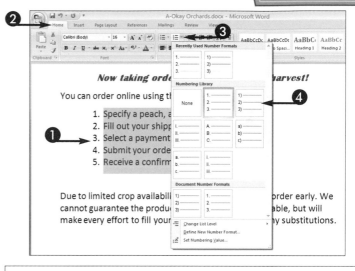

● Word applies the new style.

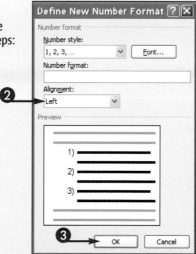

Can I customize a style?

Yes. You can create a customized style or control the positioning of bullets and numbers. Follow these steps:

1. Click the **Bullets** or **Numbering** 🔽 and then click **Define New Bullet** or **Define New Number Format**.

   The Define New Bullet or Define New Number Format dialog box appears.

2. Set any options for the format and position of the bullets or numbers.

3. Click **OK** to close the dialog box.

   Word applies the customized style.

Set Margins

You can control the margins of your document pages. By default, Word assigns a 1-inch margin at the top and bottom of a page, and a 1.25-inch margin on the left and right sides of a page in every new document that you create. You can set wider margins to fit more text on a page, or set smaller margins to fit less text on a page.

SET MARGINS USING PAGE LAYOUT TOOLS

1. Click the **Page Layout** tab on the Ribbon.

2. Click the **Margins** button.

3. Click a margin setting.

● You can click **Custom Margins** to create customized margins for a document.

● Word applies the new settings.

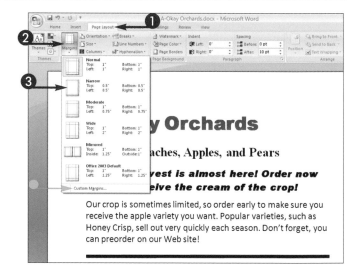

SET MARGINS USING THE RULER

① Move ▷ over the top edge of the work area and pause to display the ruler.

The ▷ changes to ↔.

② Click and drag a margin area to move a margin.

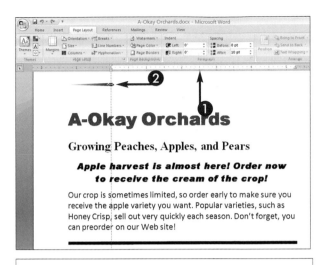

● Word immediately adjusts the margin in the document.

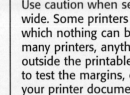

TIPS

How do I set new default margins for all of my Word documents?

If your company or organization consistently uses the same margins, you can choose those settings as the default for every new document that you open in Word. Click the **Margins** button on the Page Layout tab and click the **Custom Margins** option. This opens the Page Setup dialog box. Set the new margins using the options in the Margins tab, and then click **Default**.

I set new margins, but my printer did not follow them. Why not?

Use caution when setting margins that are too wide. Some printers have a minimum margin in which nothing can be printed. For example, with many printers, anything less than 0.25 inches is outside the printable area. Be sure to test the margins, or check your printer documentation for more information.

Format with Styles

You can use Word's styles to apply a collection of formatting specifications all at the same time. For example, if a corporate report requires specific formatting for every heading, you can assign the formatting to a style and apply it whenever you need it. This can save you time that you would otherwise spend assigning multiple formatting settings over and over again.

Word comes with a collection of preset styles that you can use. You can also customize the styles, as well as create your own new styles.

Format with Styles

APPLY A QUICK STYLE

1 Select the text that you want to format.

2 Click the **Home** tab on the Ribbon.

3 Click a style from the Styles list.

● You can click the **More** button (▾) to see the full palette of available styles.

Word applies the style.

● This example applies the Title style.

● You can click the **Change Styles** button to customize the style set, colors, or fonts.

CREATE A NEW QUICK STYLE

1. Format the text as desired and then select the text.

2. Click the **Home** tab on the Ribbon.

3. Click the **More** button (⬇) in the Styles group.

4. Click **Save Selection as a New Quick Style**.

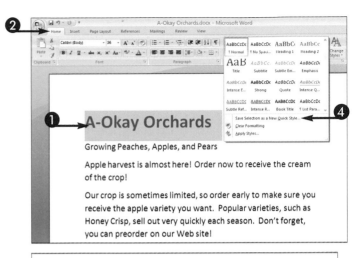

The Create New Style from Formatting dialog box appears.

5. Type a name for the style.

6. Click **OK**.

Word adds the style to the list of Quick Styles.

TIPS

How do I remove a style that I no longer need?

From the Home tab, display the full Quick Styles palette and right-click over the style that you want to remove. Click the **Remove from Quick Style Gallery** command. Word removes the style immediately from the Quick Styles list.

How do I customize an existing style?

Apply a style to your text and then leave the text selected. Click the **Change Styles** button on the **Home** tab, and then click the type of change that you want to make. For example, if you want to switch fonts, click the **Fonts** option and then select another font. If you want to change style colors, click the **Colors** option and then select another color set.

Insert a Table

You can use tables to present data in an organized fashion. For example, you can add a table to your document to display a list of items or a roster of classes. Tables are built with columns and rows that intersect to form *cells*. You can insert all types of data in table cells, including text and graphics.

After you create a table, you can use `Tab` to move from one cell to another, or you can click in the cell in which you want to add or edit data. As you type data, Word wraps the text to fit the current cell size.

Insert a Table

1 Click in the document where you want to insert a table.

2 Click the **Insert** tab on the Ribbon.

3 Click the **Table** button.

4 Drag across the number of columns and rows that you want to set for your table.

● Word previews the table as you drag over cells.

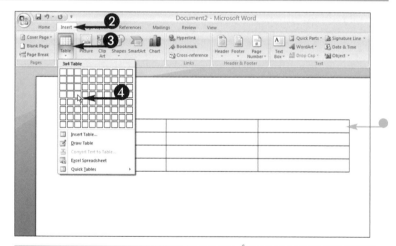

● Word adds the table to the document.

5 Click inside a cell and type your data.

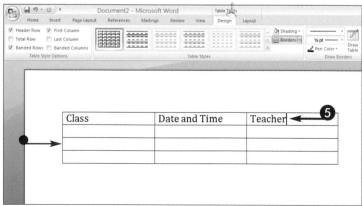

Insert a Quick Table

Word installs with a selection of preset tables that you can use in your documents. For example, you can insert a tabular-list style table, complete with subheadings, or a double table.

Insert a Quick Table

① Click the **Insert** tab on the Ribbon.

② Click the **Table** button.

③ Click **Quick Tables**.

● You can use the scroll bar to scroll through the available tables.

④ Click the table that you want to insert.

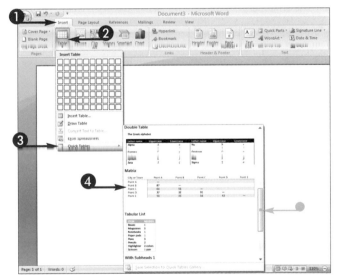

● Word adds the table to the document.

You can click inside a cell and replace the data with your own text.

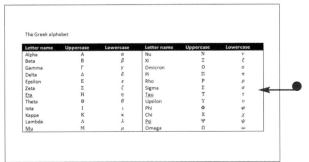

The Greek alphabet

Letter name	Uppercase	Lowercase	Letter name	Uppercase	Lowercase
Alpha	A	α	Nu	N	ν
Beta	B	β	Xi	Ξ	ξ
Gamma	Γ	γ	Omicron	O	o
Delta	Δ	δ	Pi	Π	π
Epsilon	E	ε	Rho	P	ρ
Zeta	Z	ζ	Sigma	Σ	σ
Eta	H	η	Tau	T	τ
Theta	Θ	θ	Upsilon	Υ	υ
Iota	I	ι	Phi	Φ	φ
Kappa	K	κ	Chi	X	χ
Lambda	Λ	λ	Psi	Ψ	ψ
Mu	M	μ	Omega	Ω	ω

Draw a Table

You can create a customized table by drawing the table size and controlling how the rows and columns appear in your table. Using the Table and Borders toolbar buttons, you can customize the line style, line thickness, and line color of the borders that you draw for your table cells.

Draw a Table

① Click the **Insert** tab on the Ribbon.

② Click the **Table** button.

③ Click **Draw Table**.

④ Drag across the document to draw an outside border for your table.

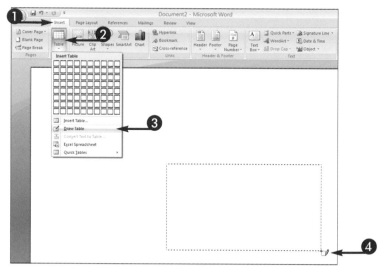

⑤ Drag an internal line to delineate a row or column in your table.

⑥ Continue adding inner lines to build your table cells.

● You can click inside a cell and type your table data.

● When you select the table, you can use the Design and Layout tabs to format and edit your table.

Note: You can find more drawing tools on the Design tab that appears after you create a table.

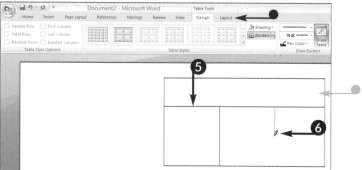

If Excel is installed on your computer, you can insert an Excel spreadsheet into your Word document. When adding an Excel spreadsheet, you can use Excel's features to add table data, including formulas and cell formatting controls.

Insert an Excel Spreadsheet

① Click the **Insert** tab on the Ribbon.

② Click the **Table** button.

③ Click **Excel Spreadsheet**.

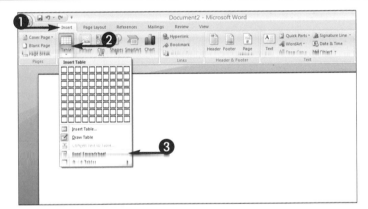

● An Excel spreadsheet appears, along with tools that are associated with the Excel program.

④ Click in a cell and type the data that you want to add.

● The Home tab displays tools for formatting your cells and data.

● The Formulas tab offers tools for building Excel formulas.

● You can click anywhere outside of the table to return to Word's tools and features.

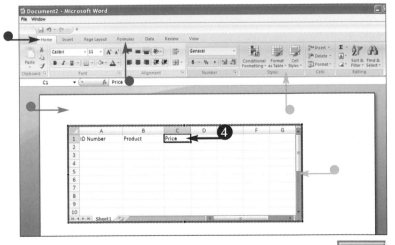

Select Table Cells

You can select table cells, rows, and columns in a table to perform editing tasks and apply formatting to all of the selected areas of the table. For example, you might select an entire column to apply bold formatting to all of the text in that column.

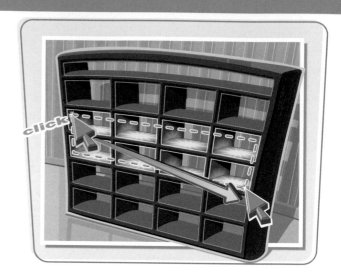

① Click and drag over the cells that you want to select.

② Release the mouse button to select everything that you dragged over.

● You can also use the **Select** tool on the Layout tab to select parts of your table.

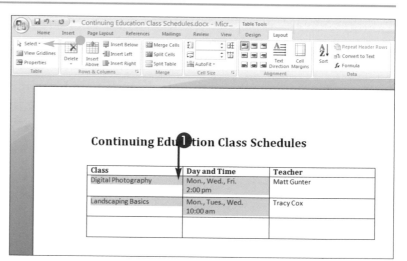

● To select a single cell, you can triple-click the cell to select everything in it.

● To select an entire column or row, you can move the mouse pointer near the border, and click.

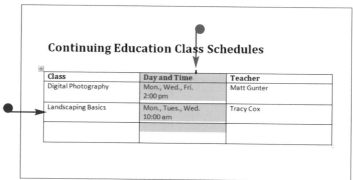

Adjust the Column Width or Row Height

After you create a table, you can control the sizing of the inner cells by adjusting the column width or row height. For example, you may need to make a cell wider to accommodate a long line of text, or you may need to make a cell large enough in depth to hold a particular graphic or chart.

Adjust the Column Width or Row Height

❶ Move the mouse pointer over the edge of the cell where you want to adjust the size.

The ⃕ changes to ‖.

❷ Click and drag the border in the desired direction to adjust the column width or row height.

If you drag the top or bottom border of a cell, the row height adjusts as you drag.

If you drag the left or right border of a cell, the column width adjusts as you drag.

❸ Release the mouse.

Word adjusts the column width or row height.

● This example widens the column.

Continuing Education Class Schedules

Class	Day and Time	Teacher
Digital Photography	Mon., Wed., Fri. 2:00	Matt Gunter
Landscaping Basics	Mon., Tues., Wed. 10:00	Tracy Cox

Continuing Education Class Schedules

Class	Day and Time	Teacher
Digital Photography	Mon., Wed., Fri. 2:00	Matt Gunter
Landscaping Basics	Mon., Tues., Wed. 10:00	Tracy Cox

Add Columns and Rows

You can add columns and rows to your Word tables to add more data. For example, you can insert a row to add another item to a list, or insert a column to add another header to a table.

1. Click in the row or column where you want to add another row or column, or select the row or column.

   If you select more than one row or column, Word duplicates the number when you activate the Insert command.

2. Click the **Layout** tab on the Ribbon.

3. Click an insertion option.

   You can click **Insert Above** or **Insert Below** to add new rows.

   You can click **Insert Left** or **Insert Right** to add new columns.

   ● Word adds a column or row to the table.

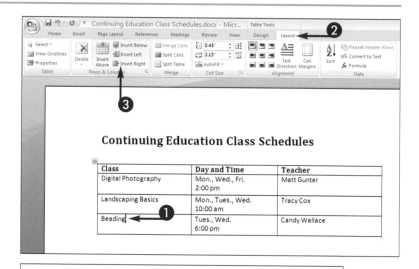

Continuing Education Class Schedules

Class	Day and Time	Teacher
Digital Photography	Mon., Wed., Fri. 2:00 pm	Matt Gunter
Landscaping Basics	Mon., Tues., Wed. 10:00 am	Tracy Cox
Beading	Tues., Wed. 6:00 pm	Candy Wallace

Continuing Education Class Schedules

Class	Day and Time	Teacher
Digital Photography	Mon., Wed., Fri. 2:00 pm	Matt Gunter
Landscaping Basics	Mon., Tues., Wed. 10:00 am	Tracy Cox
Beading	Tues., Wed. 6:00 pm	Candy Wallace

Delete Columns or Rows

You can remove a column or row that you no longer need in your table. When you remove a column or row, Word restructures the remaining cells to fill the void.

Delete Columns or Rows

① Click the row or column that you want to delete.

② Click the **Layout** tab on the Ribbon.

③ Click the **Delete** button.

④ Click a deletion option.

You can also right-click the column or row that you want to remove, and then click the **Delete** command.

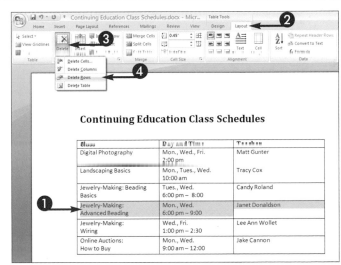

● Word deletes the column or row.

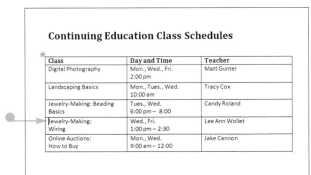

Merge Table Cells

You can combine two or more table cells to create a larger cell. For example, you might merge cells to create a title across the top of your table, or you may merge two interior cells to create one large cell for a graphic or chart.

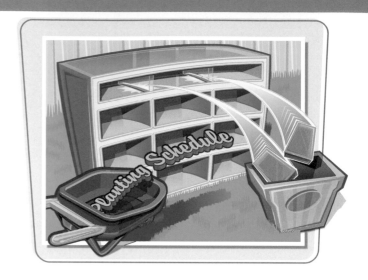

Merge Table Cells

1 Select the cells that you want to merge.

Note: See the "Select Table Cells" task, earlier in this chapter, to learn how to select cells.

2 Click the **Layout** tab on the Ribbon.

3 Click **Merge Cells**.

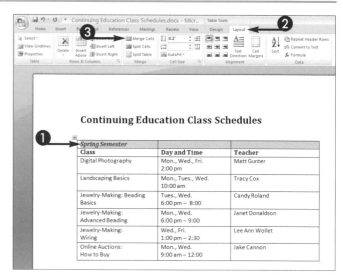

● Word creates one large cell.

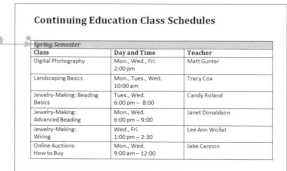

Split Table Cells

You can split table cells to create additional cells within your table. For example, you might split a cell in order to show two different choices in a column or row.

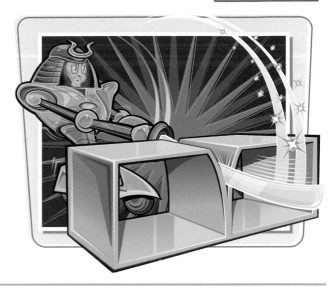

Split Table Cells

① Click inside or select the cell that you want to split.

Note: See the "Select Table Cells" task earlier in this chapter, to learn how to select cells.

② Click the **Layout** tab on the Ribbon.

③ Click **Split Cells**.

The Split Cells dialog box appears.

④ Designate how many columns or rows you want to create in the split cell.

● You can type a number, or click 🖫 to specify a number.

⑤ Click **OK**.

● Word splits the cell.

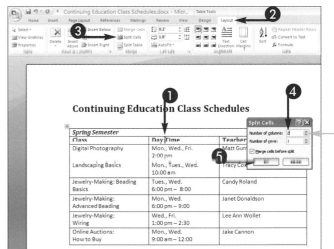

Apply Table Styles

You can add instant formatting to your Word tables by assigning one of the many formatting styles that are designed specifically for tables. Table styles offer a variety of designs that include shading and color, borders, and fonts.

Apply Table Styles

① Click anywhere in the table that you want to format.

② Click the **Design** tab on the Ribbon.

③ Click a style from the Table Styles list.

● You can click the **More** button (⬚) to display the entire palette of available styles.

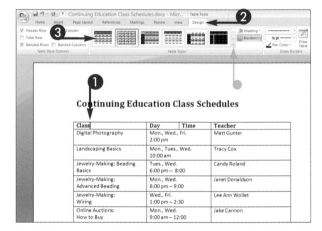

● Word applies the style.

● You can toggle table parts on or off using the Table Style Options check boxes.

● You can click these options to change the shading and borders.

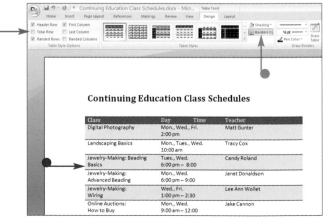

Change Cell Alignment

You can control the positioning of text within your table cells by using the alignment commands. For example, you may want to change the alignment for the column headings in a table. Word's table alignment options include the basic left, right, center, and justify alignments, as well as vertical alignments, such as bottom center or top right. By default, Word aligns your table text to the left, inside each cell.

Change Cell Alignment

① Select the cells that you want to format.

② Click the **Layout** tab on the Ribbon.

③ Click an alignment from the Alignment group.

Word applies the alignment.

● This example centers the headings in the cells.

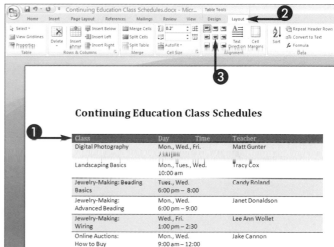

Reposition a Table

You can move a table around your document to better position it on a page. For example, you might position a smaller table off to the side of your document, or move a table to the top of a page.

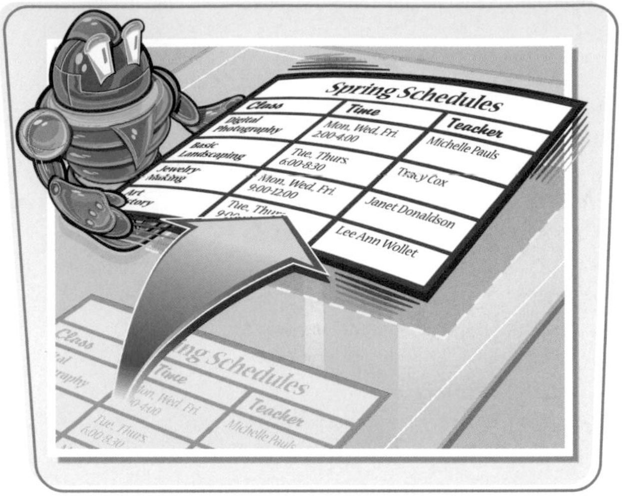

Reposition a Table

1. Move the mouse over the upper-left corner of the table.

- A selection handle appears.

  The ↖ changes to ✥ .

2. Click and drag the table handle to move the table to a new area in the document.

- A dotted line marks the table location as you move.

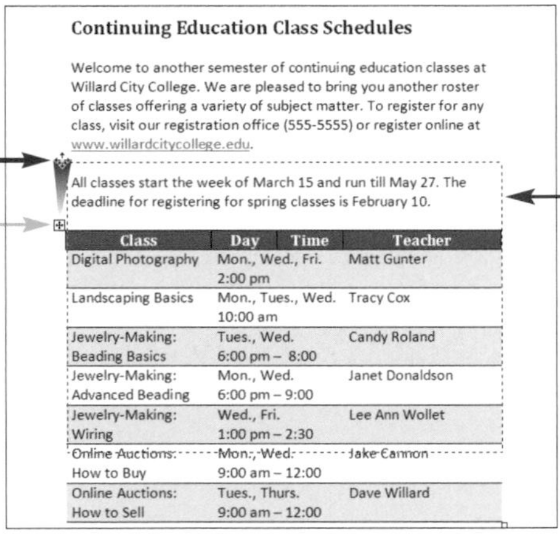

Continuing Education Class Schedules

Welcome to another semester of continuing education classes at Willard City College. We are pleased to bring you another roster of classes offering a variety of subject matter. To register for any class, visit our registration office (555-5555) or register online at www.willardcitycollege.edu.

All classes start the week of March 15 and run till May 27. The deadline for registering for spring classes is February 10.

Class	Day Time	Teacher
Digital Photography	Mon., Wed., Fri. 2:00 pm	Matt Gunter
Landscaping Basics	Mon., Tues., Wed. 10:00 am	Tracy Cox
Jewelry-Making: Beading Basics	Tues., Wed. 6:00 pm – 8:00	Candy Roland
Jewelry-Making: Advanced Beading	Mon., Wed. 6:00 pm – 9:00	Janet Donaldson
Jewelry-Making: Wiring	Wed., Fri. 1:00 pm – 2:30	Lee Ann Wollet
Online Auctions: How to Buy	Mon., Wed. 9:00 am – 12:00	Jake Cannon
Online Auctions: How to Sell	Tues., Thurs. 9:00 am – 12:00	Dave Willard

3. Release the mouse button.

   Word moves the table.

***Note:** You can control the text wrap around a table using the Table Properties dialog box. With the table selected, click the **Properties** button on the Layout tab to open the dialog box. Click the **Table** tab to view the text-wrapping options.*

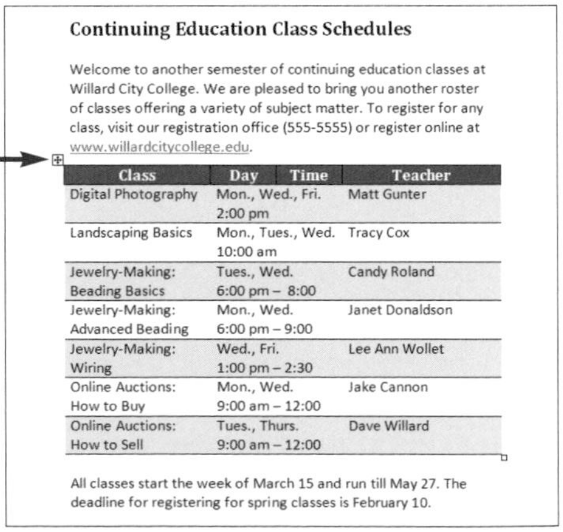

Continuing Education Class Schedules

Welcome to another semester of continuing education classes at Willard City College. We are pleased to bring you another roster of classes offering a variety of subject matter. To register for any class, visit our registration office (555-5555) or register online at www.willardcitycollege.edu.

Class	Day Time	Teacher
Digital Photography	Mon., Wed., Fri. 2:00 pm	Matt Gunter
Landscaping Basics	Mon., Tues., Wed. 10:00 am	Tracy Cox
Jewelry-Making: Beading Basics	Tues., Wed. 6:00 pm – 8:00	Candy Roland
Jewelry-Making: Advanced Beading	Mon., Wed. 6:00 pm – 9:00	Janet Donaldson
Jewelry-Making: Wiring	Wed., Fri. 1:00 pm – 2:30	Lee Ann Wollet
Online Auctions: How to Buy	Mon., Wed. 9:00 am – 12:00	Jake Cannon
Online Auctions: How to Sell	Tues., Thurs. 9:00 am – 12:00	Dave Willard

All classes start the week of March 15 and run till May 27. The deadline for registering for spring classes is February 10.

Resize a Table

You can resize a table to adjust its appearance in a Word document. For example, you may need to enlarge a table to make it more legible, or you may need to reduce the table size to fit it in with other text on the page.

Resize a Table

① Move the mouse over any area of the table.

● A sizing handle appears in the lower-right corner of the table.

The ⌖ changes to +.

② Click and drag the resizing handle to enlarge or reduce the table size.

Note: If you make the table too small, Word shortens the table width but tries to fit all of the text in each cell by increasing the table depth.

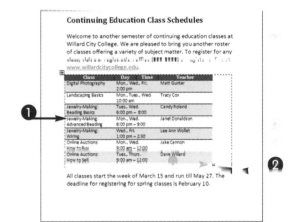

③ Release the mouse button.

Word resizes the table.

Note: You can control the text wrap around a table using the Table Properties dialog box. With the table selected, click the **Properties** button on the Layout tab to open the dialog box. Click the **Table** tab to view text-wrapping options.

Assign a Theme

You can use Word's themes to quickly add a professional look to your documents. Themes are predesigned sets of formatting that include backgrounds, color schemes, and fonts. Because themes are shared among the Office programs, you can use a theme in your Word document to match the same theme in worksheets that you create with Excel, or slides that you create in PowerPoint.

If you assign Word's styles, such as headings and subtitles, you can see the difference that an applied theme can make. The theme is even more pronounced when you assign a background color to a page.

Assign a Theme

APPLY A THEME

① Click the **Page Layout** tab on the Ribbon.

② Click the **Themes** button.

③ Click a theme.

● Word immediately applies the theme to the current document.

● You can use these tools to change the formatting of the theme's colors, fonts, and effects.

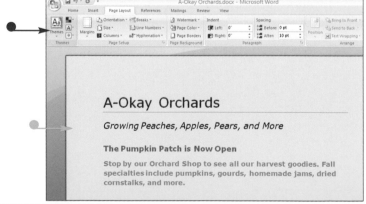

CREATE A CUSTOM THEME

① Apply a theme and edit the formatting to create the theme that you want to save.

② Click the **Page Layout** tab on the Ribbon.

③ Click the **Themes** button.

④ Click **Save Current Theme**.

The Save Current Theme dialog box appears.

⑤ Type a unique name for the theme.

● By default, Word saves the theme to the Document Themes folder so that it is accessible in the Themes Gallery.

⑥ Click **Save**.

Word saves the theme and adds it to the list of available themes.

TIPS

How do I apply a background color to my document?

To add a background color, click the **Page Layout** tab on the Ribbon and then click the **Page Color** button in the Page Background group of controls. When you click a color from the palette, Word immediately assigns it to the page.

Where can I find more themes to use with my Word documents?

You can visit the Office Web site to look for more themes that you can download onto your computer. Click the **Page Layout** tab, click **Themes**, and then click **Search Office Online**. If you are connected to the Internet, your browser opens and displays your default Web page to the Office Web site. You can then download any themes that you find and add them to the Document Themes folder, which is the default folder for all of the Office themes.

Add
Borders

You can add borders to your document text to add emphasis or make the document aesthetically appealing. For example, you can add a border to a paragraph to bring attention to the text. You can also add a border to the entire document page.

You should not add too many effects, such as borders, to your document because it will become difficult to read.

Add Borders

ADD A BORDER

① Click anywhere in the text, or select the text to which you want to add a border.

② Click the **Home** tab on the Ribbon.

③ Click the **Borders** button (⊞).

④ Click a border.

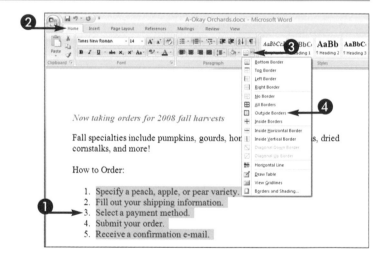

● Word applies the border to the text.

ADD A PAGE BORDER

1 Click the **Page Layout** tab on the Ribbon.

2 Click the **Page Borders** button.

● The Borders and Shading dialog box appears, and displays the Page Border tab.

3 Click the type of border that you want to add.

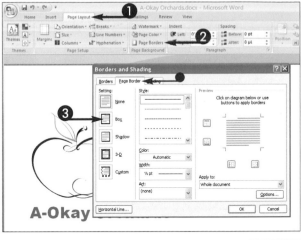

● You can use these settings to select a different border line style, color, and width.

● You can set a graphical border using this option.

● The Preview area displays a sample of the selections.

4 Click **OK**.

● Word applies the border to the page.

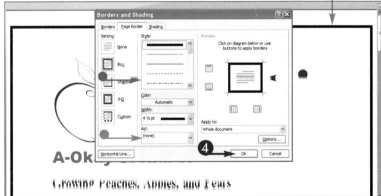

TIPS

How do I add shading to my text instead of a border?

To add shading behind a block of text, you can use the **Shading** tool (🖌), which is located on the Home tab with the Paragraph group of tools. Simply click the **Shading** button (🖌) and click a color to apply. Word immediately applies the shading to the selected text. To learn more about this feature, see the "Apply Color Shading" task in Chapter 5.

How do I create a custom border?

You can use the Custom setting in the Borders and Shading dialog box to create a custom border. For example, you might make each border line a different color or line thickness, or you might apply two different line styles to a border. To create a custom border, click the **Borders** button (▦) on the Home tab, and then click Borders and Shading. Next, click the **Custom** setting on the Borders tab and assign the options that you want to apply to the first line. Then click in the **Preview** area where you want the line to appear. You can repeat this process for each line that you want to add. When finished, click **OK** to apply the effects.

Create Columns

You can create columns in Word to present your text in a format similar to a newspaper or magazine. For example, if you are creating a brochure or newsletter, you can use columns to make text flow from one block to the next.

Create Columns

CREATE QUICK COLUMNS

1. Select the text that you want to place into columns.

2. Click the **Page Layout** tab on the Ribbon.

3. Click the **Columns** button.

4. Click the number of columns that you want to assign.

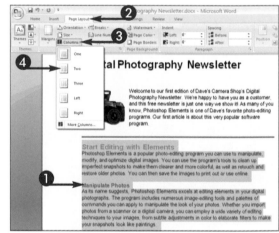

● Word immediately places the selected text into the number of columns that you specify.

CREATE CUSTOM COLUMNS

① Select the text that you want to place into columns.

② Click the **Page Layout** tab on the Ribbon.

③ Click the **Columns** button.

④ Click **More Columns**.

The Columns dialog box appears.

⑤ Click a preset for the type of column style that you want to apply.

● You can also specify the number of columns here.

● You can set an exact column width and spacing here.

● You can specify whether the columns apply to the selected text or the entire document.

● You can include a vertical line separating the columns.

⑥ Click **OK**.

Word applies the column format to the selected text.

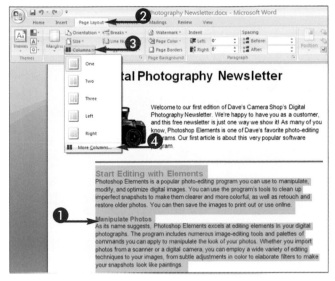

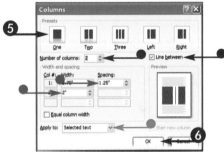

TIPS

How do I wrap column text around a picture?

You can control the text wrap for any object that you place in a Word document. To do so, right-click the picture or other object that you want to wrap, click the **Text Wrapping** command, and then click the type of wrapping that you want to apply. For example, Tight wrapping allows column text to flow neatly around the image, regardless of where you move the image in the column area. You can also control text wrapping for a selected object by using the Text Wrapping button on the Format tab.

How do I create a break within a column?

You can add a column break by first clicking where you want the break to occur and then pressing `Ctrl` + `Shift` + `Enter`. To remove a break, select it and press `Delete`. To return to a one-column format, click the **Columns** button on the Page Layout tab, and then select the single-column format.

Add Headers and Footers

You can use headers and footers to add text that appears at the top or bottom of every page. Headers and footers are useful for ensuring that every page prints with a page number, document title, author name, or date. Header text appears at the very top of the page outside the text margin. Footers appear at the very bottom of the page.

Headers and footers are built with *fields* that hold places for information that updates, such as page numbers or dates.

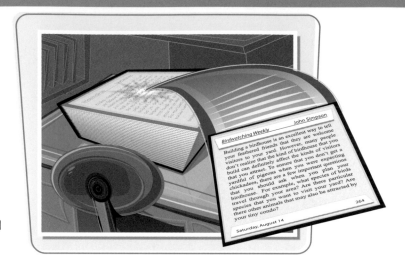

Add Headers and Footers

ADD A HEADER OR FOOTER

❶ Click the **Insert** tab on the Ribbon.

❷ Click the **Header** button to add a header, or click the **Footer** button to add a footer.

❸ Click the type of header or footer that you want to add.

This example creates header text.

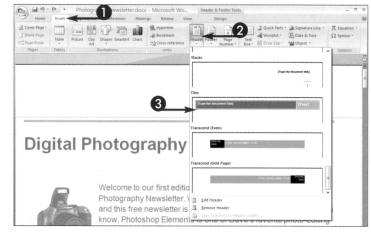

❹ To create header text, click the field in the header area and type your text.

● You can click the **Quick Parts** button to insert additional fields.

● You can insert more headers and footers using these controls.

❺ Click the **Close Header and Footer** button.

Word closes the Header and Footer tools.

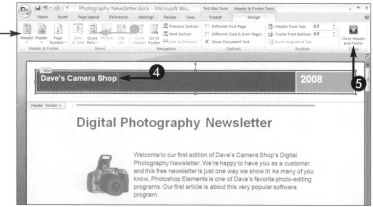

● Word displays the header or footer on the document page.

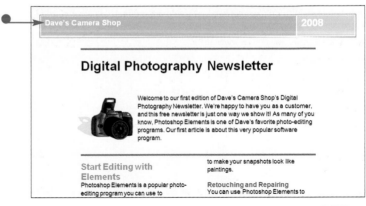

EDIT A HEADER OR FOOTER

① Click the **Insert** tab on the Ribbon.

② Click the **Header** or **Footer** button.

③ Click **Edit Header** or **Edit Footer**.

Word displays the Header and Footer tools, and you can now edit the header or footer text.

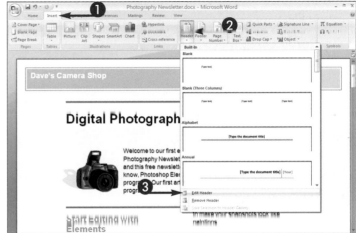

Can I remove a header or footer from the first page and keep it for the remaining pages?

Yes. To do so, click the **Header** or **Footer** button on the Insert tab, and then click **Edit Header** or **Edit Footer**. Next, click the **Different First Page** check box in the Options group (☐ changes to ☑). If you want to remove the header or footer for odd or even pages, click the **Different Odd & Even Pages** check box.

How do I remove a header or footer that I no longer want?

Click the **Insert** tab on the Ribbon and click either the **Header** or **Footer** button. Then click the **Remove Header** or **Remove Footer** command at the bottom of the menu. Word immediately removes the header or footer from your document.

Insert Comments

You can add comments to your documents to make a note to yourself about a particular section or task, or as a note for other users to see. For example, if you share your documents with other users, you can use comments to leave feedback about the text without typing directly in the document. Word displays comments in a balloon or in the Reviewing pane.

Comments are especially important if you and your colleagues use Word's tracking and revision features. To learn more about tracking and reviewing document changes, see Chapter 8.

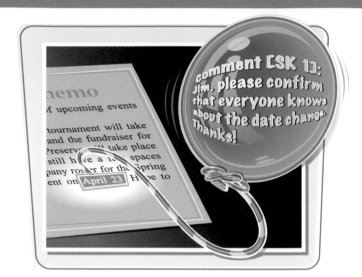

Insert Comments

ADD A COMMENT

① Click where you want to insert a comment, or select the text.

② Click the **Review** tab on the Ribbon.

③ Click the **New Comment** button.

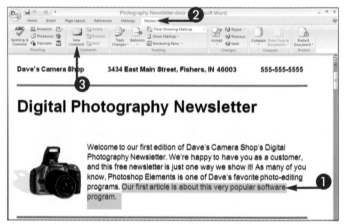

● A comment balloon appears.

④ Type your comment.

● You can use the **Previous** and **Next** buttons to navigate between comments.

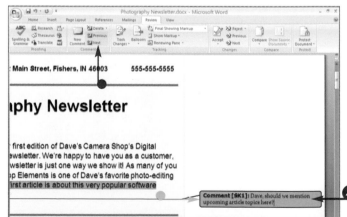

VIEW COMMENTS IN THE REVIEWING PANE

1 Click the **Review** tab on the Ribbon.

2 Click the **Reviewing Pane** button.

● Word displays the Reviewing pane, and lists all of the comments associated with the document.

You can click the **Reviewing Pane** button again to hide the pane.

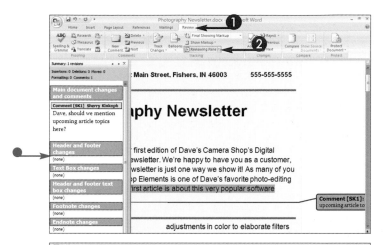

DELETE A COMMENT

1 Click the comment that you want to remove.

2 Click the **Delete** button on the Review tab.

You can also right-click over a comment and click **Delete**.

Word deletes the comment.

TIPS

How do I change the name used in my comments?

Click the **Review** tab on the Ribbon, and then click the **Track Changes** button. Click the **Change User Name** command to display the Word Options dialog box. Click to display the **Personalize** tab, click in the **User Name** text box, and then type a new name for your comments. Click **OK** to apply the change.

How do I respond to a comment?

You can respond to a comment by typing a new comment adjacent to the existing comment. Navigate to the comment using the Previous or Next buttons on the Review tab, and then click the **New Comment** button. Word inserts a new comment.

Insert Footnotes and Endnotes

You can add footnotes and endnotes to your document to include additional information. Footnotes and endnotes help identify sources or references to other materials. Footnotes appear at the bottom of a page, while endnotes appear at the end of the document.

Insert Footnotes and Endnotes

INSERT A FOOTNOTE

1 Click where you want to insert the footnote number.

2 Click the **References** tab on the Ribbon.

3 Click the **Insert Footnote** button.

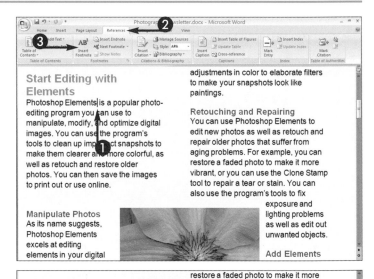

4 Type the note text.

● To return to the reference mark in the document, you can double-click the footnote number.

You can repeat these steps to add more footnotes.

INSERT AN ENDNOTE

1 Click the **References** tab on the Ribbon.

2 Click the **Insert Endnote** button.

3 Type your note text at the bottom of the last page of the document.

● The endnote number appears automatically.

To return to the reference mark in the document, you can double-click the endnote number.

How can I reset the footnote number in my document?

If you need to reset the number, perhaps for a new chapter in the document, you can open the Footnote and Endnote dialog box and specify a start number. Click the **References** tab on the Ribbon and click the **Footnote & Endnote Dialog** button (□) in the bottom-right corner of the Footnotes group. The Footnote and Endnote dialog box appears. Next, click inside the **Start at** text box and type a number, or use the spin arrow button (□) to set a new number. Click **Apply** to apply the changes to the document.

What other referencing tools can I use in Word?

The References tab offers several other referencing tools that you can apply to your documents, such as indexing features, citation and bibliography tools, captioning tools, and cross-reference features. For example, you can use the Insert Caption button to set a caption for a figure or table in your document. See the Word Help files to learn more about the other available referencing tools.

Insert Page Numbers and Page Breaks

You can add page numbers and page breaks to your documents to make the pages more manageable. For example, adding page numbers to longer documents can help you keep the pages in order after printing. Adding page breaks can help you control which text appears on which page of the document. Page numbers are added to the header or footer area of the document.

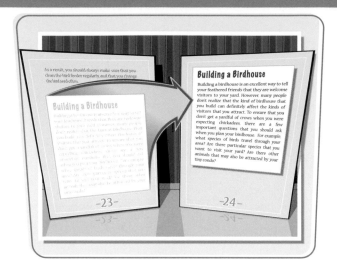

Insert Page Numbers and Page Breaks

INSERT PAGE NUMBERS

1. Click the **Insert** tab on the Ribbon.
2. Click the **Page Number** button.
3. Click a location for the page numbers.
4. Click a page number style.

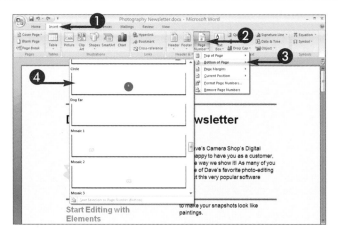

- Word assigns page numbers to your document.

5. Click **Close Header and Footer** to exit the header or footer area.

Note: See the "Add Headers and Footers" task to learn more.

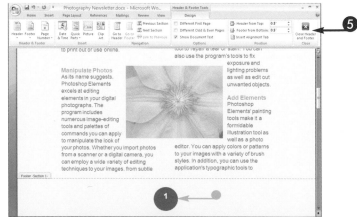

INSERT PAGE BREAKS

1 Click in the document where you want to insert a page break.

2 Click the **Insert** tab on the Ribbon.

3 Click the **Page Break** button.

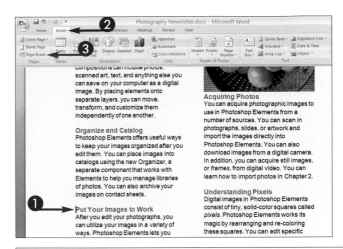

● Word assigns the page break.

Is there a faster way to insert a page break?

Yes. You can use keyboard shortcuts to quickly insert a page break as you type in your document. You can insert a manual page break by pressing Ctrl + Enter . You can also insert a soft break by pressing Shift + Enter .

Can I change the number style that is used in my document's page numbers?

Yes. Click the **Page Number** button on the Insert tab, and then click **Format Page Numbers**. This opens the Page Number Format dialog box. You can change the number style to Roman numerals, alphabetical numbering, and more. You can also include chapter numbers with your page numbers.

Add a Watermark

You can add a watermark to your document pages to appear faintly behind the text of your printed documents. For example, you might add a watermark to your memo that reads CONFIDENTIAL or URGENT. Watermarks can be text or pictures.

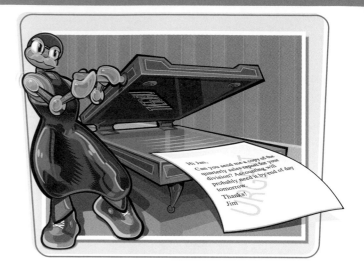

APPLY A WATERMARK

1 Click the **Page Layout** tab on the Ribbon.

2 Click the **Watermark** button.

3 Click the watermark that you want to apply.

● You can use the scroll bar to scroll through all of the available choices.

● Word adds the watermark to every page in your document.

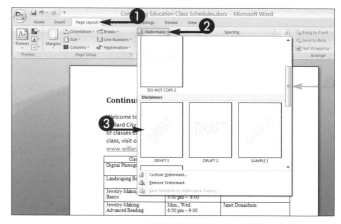

CREATE A CUSTOM WATERMARK

1. Click the **Page Layout** tab on the Ribbon.

2. Click the **Watermark** button.

3. Click **More Watermarks**.

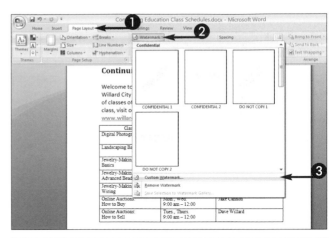

The Printed Watermark dialog box appears.

4. Click the type of watermark that you want to create (○ changes to ◉), and set any options for the watermark.

5. Click **Apply** to see a preview of the effect.

6. Click **Close**.

● Word adds the watermark to every page in your document.

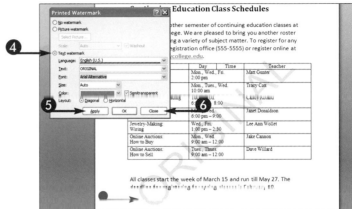

 TIPS

How do I remove a watermark that I no longer want?

Click the **Page Layout** tab on the Ribbon and then click the **Watermark** button. Click **Remove Watermark**. Word removes the watermark from the document.

How do I assign a picture as a watermark?

To set a picture watermark instead of a text watermark, click the **Picture watermark** option (○ changes to ◉) in the Printed Watermark dialog box, and then click **Select Picture** to open the Insert Picture dialog box. Locate the file that you want to use and then return to the Printed Watermark dialog box to set any additional options for the image.

Find and
Replace Text

You can use Word's Find tool to search your document for a particular word or phrase. You can use the Replace tool to replace instances of a word or phrase with other text. For example, you may need to search through a long document to replace a reference with another name.

Find and Replace Text

FIND TEXT

1 Click at the beginning of your document.

2 Click the **Home** tab on the Ribbon.

3 Click the **Find** button.

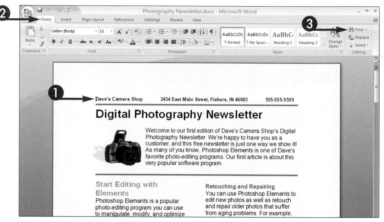

● The Find and Replace dialog box appears, displaying the Find tab.

4 Type the text that you want to find.

5 Click **Find Next** or press Enter .

● Word searches the document and finds the first occurrence of the text.

You can click **Find Next** again to search for the next occurrence.

6 When finished, click **Cancel**.

Note: If Word displays a prompt box when the last occurrence is found, click OK.

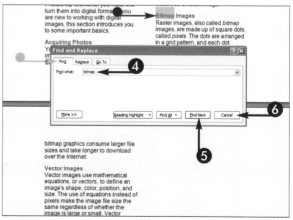

REPLACE TEXT

1 Click at the beginning of your document.

2 Click the **Home** tab on the Ribbon.

3 Click the **Replace** button.

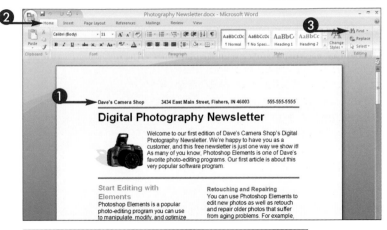

4 In the Replace tab of the Find and Replace dialog box, type the text that you want to find.

5 Type replacement text.

6 Click **Find Next**.

● Word locates the first occurrence.

7 Click **Replace** to replace the occurrence.

● To replace every occurrence in the document, you can click **Replace All**.

8 When finished, click **Cancel**.

Note: If Word displays a prompt box when the last occurrence is found, click **OK**.

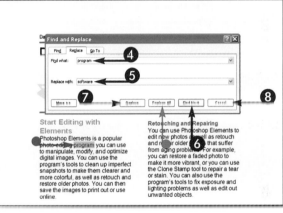

TIPS

Where can I find detailed search options?

You can click **More** in the Find and Replace dialog box to reveal additional search options that you can apply. For example, you can search for matching text case, whole words, and more. You can also search for specific formatting or special characters by clicking **Format** and **Special**. To hide the additional search options, click **Less**.

How can I search for and delete text?

You can search for a particular word or phrase using the Find and Replace dialog box, and remove the text completely from the document. Start by typing the text in the Find what text field. Leave the Replace with text field empty. When you activate the search, Word looks for the text and deletes it without adding new text to the document.

Check Spelling and Grammar

You can use Word's Spelling and Grammar check features to review your document for spelling and grammatical errors. Although both features are helpful, they are never a substitute for good proofreading with your own eyes. Both features can catch some errors, but not all, so you should take time to read over your documents for misspellings.

By default, Word automatically checks for spelling and grammar problems. Misspellings appear underlined with a red wavy line. Potential grammar errors are underlined with a green wavy line.

Check Spelling and Grammar

CORRECT A MISTAKE

1 When you encounter a spelling or grammar problem, right-click the underlined text.

The menu that appears shows possible corrections.

2 Click a correction from the menu.

● To ignore the error, you can click **Ignore** or click **Ignore All** for all instances of the error.

● To add the word to the built-in dictionary, you can click **Add to Dictionary**.

RUN THE SPELL CHECKER

1 Click the **Review** tab on the Ribbon.

2 Click the **Spelling & Grammar** button.

To check only a section of your document, you can select the section before activating the spell check.

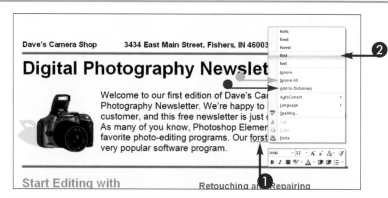

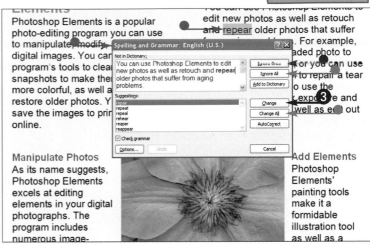

- Word searches the document for any mistakes and displays the Spelling and Grammar dialog box if it finds an error.

3 Click **Change** to make a correction.

- To correct all of the misspellings of the same word, you can click **Change All**.

- To ignore the error one time, you can click **Ignore Once**.

- To ignore every occurrence, you can click **Ignore All** or **Ignore Rule**.

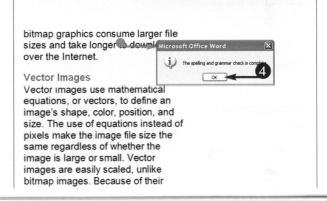

- When the spell check is complete, a prompt box appears.

4 Click **OK**.

 TIP

How do I turn the automatic spelling and grammar checking off?

To turn off the automatic checking features, open the Word Options dialog box. Then, follow these steps:

1 Click the **Office** button.

2 Click the **Word Options** button.

The Word Options dialog box appears.

3 Click the **Proofing** tab.

4 Under the When Correcting Spelling in Word options, click **Check spelling as you type** (☑ changes to ☐).

5 Under the When Correcting Grammar in Word options, click **Mark grammar errors as you type** (☑ changes to ☐).

6 Click **OK**.

Word turns off the automatic checking features.

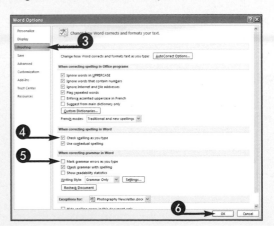

Work with AutoCorrect

You can use the AutoCorrect feature to quickly correct words that you commonly misspell. For example, if you continually mistype the same term, you can add the word to the AutoCorrect dictionary. The next time you mistype the word, AutoCorrect fixes your mistake for you.

You may have already noticed the AutoCorrect feature working as you typed in a document. This feature performs corrections automatically. Although AutoCorrect comes with a list of preset misspellings, the list is not comprehensive. To speed up your own text entry tasks, you can add your own problem words to the list.

Work with AutoCorrect

ADD A MISSPELLING

① Click the **Office** button.

② Click **Word Options**.

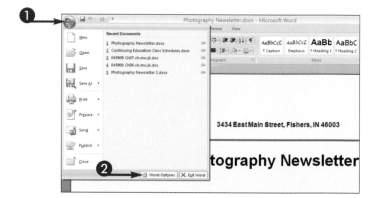

The Word Options dialog box appears.

③ Click the **Proofing** tab.

④ Click **AutoCorrect Options**.

● The AutoCorrect dialog box appears, displaying the AutoCorrect tab.

⑤ Type the common misspelling in the Replace text field.

Be sure to type the word exactly as you normally misspell it.

⑥ Type the correct spelling in the With text field.

⑦ Click **Add**.

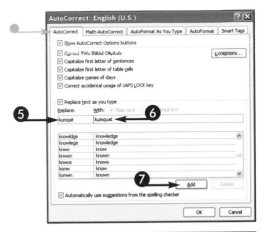

● AutoCorrect adds the word to the list.

You can repeat Steps **5** to **7** to add more words to the list, as needed.

⑧ Click **Close** to exit the dialog box.

⑨ Click **OK** to exit the Word Options dialog box.

The next time that you misspell the word, AutoCorrect corrects it for you.

Note: *If you type text that you do not want to be corrected, press* Ctrl *+* Z *to undo AutoCorrect before you continue typing anything else.*

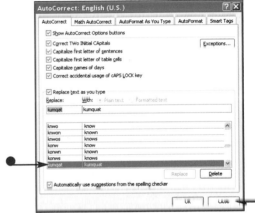

TIPS

How do I remove or edit a word from the AutoCorrect list?

Open the AutoCorrect dialog box as shown in this task and display the AutoCorrect tab. Click the word that you want to remove, and then click **Delete**. To edit a word, select it from the list and make your change to the Replace or With text fields. Click **OK** to exit the dialog box and apply your changes.

Can I customize how the AutoCorrect feature works?

Yes. You can select or deselect search options for AutoCorrect, such as typing two initial caps or capitalizing the first letter of a sentence. To control any of the AutoCorrect options, you must first open the AutoCorrect dialog box, as shown in the steps in this task. You can find the options in the AutoCorrect tab. You can also turn the AutoCorrect feature off by clicking the **Replace text as you type** check box (☑ changes to ☐). Click **OK** to exit the dialog box and apply your changes.

Use the Thesaurus

You can use the Word Thesaurus to help you find just the right word to use in your document. The Thesaurus is just one of several research tools that you can use to build better documents.

❶ Select the word that you want to look up.

❷ Click the **Review** tab on the Ribbon.

❸ Click the **Thesaurus** button.

● The Research task pane opens and displays suggested replacements for the word.

● To replace the selected word with a word from the Thesaurus, you can click the word, click ⌄, and then click **Insert**.

● You can click the **Close** button (⨯) to close the pane.

Before sending or sharing your documents with others, you can check them over for different types of hidden or personal data. When you save a document, certain hidden information, called metadata, is saved with the file. This information can include data about your company or other information that you may not want made public. By removing metadata, you can keep your file secure.

Metadata
The Acme Company
George Gomez, Marketing Di...
Alice Fewmet, Project...

Hi George:
Please submit a list of suggestio
our marketing campaign at the
Quarterly meeting on Sept 10.
You and your team always hav
great ideas....we'll be looking fo
...ing your presentation.
thanks,

Check Your Document for Hidden or Personal Data

① Click the **Office** button.

② Click **Prepare**.

③ Click **Inspect Document**.

The Document Inspector dialog box appears.

④ Click the types of data that you want to search (☐ changes to ☑).

⑤ Click **Inspect**.

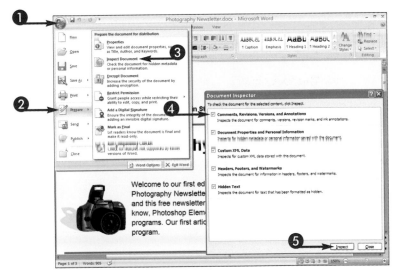

The Document Inspector checks the document and displays any inspection results.

⑥ Click **Remove All** to remove the information.

⑦ Click **Close**.

Track and Review Document Changes

If you work in an environment in which you share your Word documents with others, you can use the track and review features to help you keep track of who adds changes to the file. For example, you can see what edits others have made, including formatting changes and text additions or deletions.

The tracking feature changes the color for each person's edits, making it easy to see who changed what in the document. When you review the document, you can choose to accept or reject the changes.

Track and Review Document Changes

TURN ON TRACKING

① Click the **Review** tab on the Ribbon.

② Click the **Track Changes** button.

③ Click **Track Changes**.

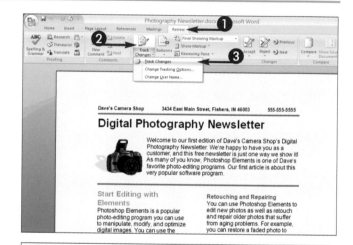

Word activates the Track Changes feature.

④ Edit the document.

● Any changes that you make appear underlined and in color.

● Word marks the deleted text with a strikethrough.

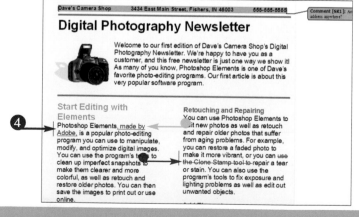

REVIEW CHANGES

1 Click the top of the document.

2 Click the **Review** tab on the Ribbon.

3 Click the **Reviewing Pane** button.

● The Reviewing pane opens.

The Reviewing pane shows each person's edits, including the user's name and when they added any edits and comments.

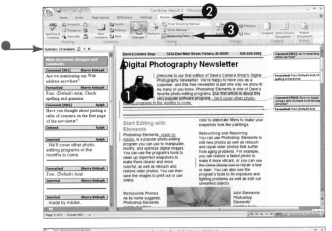

4 Click the **Next** button.

● Word displays the next edit.

● You can click the **Accept** button to add the change to the final document.

● You can click the **Reject** button to reject the change.

5 When you complete the review, click the **Track Changes** button to turn the feature off.

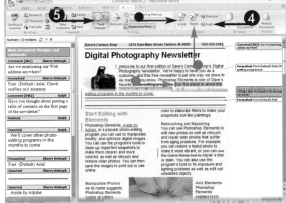

TIPS

How can I customize the markup options?

You can customize what color appears for your edits by using the Change Tracking Options dialog box. On the **Review** tab, click the **Track Changes** button, and then click **Change Tracking Options**. This opens the Track Changes dialog box, where you can make changes to the tracking color, formatting, and more.

Can I control which markup elements appear in a document?

Yes. You can click the **Show Markup** button on the Reviewing tab to select which elements you want to include in the review. For example, you may want to hide comments or review marks for a particular user.

E-mail a Document

You can e-mail a document without leaving the Word program. If you use Microsoft Outlook as your e-mail editor, you can use the program's features to insert e-mail addresses and send a Word document as an e-mail message.

You may need to log on to your Internet account before sending an e-mail message from Word.

E-mail a Document

① Click the **Office** button.

② Click **Send**.

③ Click **E-mail**.

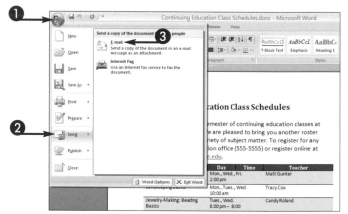

An Outlook message window appears with the current document attached.

④ Type the recipient's e-mail address.

● You can click **To** to access the Outlook Address Book and retrieve an address.

When typing more than one e-mail address, use a semicolon (;) to separate them.

● You can replace the default subject title with another title.

● You can type a brief introduction about the message here.

⑤ Click the **Send** button.

Outlook sends the message.

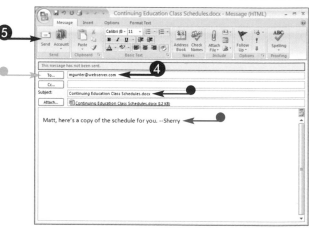

You can change the size of your document page to print to a particular size of paper. For example, if you need to print your memo on legal size paper, you can use the Page Setup dialog box to switch to the Legal or Executive paper size. By default, Word sets the paper to Letter size.

Change Paper Size

❶ Click the **Page Layout** tab on the Ribbon.

❷ Click the **Size** button.

❸ Click a paper size.

Note: To learn more about printing with Office, see Chapter 2.

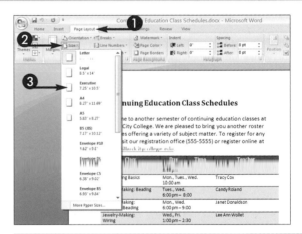

● Word applies the sizing to your document.

● To change the page orientation, click **Orientation** and choose an orientation setting.

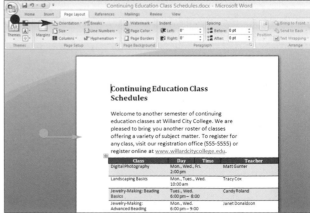

You can create instant envelopes in Word based on the information in a document. For example, when typing a letter, you can use the address from the document to create and print an envelope.

Print an Envelope

① Select the text that you want to use as the address.

② Click the **Mailings** tab on the Ribbon.

③ Click the **Envelopes** button.

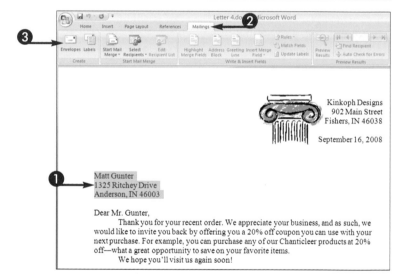

The Envelopes and Labels dialog box appears.

④ Click the **Envelopes** tab if it is not already displayed.

⑤ Type the return address, if needed.

To accommodate preprinted envelopes, Word does not display a return address.

⑥ Click **Options**.

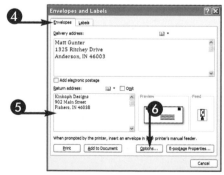

The Envelope Options dialog box appears, displaying the Envelope Options tab.

⑦ Click the **Envelope size** 🔽 to choose an envelope size.

● You can change the font or positioning of addresses, if needed.

⑧ Click **OK**.

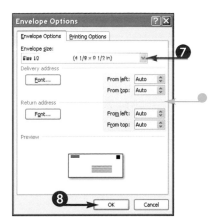

⑨ Click **Print**.

Word sends your envelope text to the printer.

● Depending on your printer setup, the Feed area indicates how to feed the envelope into the printer.

Note: *See your printer documentation to learn how to print envelopes.*

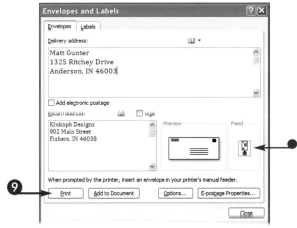

Can I save the envelope information for later use?

Yes. You can save the delivery and return address information along with the document to use at a later time. Click **Add to Document** in the Envelopes and Labels dialog box. The next time you open the file and the dialog box, the information is already entered and ready to print.

How do I print labels?

You can use the Envelopes and Labels dialog box to print labels. From the **Mailings** tab on the Ribbon, click the **Labels** button to open the Envelopes and Labels dialog box with the Labels tab displayed. You can create an address label, and print either one or multiple copies of the label. You can choose to print the return address or the delivery address on your label. You can also choose a label type by clicking **Options**, and then selecting a label size from the Label Options dialog box.

PART

Part III: Excel

Excel is a powerful spreadsheet program you can use to enter and organize data, and perform a wide variety of number crunching tasks. You can use Excel strictly as a program for manipulating numerical data, or you can use it as a database program to organize and track large quantities of data. In this part, you learn how to enter data into worksheets and tap into the power of Excel's formulas and functions to perform mathematical calculations and analysis.

Enter Cell Data

You can enter data into any cell within an Excel worksheet. When you click a cell, it immediately becomes the active cell in the worksheet, and any data that you type appears within the active cell. You can type data directly into the cell, or you can enter data using the Formula bar.

Data can be either text, such as row or column labels, or numbers, which are called *values*. Values also include formulas. Excel automatically left-aligns text data in a cell and right-aligns values. By default, Excel recognizes numerical dates and times that you enter as values, and assigns right alignment.

Enter Cell Data

TYPE INTO A CELL

1 Click the cell that you want to use.

The active cell always appears highlighted with a thicker border than the other cells.

● To add data to another worksheet in your workbook, you can simply click the worksheet tab to display the worksheet.

● To magnify your view of the worksheet, you can click and drag the Zoom slider.

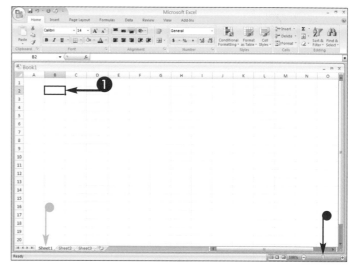

2 Type your data.

● The data appears both in the cell and in the Formula bar.

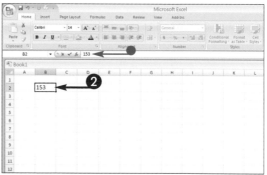

TYPE DATA IN THE FORMULA BAR

① Click the cell that you want to use.

② Click in the Formula bar.

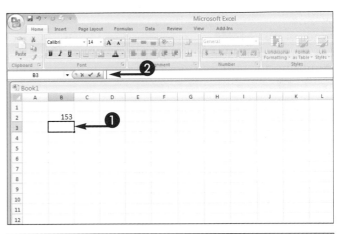

③ Type your data.

● The data appears both in the Formula bar and in the cell.

④ Click **Accept** (☑) or press **Enter** to enter the data.

● To cancel an entry, you can click **Cancel** (☒).

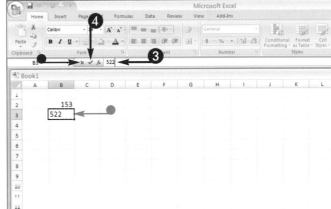

TIPS

What if the data that I type is too long to fit in my cell?

Long text entries appear truncated when you type data into adjoining cells. You can remedy this by resizing the column to fit the data, or by turning on the cell's text wrap feature, which wraps the text to fit in the cell and remain visible. Text wrapping causes the cell depth to increase. To learn how to resize columns, see the "Resize Columns and Rows" task. To learn how to turn on the text wrap feature, see the "Turn On Text Wrapping" task.

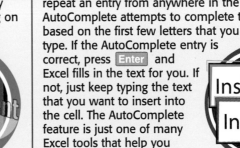

When I start typing in a cell, Excel tries to fill in the text for me. Why?

Excel's AutoComplete feature is automatic. If you repeat an entry from anywhere in the same column, AutoComplete attempts to complete the entry for you, based on the first few letters that you type. If the AutoComplete entry is correct, press **Enter** and Excel fills in the text for you. If not, just keep typing the text that you want to insert into the cell. The AutoComplete feature is just one of many Excel tools that help you speed up your data entry tasks.

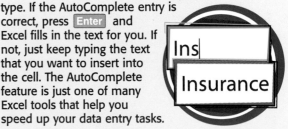

Select Cells

You can select cells in Excel to perform editing, mathematical, and formatting tasks. Selecting a single cell is easy: You just click the cell. To select a group of cells, called a *range*, you can use your mouse or keyboard. For example, you might apply formatting to a range of cells rather than format each cell individually.

You can learn more about working with a range of cells in Chapter 11.

SELECT A RANGE OF CELLS

1. Click the first cell in the range of cells that you want to select.

2. Click and drag across the cells that you want to include in the range.

   The ⇧ changes to ⬧.

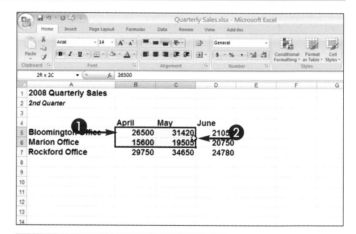

3. Release the mouse button.

● Excel selects the cells.

● To select all of the cells in the worksheet, you can click here.

   You can select multiple noncontiguous cells by pressing and holding **Ctrl** while clicking cells.

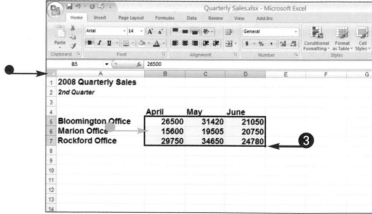

SELECT A COLUMN OR ROW

① Move the mouse over the header of the column or row that you want to select.

The ⌖ changes to ⬇.

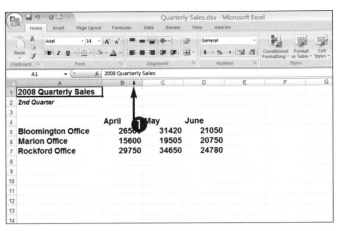

② Click the column or row.

● Excel selects the entire column or row.

To select multiple columns or rows, you can click and drag across the column or row headings.

You can select multiple noncontiguous columns or rows by pressing and holding Ctrl while clicking column or row headings.

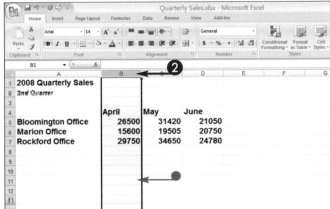

TIPS

How do I select data inside a cell?

To select a word or number inside a cell, you can click in front of the text in the Formula bar, and then drag over the characters or numbers that you want to select. You can also select data directly in a cell. If a cell contains several words, you can double-click a word to select it.

How do I use my keyboard to select cells?

You can use the arrow keys to navigate to the first cell in the range. Next, press and hold Shift while using an arrow key to select the range, such as ← or ↓. Excel selects any cells that you move over using the keyboard navigation keys.

Faster Data Entry with AutoFill

You can use Excel's AutoFill feature to help you automate data entry tasks. You can use AutoFill to add duplicate entries or a data series to your worksheet cells, such as labels for Monday, Tuesday, Wednesday, and so on. You can create your own custom data lists, as well as use built-in lists of common entries such as days of the week, months, and number series.

When you make a cell active in the worksheet, a small fill handle appears in the lower-right corner of the selector. You can use the fill handle to create an AutoFill series.

Faster Data Entry with AutoFill

AUTOFILL A TEXT SERIES

① Type the first entry in the text series.

② Click and drag the cell's fill handle across or down the number of cells that you want to fill.

The ⌖ changes to **+**.

You can also use AutoFill to copy the same text to every cell that you drag over.

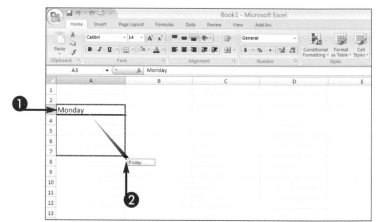

③ Release the mouse button.

● AutoFill fills in the text series.

● An AutoFill smart tag (⊞) may appear, offering additional options that you can assign to the data.

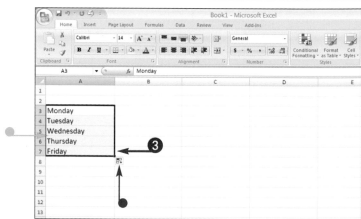

AUTOFILL A NUMBER SERIES

1 Type the first entry in the number series.

2 In an adjacent cell, type the next entry in the number series.

3 Select both cells.

Note: See the "Select Cells" task to learn more.

4 Click and drag the fill handle across or down the number of cells that you want to fill.

The ⟲ changes to +.

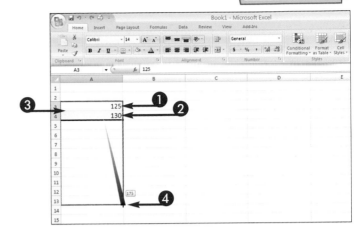

5 Release the mouse button.

● AutoFill fills in the number series.

● An AutoFill smart tag (⊞) may appear, offering additional options that you can assign to the data.

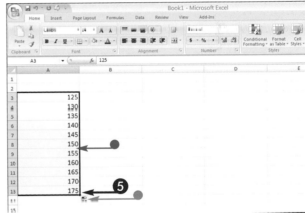

TIP

How do I create a custom list?
To add your own custom list to AutoFill's list library, first create the custom list in your worksheet cells. Then follow these steps:

1 Select the cells containing the list that you want to save.

2 Click the **Office** button.

3 Click the **Excel Options** button.

4 In the Excel Options dialog box, click the **Popular** tab.

5 Click the **Edit Custom Lists** button.

6 In the Custom Lists dialog box, click **Import**, and Excel adds the series to the custom lists.

● You can also create a new list by clicking **Add** and typing your list here.

7 Click **OK** to close both dialog boxes.

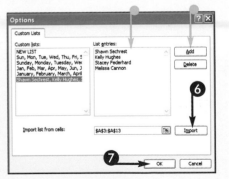

Add Columns and Rows

You can add columns and rows to your worksheets to add more data. For example, you may need to add a column in the middle of several existing columns to add data that you left out the first time you created the workbook.

ADD A COLUMN

1 Click the heading of the column to the right of where you want to insert a new column.

Note: See the task "Select Cells" task, earlier in this chapter, to learn how to select columns and rows.

2 Click the **Home** tab on the Ribbon.

3 Click the **Insert** ⬛.

4 Click **Insert Sheet Columns**.

You can also right-click a column heading and click **Insert**.

● Excel adds a column.

● A smart tag icon (⬛) may appear when you insert a column, and you can click the icon to view a list of options that you can assign.

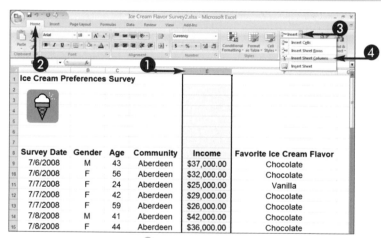

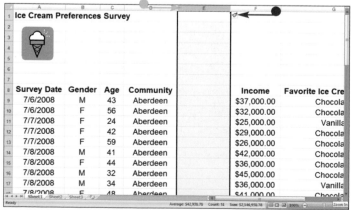

ADD A ROW

1. Click the heading of the row below where you want to insert a new row.

***Note:** See the "Select Cells" task, earlier in this chapter, to learn how to select columns and rows.*

2. Click the **Home** tab on the Ribbon.
3. Click the **Insert** ▾.
4. Click **Insert Sheet Rows**.

   You can also right-click a row heading and click **Insert**.

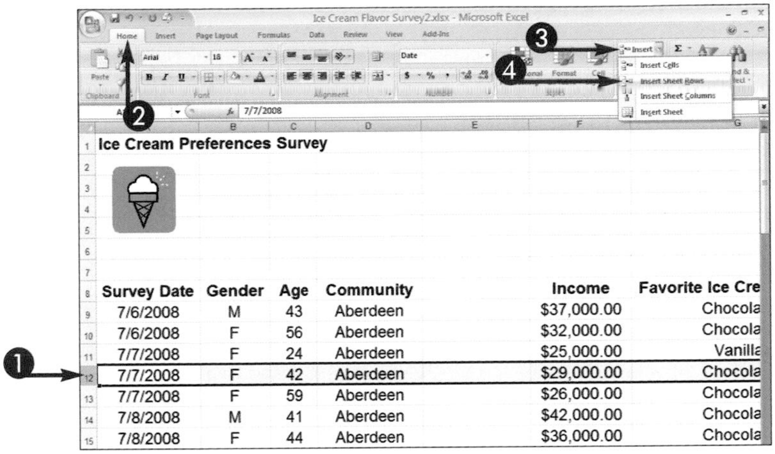

- Excel adds a row.
- A smart tag icon may appear (), and you can click the icon to view a list of options that you can assign.

  You can also right-click the row and click **Insert**.

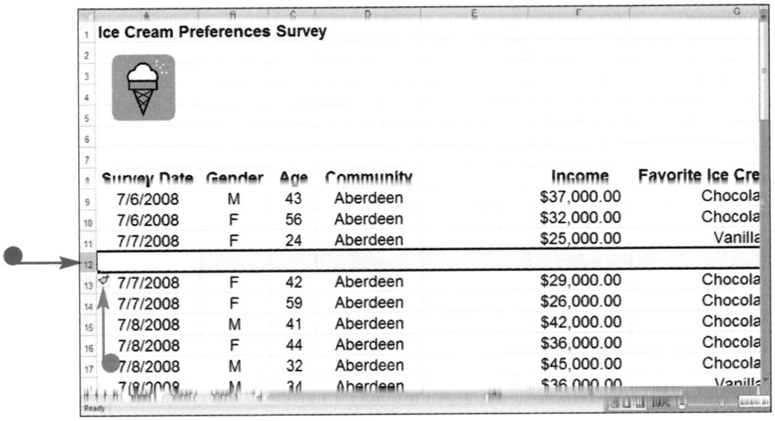

TIPS

Can I insert a multiple number of columns and rows?

Yes. First, select two or more columns and rows in the worksheet and then activate the **Insert** command as shown in the steps in this task. Excel adds the same number of new columns and rows as the number that you originally selected. You can also right-click the selected columns or rows, and then click **Insert** to insert multiple columns or rows into your worksheet.

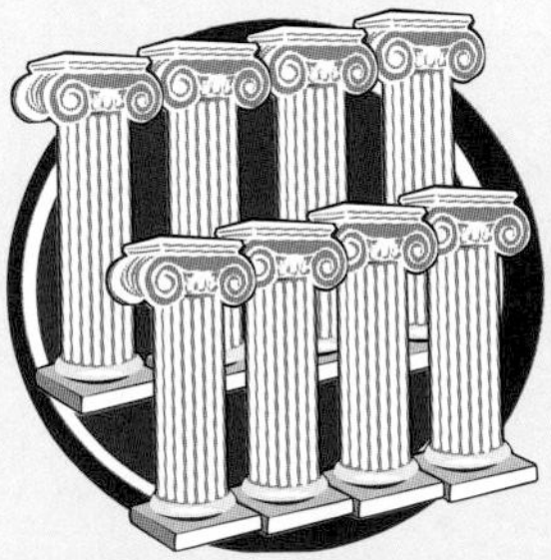

Can I insert columns or rows using the Insert dialog box?

Yes. If you click a cell and click the **Insert** ▾ on the Home tab and click **Insert Cells**, the Insert dialog box appears. You can click the **Entire Row** or **Entire Column** options (○ changes to ◉). When you click **OK** to exit the dialog box, Excel immediately adds a single row or column below or to the right of the active cell.

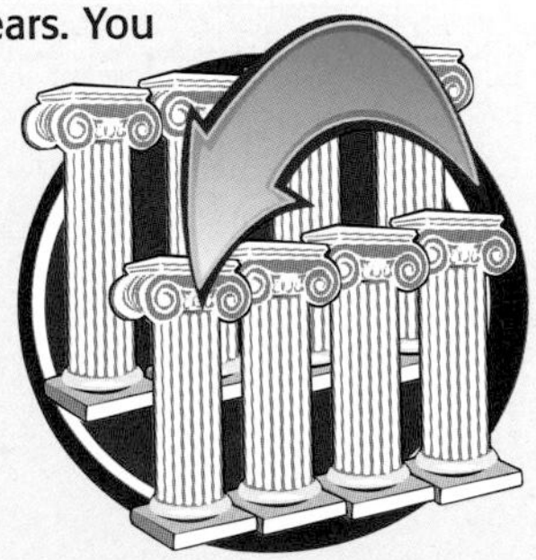

Delete Columns and Rows

You can remove columns or rows that you no longer need in your worksheet. For example, you may want to remove a row of obsolete data. When you delete an entire column or row, Excel deletes any existing data within the selected cells. Excel also moves over the other columns and rows to fill the space left by the deletion.

Delete Columns and Rows

DELETE A COLUMN

① Click the heading of the column that you want to delete.

Note: See the "Select Cells" task, earlier in this chapter, to learn how to select columns and rows.

② Click the **Home** tab on the Ribbon.

③ Click the **Delete** ▾.

④ Click **Delete Sheet Columns**.

You can also click the **Delete** button rather than the down arrow to delete a column.

Note: If you press `Delete`*, Excel deletes the column's contents instead of the entire column.*

● Excel deletes the column.

You can also right-click a column heading and click **Delete** to remove a column.

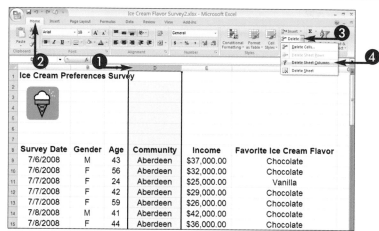

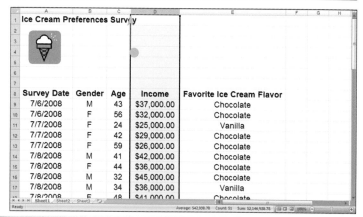

DELETE A ROW

1 Click the heading of the row that you want to delete.

Note: See the "Select Cells" task, earlier in this chapter, to learn how to select columns and rows.

2 Click the **Home** tab on the Ribbon.

3 Click the **Delete** ▾.

4 Click **Delete Sheet Rows**.

You can also click the **Delete** button rather than the down arrow to delete rows.

Note: If you press **Delete** *, Excel deletes the row's contents instead of the entire row.*

● Excel deletes the row.

You can also right-click a row heading and click **Delete** to remove the row.

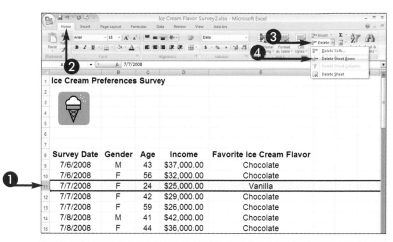

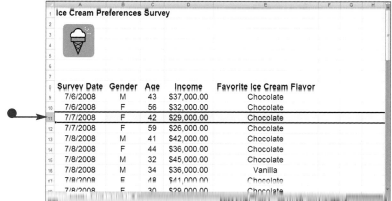

How do I delete an entire worksheet from my workbook?

To remove a worksheet, right-click the worksheet tab, and then click **Delete** from the shortcut menu. If the sheet contains any existing data, Excel prompts you to confirm the deletion by clicking the **Delete** button. To learn more about adding and deleting worksheets from a workbook file, see Chapter 10.

I accidentally deleted a column that I need. How do I reinsert it?

If you click the **Undo** button (🔄) on the Quick Access toolbar immediately after deleting a row or column, you can undo the action. Excel reinserts the row or column, including any data that it contained.

Resize Columns and Rows

You can resize your worksheet's columns and rows to accommodate text or make the worksheet more aesthetically appealing.

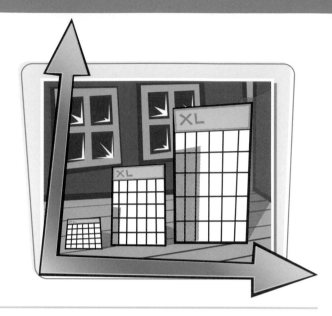

1 Move the mouse pointer over the heading of the border of the column or row that you want to resize.

The ⌖ changes to ✛.

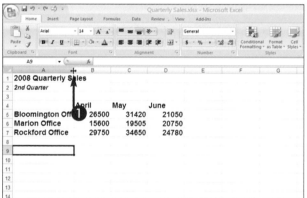

2 Click and drag the border to the desired size.

● A dotted line marks the new border of the column or row as you drag.

3 Release the mouse button.

Excel resizes the column or row.

● You can also click the **Format** button on the Home tab, and then click **AutoFit Selection** to quickly resize a highlighted column to fit existing text.

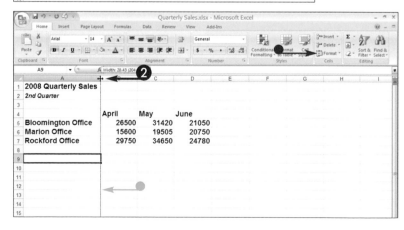

Turn On
Text Wrapping

By default, long lines of text that you type into a cell remain on one line. You can turn on the cell's text-wrapping option to make text wrap to the next line and fit into the cell without truncating the text. Text wrapping makes the row size taller to fit the number of lines that wrap.

Turn On Text Wrapping

① Click the cell that you want to edit.

Note: *You can also apply text wrapping to multiple cells. See the "Select Cells" task, earlier in this chapter, to learn how to select multiple cells for a task.*

② Click the **Home** tab on the Ribbon.

③ Click the **Wrap Text** (▦) button.

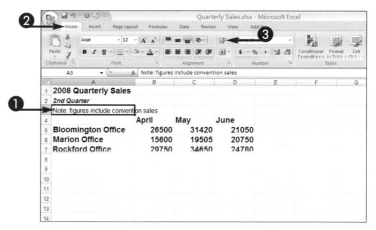

● Excel applies text wrapping to the cell.

Note: *See the previous task, "Resize Columns and Rows," to learn how to adjust cell depth and width to accommodate your text.*

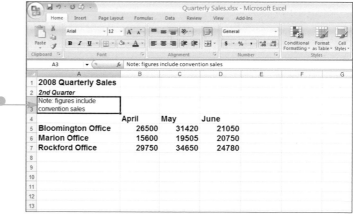

Center Data Across Columns

You can center a title or heading across a range of cells in your worksheet. For example, you may want to include a title across multiple columns of labels. You can use the Merge and Center command to quickly create a merged cell to hold the title text.

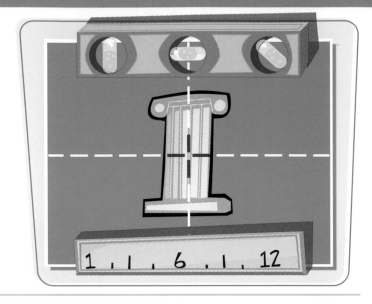

① Select the cell containing the text that you want to center, and the cells that you want to center the text across.

Note: *See the "Select Cells" task, earlier in this chapter, to learn how to select columns and rows.*

② Click the **Home** tab on the Ribbon.

③ Click the **Merge and Center** button (⬚).

You can also click the **Merge and Center** ⬚ to select from several different merge commands.

● Excel merges the cells and centers the text.

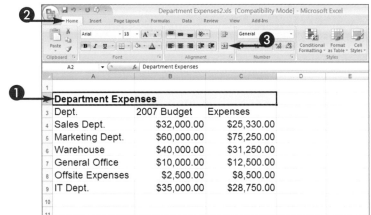

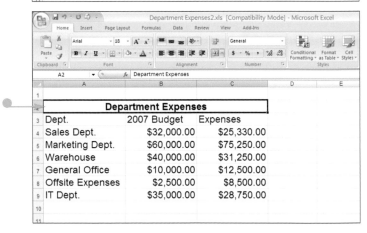

Freeze a Column or Row

You can freeze a column or row to keep the labels in view as you scroll through larger worksheets. As a result, you cannot scroll the area that you freeze, but you can scroll the unfrozen areas of the worksheet.

Freeze a Column or Row

1 Click to the right of the column or below the row that you want to freeze.

Note: To freeze only a row or column, click the row or column heading rather than a cell.

2 Click the **View** tab on the Ribbon.

3 Click the **Freeze Panes** □.

4 Click **Freeze Panes**.

You can also choose to freeze a row or column headings or a column of row titles.

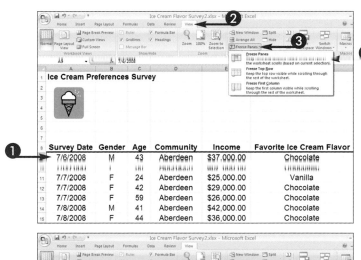

● Excel freezes the areas above or to the left of where you applied the Freeze Panes command.

You can scroll the area below or to the right of the frozen pane.

● To unlock the columns and rows, you can click the **Freeze Panes** □, and then click **Unfreeze Panes**.

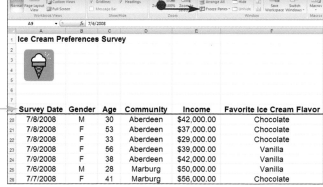

Remove Data or Cells

You can delete Excel data that you no longer need. When you decide to delete data, you can choose whether you want to remove the data and keep the cells or delete the cells entirely. When you delete a cell's contents, Excel removes only the data. When you delete a cell, Excel removes the cell as well as its contents. The existing cells in your worksheet shift over to fill any gap in the worksheet structure.

Remove Data or Cells

DELETE DATA

1 Select the cell or cells containing the data that you want to remove.

Note: See the "Select Cells" task, earlier in this chapter, to learn how to select cells.

2 Press **Delete**.

Excel deletes the data from the cell, but the cell remains.

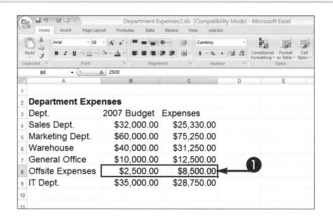

DELETE CELLS

1 Select the cell or cells that you want to remove.

Note: See the "Select Cells" task, earlier in this chapter, to learn how to select cells.

2 Click the **Home** tab.

3 Click the **Delete** ▾.

4 Click **Delete Cells**.

You can also right-click the selected cells and then click the **Delete** command.

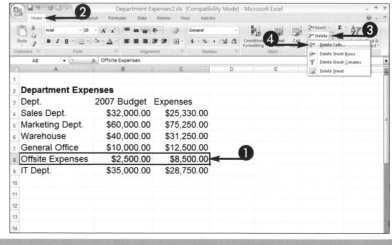

The Delete dialog box appears.

5 Click a deletion option (○ changes to ◉).

6 Click **OK**.

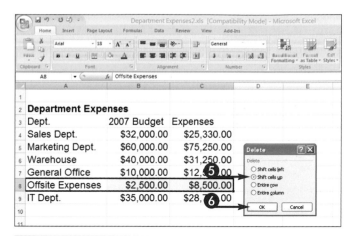

● Excel removes the cells and their content from the worksheet.

Other cells shift over or up to fill the void of any cells that you remove from your worksheet.

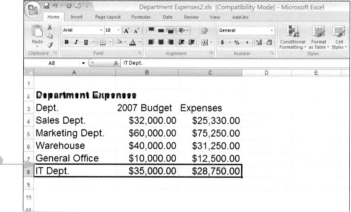

TIP

Can I remove a cell's formatting without removing the content?

Yes. You can use the Clear command to remove formatting, contents, or comments from your worksheet cells. To activate the command, select the cell or cells that you want to edit and click the **Home** tab on the Ribbon. Click the **Clear** button (⬚) ▾. A submenu appears. Click **Clear Formats** to remove all of the formatting in the cell. Click **Clear Contents** to remove all of the cell's data. Click **Clear Comments** to remove any comments assigned to the cell. To remove all formatting, contents, and comments at the same time, click **Clear All**.

Assign Worksheet Names

You can name your Excel worksheets to help identify their content. For example, if your workbook contains four worksheets, each detailing a different sales quarter, then you can give each worksheet a unique name, such as Quarter 1, Quarter 2, and so on.

Assign Worksheet Names

1 Double-click the worksheet tab that you want to rename.

Excel highlights the current name.

You can also right-click the worksheet name and click **Rename**.

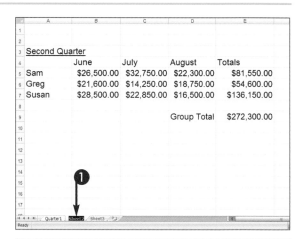

2 Type a new name for the worksheet.

3 Press Enter.

Excel assigns the new worksheet name.

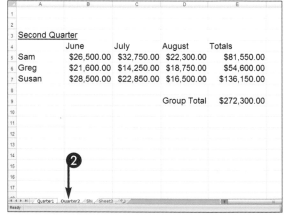

You can delete a worksheet that
you no longer need in your
workbook. You should always
check the worksheet's contents
before deleting it to avoid
removing any important data. As
soon as you delete a worksheet,
Excel permanently removes it
from the workbook file.

1 Right-click the worksheet tab.

2 Click **Delete**.

● You can also click the **Delete** ⏷ on the
Home tab and then click **Delete Sheet**.

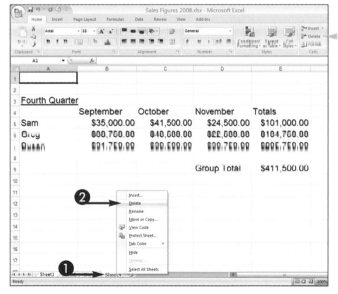

If the worksheet is blank, Excel deletes it
immediately.

If the worksheet contains any data,
Excel prompts you to confirm the
deletion.

3 Click **Delete**.

Excel deletes the worksheet.

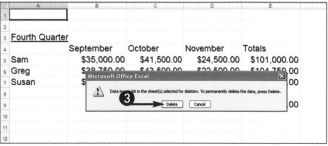

Add a Worksheet

You can add a worksheet to your workbook to create another worksheet in which to enter data. By default, every Excel workbook opens with three worksheets. You can add more worksheets as you need them.

You can move worksheets to reposition their order. See the next task, "Move a Worksheet," for more information.

① Click the **Insert Worksheet** button (⊡).

You can also right-click a worksheet tab and click **Insert** to open the Insert dialog box, where you can choose to insert a worksheet.

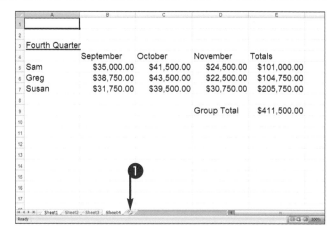

● Excel adds a new worksheet and gives it a default worksheet name.

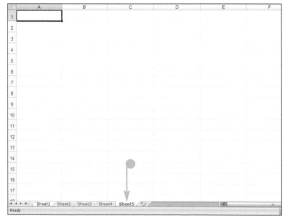

You can move a worksheet within a workbook to rearrange the worksheet order. For example, you may want to position the worksheet that you use most often as the first worksheet in the workbook.

① Click the tab of the worksheet that you want to move.

② Drag the worksheet to a new position in the list of worksheets.

The ⬚ changes to ⬚.

● A small black triangle icon keeps track of the worksheet's location in the group while you drag.

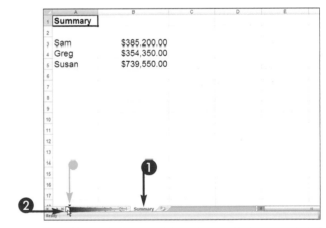

③ Release the mouse button.

● Excel moves the worksheet.

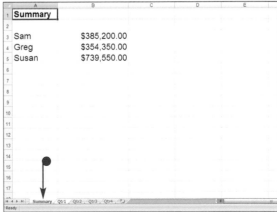

Copy a Worksheet

You can copy a worksheet within a workbook. For example, you may want to copy a worksheet to use as a starting point for data that is new, yet similar.

1 Click the worksheet tab that you want to copy.

2 Press and hold `Ctrl`.

The ⌀ changes to ⌀.

3 Drag the worksheet copy to a new position in the list of worksheets.

● A small, black triangle icon keeps track of the worksheet's location in the group while you drag.

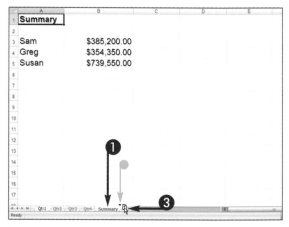

4 Release the mouse button.

● Excel copies the worksheet as a new worksheet in the workbook and gives it a default name to indicate that it is a copy.

Note: *Excel names worksheet copies sequentially with a number, starting with (2), after the worksheet name.*

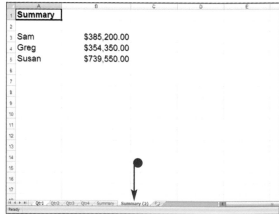

Format the Worksheet Tab Color

You can add color to your worksheet tabs to help distinguish one worksheet from another. The color that you add to a tab appears in the background, behind the worksheet tab name. By default, all worksheet tabs are white unless you assign another color.

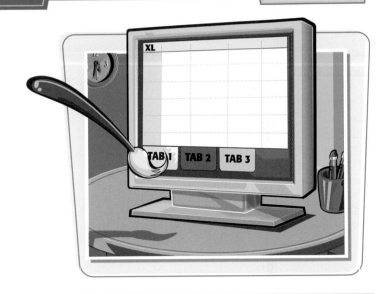

Format the Worksheet Tab Color

① Right-click the worksheet tab that you want to format.

② Click **Tab Color**.

③ Click a color.

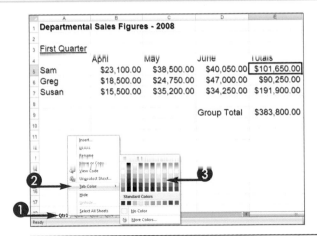

● Excel assigns the color to the tab.

● To see the new tab color, you can click another worksheet tab.

Note: You can set the tab color to No Color to return it to the default state.

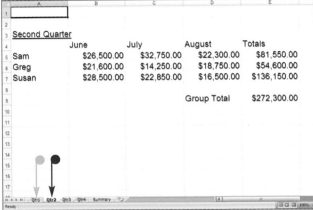

Find and Replace Data

You can use Excel's Find tool to search through your worksheet for a particular number, formula, word, or phrase. You can use the Replace tool to replace instances of text or numbers with other data. For example, you may need to sort through a long worksheet to replace a reference with another name.

Find and Replace Data

FIND DATA

1 Click the **Home** tab on the Ribbon.

2 Click the **Find & Select** button.

3 Click **Find**.

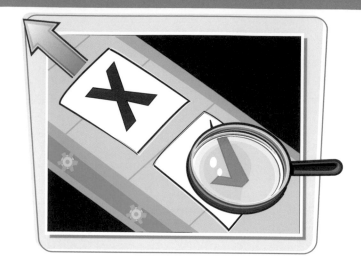

● The Find and Replace dialog box appears, displaying the Find tab.

4 Type the data that you want to find.

5 Click **Find Next**.

● Excel searches the worksheet and finds the first occurrence of the data.

You can click **Find Next** again to search for the next occurrence.

6 When finished, click **Close** to close the dialog box.

Note: *Excel may display a prompt box when the last occurrence is found. Click **OK**.*

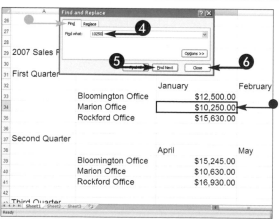

REPLACE DATA

1 Click the **Home** tab on the Ribbon.

2 Click the **Find & Select** button.

3 Click **Replace**.

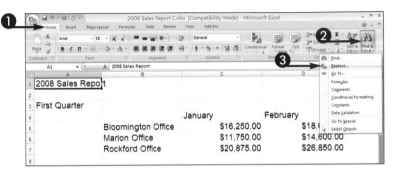

● The Find and Replace dialog box appears, displaying the Replace tab.

4 Type the data that you want to find.

5 Type the replacement data.

6 Click **Find Next**.

● Excel locates the first occurrence of the data.

7 Click **Replace** to replace it.

● You can click **Replace All** to replace every occurrence in the worksheet.

8 When finished, click **Close**.

*Note: Excel may display a prompt box when the last occurrence is found. Click **OK**.*

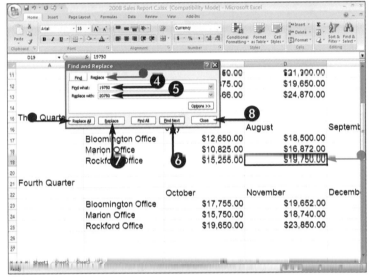

Where can I find detailed search options?

You can click the **Options** button in the Find and Replace dialog box to reveal additional search options that you can apply. For example, you can search by rows or columns, matching data, and more. You can also search for specific formatting or special characters using Format options. To hide the additional search options, click the **Options** button again.

How can I search for and delete data?

You can search for a particular word, number, or phrase using the Find and Replace dialog box, and remove the data completely from the worksheet. Start by typing the text in the Find what field. Leave the Replace with field empty. When you activate the search, Excel looks for the data, and deletes it without adding new data to the worksheet.

Sort Data

You can sort your Excel data to reorganize the information. This technique is particularly useful when using Excel to create database tables, which are lists of related data. For example, you might want to sort a client table to list the names alphabetically. An ascending sort lists records from A to Z, and a descending sort lists records from Z to A. In the case of numbers, an ascending sort lists numbers from lowest to highest, while a descending sort lists numbers from highest to lowest.

Sort Data

PEFORM A QUICK SORT

① Click in the field name, or heading, that you want to sort.

② Click the **Home** tab on the Ribbon.

③ Click the **Sort & Filter** button.

④ Click an ascending or descending sort command.

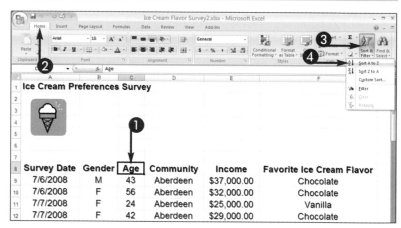

● Excel sorts the records based on the field that you specified.

● If you do not want Excel to sort the records permanently, click the **Undo** button (🔄) on the Quick Access toolbar to return the list to its original state.

PERFORM A CUSTOM SORT

1 Click in the field name, or heading, that you want to sort.

2 Click the **Home** tab on the Ribbon.

3 Click the **Sort & Filter** button.

4 Click **Custom Sort**.

The Sort dialog box appears.

5 Click the first **Sort by** ⬇ and select the primary field to sort by.

● By default, the Sort On field is set to values. To sort on another setting, you can click the **Sort On** ⬇ and choose a setting.

6 Click the **Order** ⬇ to sort the field in ascending or descending order.

To specify additional sort fields, repeat Steps **5** and **6**.

7 Click **OK**.

● Excel sorts the data.

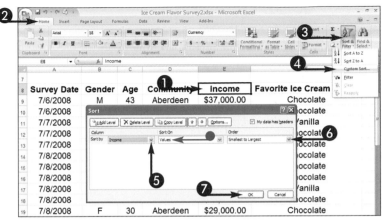

What are database tables, and how do I use them in Excel?

A database is a collection of related information, such as an address book. You can create a variety of database lists in Excel to manage sales contacts, inventory, household valuables, and more. An entire database list of information is called a *table*. You use *fields* to break down your list into manageable pieces. Fields are typically the columns that you use to define each part of your list, such as name, address, and phone number. You use rows to enter each database entry for your list of data. Database entries are called *records*.

Can I sort data in rows?

Yes. If the listed data is across a row instead of down a column, you can activate the Sort left to right option. Open the Sort dialog box as shown in this task, and click the **Options** button. In the Sort Options dialog box that appears, click the **Sort left to right** option (○ changes to ◉).

Filter Data with AutoFilter

When using Excel as a database, you can use an AutoFilter to view only portions of your data. Unlike a sort, which sorts the entire table, a filter selects certain records to display based on your criteria, while hiding records that do not match the criteria.

You can refer to the previous task to learn how to sort data in Excel.

Filter Data with AutoFilter

① Select the field names for the data that you want to filter.

② Click the **Home** tab on the Ribbon.

③ Click the **Sort & Filter** button.

④ Click **Filter**.

● Excel adds drop-down arrow buttons (▼) to your field names.

⑤ Click ▼.

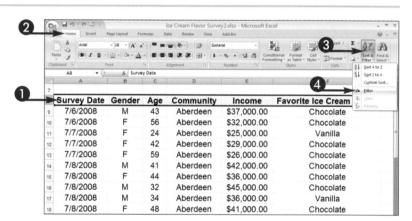

6 Click a filter type.

You can filter the table based on a particular field.

7 Click **OK**.

● Excel filters the table.

To view all of the records again, you can display the filter list and click **Select All**. You can also click the **Clear Filter** command to clear the filter.

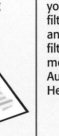

Are there other filtering tasks that I can perform?

Yes. For real filtering power, you can use Microsoft Access. You can turn any Excel spreadsheet into an Access database and use the many filtering and sorting tools that are available in Access. To learn more about creating filters in Access, see Chapter 21.

In what ways can I customize a filter?

In the Filter drop-down list, click **Text Filters** or **Number Filters**, and then click **Custom** to open the Custom AutoFilter dialog box. Here you can further customize the filter by selecting operators and values to apply on the filtered data. To learn more about customizing AutoFilters, see Excel's Help files.

Insert a Comment

You can add comments to your worksheets to make a note to yourself about a particular cell's contents, or as a note for other users to see. For example, if you share your workbooks with other users, you can add comments to leave feedback about the data without typing directly in the worksheet. Excel displays comments in a balloon.

ADD A COMMENT

1. Click the cell to which you want to add a comment.

2. Click the **Review** tab on the Ribbon.

3. Click the **New Comment** button.

   You can also right-click the cell and click **New Comment**.

A comment balloon appears.

4. Type your comment text.

5. Click anywhere outside the comment balloon to deselect the comment.

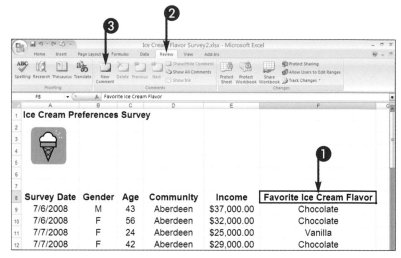

● Cells that contain comments display a tiny red triangle in the corner.

7				
8	Age	Community	Income	Favorite Ice Cream Flavor
9	43	Aberdeen	$37,000.00	Chocolate
10	56	Aberdeen	$32,000.00	Chocolate
11	24	Aberdeen	$25,000.00	Vanilla
12	42	Aberdeen	$29,000.00	Chocolate
13	59	Aberdeen	$26,000.00	Chocolate
14	41	Aberdeen	$42,000.00	Chocolate
15	44	Aberdeen	$36,000.00	Chocolate
16	32	Aberdeen	$45,000.00	Chocolate
17	34	Aberdeen	$36,000.00	Vanilla
18	48	Aberdeen	$41,000.00	Chocolate

Sheet1 Sheet2 Sheet3
Ready

VIEW A COMMENT

1 Position the mouse pointer over the upper-right corner of the cell.

● The comment balloon appears, displaying the comment.

7				
8	Age	Community	Income	Favorite Ice Cream Flavor
9	43	Aberdeen	$37,000.00	Chocolate
10	56	Aberdeen	$32,000.00	Chocolate
11	24	Aberdeen	$25,000.00	Vanilla
12	42	Aberdeen	$29,000.00	Chocolate
13	59	Aberdeen	$26,000.00	Chocolate
14	41	Aberdeen	$42,000.00	Chocolate
15	44	Aberdeen	$36,000.00	Chocolate
16	32	Aberdeen	$45,000.00	Chocolate
17	04	Aberdeen	000,000.00	Vanilla
18	48	Aberdeen	$41,000.00	Chocolate

Sherry Kinkoph:
Include strawberry on next year's survey

Sheet1 Sheet2 Sheet3
Cell F8 commented by Sherry Kinkoph

TIPS

How do I remove a comment?
To remove a comment that you no longer want to associate with a cell, right-click the cell containing the comment to display a shortcut menu. Click **Delete Comment**. Excel immediately removes the comment from the cell.

How do I respond to and edit another user's comment?
If the worksheet's tracking features are turned on, you can add a comment to another user's comment. Excel's tracking features enable you to see the edits that each user makes to the workbook. After all of the edits are completed, you can decide which edits to accept or reject to create a final file. To turn on workbook tracking, click the **Review** tab on the Ribbon, click the **Track Changes** , and then click **Highlight Changes**. See the next task, "Track and Review Workbook Changes," to learn more.

Track and Review Workbook Changes

If you work in an environment in which you share your Excel workbooks with others, you can use the tracking and reviewing features to help you keep track of who adds changes to the files. For example, you can see what edits others have made, including formatting changes and data additions or deletions.

The tracking feature changes the color for each person's edits, making it easy to see who changed what in the workbook. When you review the workbook, you can choose to accept or reject the changes.

Track and Review Workbook Changes

TURN ON TRACKING

① Click the **Review** tab on the Ribbon.

② Click the **Track Changes** ▪.

③ Click **Highlight Changes**.

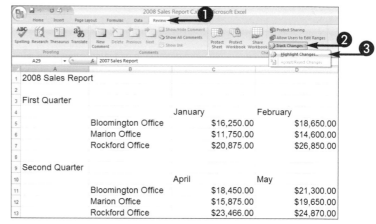

The Highlight Changes dialog box appears.

④ Click the **Track changes while editing** option (☐ changes to ☑).

This option automatically creates a shared workbook file if you have not already activated the share workbook feature.

● You can click an option to choose when, by whom, or where you track changes (☐ changes to ☑).

● You can leave this option checked (☑) to view changes in the file.

⑤ Click **OK**.

Excel prompts you to save the file.

6 Click **OK**.

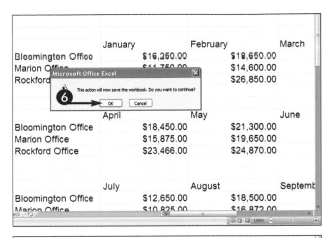

Excel activates the tracking feature.

● Excel highlights any changes in the worksheet.

● To view details about a change and the author, you can move the mouse over the highlighted cell.

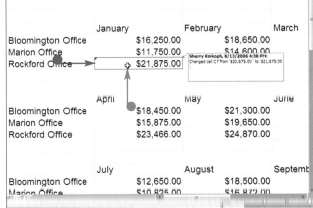

Is there a way to view all of the changes at the same time when reviewing a workbook?

Yes. Click the **Track Changes** ⊡ on the Ribbon and then click **Highlight Changes**. In the Highlight Changes dialog box that appears, you can click the **List changes on a new sheet** check box (☐ changes to ☑). This opens a special History sheet in the workbook for viewing each edit. The History sheet breaks down the details of each edit, including the date, time, and author. You can use the filters to change the list of edits. When you save the workbook, Excel deletes the History sheet.

Can I remove a user from a shared workbook?

Yes. You can open the Share Workbook dialog box and view which users are using the file. Click the **Review** tab on the Ribbon, and then click the **Share Workbook** button to open the dialog box. You can then remove a user by clicking his or her name and then clicking **Remove User**.

continued

When you activate the reviewing process, Excel goes through each change in the worksheet and allows you to accept or reject the edit. When the review is complete, you can turn the tracking feature off.

Track and Review Workbook Changes *(continued)*

REVIEW CHANGES

1 Click the **Review** tab on the Ribbon.

2 Click the **Track Changes** ☑.

3 Click **Accept/Reject Changes**.

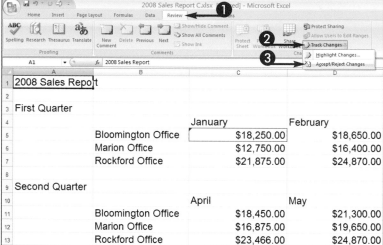

Excel prompts you to save the file.

4 Click **OK**.

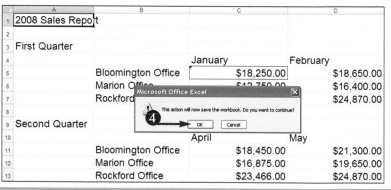

The Select Changes to Accept or Reject dialog box appears.

5 Click options for which changes you want to view (☐ changes to ☑).

6 Click **OK**.

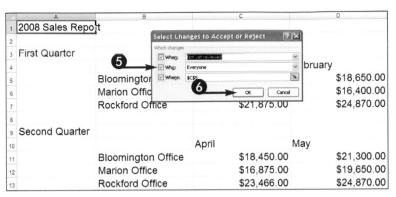

The Accept or Reject Changes dialog box appears.

7 Specify an action for each edit.

● You can click **Accept** to add the change to the final worksheet.

● To reject the change, you can click **Reject**.

● You can click one of these options to accept or reject all of the changes at the same time.

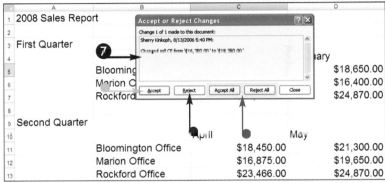

 TIPS

Are there certain edits that Excel does not track or highlight?

Yes. Excel's tracking feature does not keep track of changes in worksheet names, inserted or deleted worksheets, or hidden rows or columns. In addition, some of Excel's features do not work with shared workbooks, such as grouping data, recording and assigning macros, or inserting pictures or hyperlinks. For a complete list of changes and features that are supported with shared workbooks, see Excel's Help files.

How do I turn off the tracking feature?

Click the **Review** tab on the Ribbon, and then click the **Track Changes** . Click the **Highlight Changes** command to open the Highlight Changes dialog box. Next, click the **Track changes while editing** check box (☑ changes to ☐). When you click **OK**, Excel turns the feature off.

Change Page Setup Options

You can assign page setup options, such as page orientation, margins, paper size, and more using the tools on the Page Layout tab on the Ribbon. For example, if your workbook data appears too wide to fit on a regular 8½-by-11 sheet, then you can change the page orientation to Landscape to fit more data on the page horizontally. You can also insert your own page breaks to control the placement of data on a printed page.

CHANGE THE PAGE ORIENTATION

1 Click the **Page Layout** tab on the Ribbon.

2 Click the **Orientation** button.

3 Click **Portrait** or **Landscape**.

Note: Portrait is the default orientation.

Excel applies the new orientation.

● This example applies Landscape, and Excel marks the edge of the page with a dotted line.

● You can click the **Margins** button to set up page margins.

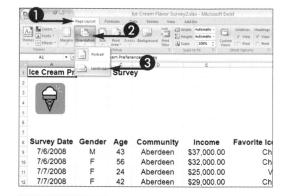

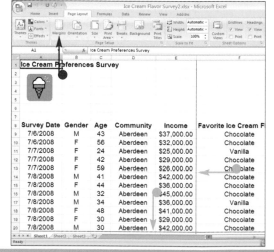

INSERT A PAGE BREAK

1️⃣ Click the cell or row above which you want to insert a page break.

2️⃣ Click the **Page Layout** tab on the Ribbon.

3️⃣ Click the **Breaks** button.

4️⃣ Click **Insert Page Break**.

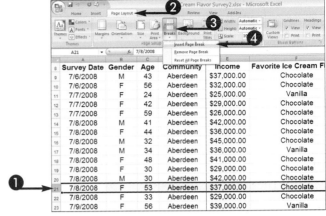

● Excel inserts a page break.

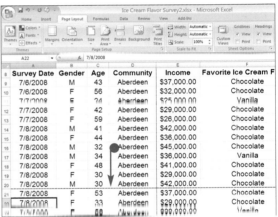

How do I define a print area?

You can assign a print area to print only a certain portion of a worksheet. For example, you may want to print only a range of cells. You can define a print area to prevent Excel from printing the entire worksheet every time you print. To do so, first select the cells that you want to define as the print area, and then click the **Page Layout** tab on the Ribbon. Next, click the **Print Area** button and click the **Set Print Area** command. Excel defines the print area.

How do I print a spreadsheet with gridlines?

By default, the gridlines that you see on a worksheet do not print out with the cell data. You can turn gridlines on for printing purposes. To do so, simply click the **Gridlines Print** check box on the Page Layout tab (☐ changes to ☑). A check mark in the check box indicates that the feature is on.

Understanding Formulas

You can use formulas to perform all kinds of calculations on your Excel data. You can build formulas using mathematical operators, values, and cell references. For example, you can add the contents of a column of monthly sales totals to determine the cumulative sales total. If you are new to writing formulas, this task explains all of the basics required to build your own formulas in Excel.

Formula Structure

Ordinarily, when you write a mathematical formula, you write the values and the operators, followed by an equal sign, such as 2+2=. In Excel, formula structure works a bit differently. All Excel formulas begin with an equal sign (=), such as =2+2. The equal sign immediately tells Excel to recognize any subsequent data as a formula rather than as a regular cell entry.

Referencing Cells

Although you can enter specific values in your Excel formulas, you can also easily reference data in specific cells. For example, you can add two cells together or multiply the contents of one cell by a value. Every cell in a worksheet has a unique address, also called a cell reference. By default, cells are identified by their specific column letter and then by their row number, and so cell D5 identifies the fifth cell down in column D. To help make your worksheets easier to use, you can also assign your own unique names to cells. For example, if a cell contains a figure totaling weekly sales, then you might name the cell Sales.

Cell Ranges

A group of related cells in a worksheet is called a range. Excel identifies a cell range by the anchor points in the upper-left and lower-right corners of the range. The range reference includes both anchor points separated by a colon. For example, the range name A1:B3 includes cells A1, A2, A3, B1, B2, and B3. You can also assign unique names to your ranges to make it easier to identify their contents. Range names must start with a letter or underscore, and can include uppercase and lowercase letters. Spaces are not allowed in range names.

Mathematical Operators

You can use mathematical operators in Excel to build formulas. Basic operators include the following:

Operator	Operation
+	Addition
-	Subtraction
*	Multiplication
/	Division
%	Percentage
^	Exponentiation

Operator	Operation
=	Equal to
<	Less than
≤	Less than or equal to
>	Greater than
≥	Greater than or equal to
<>	Not equal to

Operator Precedence

Excel performs a series of operations from left to right, but also gives some operators precedence over others, as follows:

First	All operations enclosed in parentheses
Second	Exponential equations
Third	Multiplication and division
Fourth	Addition and subtraction

When you are creating equations, the order of operations determines the results. For example, if you want to determine the average of values in A2, B2, and C2, and you enter the equation =A2+B2+C2/3, you will calculate the wrong answer. This is because Excel divides the value in cell C2 by 3 and then adds that result to A2 + B2. Following operator precedence, division takes precedence over addition. The correct way to write the formula is =(A2+B2+C2)/3. By enclosing the values in parentheses, Excel adds the cell values first before dividing them by 3.

Reference Operators

You can use Excel's reference operators to control how a formula groups cells and ranges in order to perform calculations. For example, if your formula needs to include the cell range D2:D10 and cell E10, you can instruct Excel to evaluate all of the data contained in these cells using a reference operator. Your formula might look like this: =SUM(D2:D10,E10).

Operator	Example	Operation
:	=SUM(D3:E12)	Range operator. Evaluates the reference as a single reference, including all of the cells in the range from both corners of the reference.
,	=SUM(D3:E12,F3)	Union operator. Evaluates the two references as a single reference.
[space]	=SUM(D3:D20 D10:E15)	Intersect operator. Evaluates the cells common to both references.
[space]	=SUM(Totals Sales)	Intersect operator. Evaluates the intersecting cell or cells of the column labeled Totals and the row labeled Sales.

Create Formulas

You can write a formula to perform a calculation on data in your worksheet cells. All formulas begin with an equal sign (=) in Excel. You can reference values in cells by entering the cell name, also called a cell reference. For example, if you want to add the contents of cells C3 and C4 together, your formula looks like this: =C3+C4.

You can create a formula in the Formula bar at the top of the worksheet. Formula results appear in the cell to which you assign a formula.

Create Formulas

① Click in the cell to which you want to assign a formula.

② Type **=**.

● Excel displays the formula in the Formula bar and in the active cell.

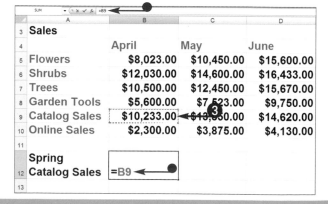

③ Click the first cell that you want to reference in the formula.

● Excel inserts the cell reference into the formula.

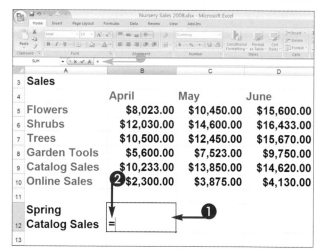

④ Type an operator for the formula.

Note: *See the previous task "Understanding Formulas" to learn more about mathematical operators.*

⑤ Click the next cell that you want to reference in the formula.

● Excel inserts the cell reference into the formula.

⑥ Press **Enter** .

● You can also click **Accept** (☑) on the Formula bar to accept the formula.

● You can click **Cancel** (☒) to cancel the formula.

● The formula results appear in the cell.

To view the formula in the Formula bar, you can simply click in the cell.

● The Formula bar displays any formula assigned to the active cell.

Note: *If you change any of the values in the cells referenced in your formula, the formula results automatically update to reflect the changes.*

	A	B	C	D
				=B9+C9
3	**Sales**			
4		April	May	June
5	Flowers	$8,023.00	$10,450.00	$15,600.00
6	Shrubs	$12,030.00	$14,600.00	$16,433.00
7	Trees	$10,500.00	$12,450.00	$15,670.00
8	Garden Tools	$5,600.00	$7,523.00	$9,750.00
9	Catalog Sales	$10,233.00	$13,850.00	$14,620.00
10	Online Sales	$300.00	$3,875.00	$4,130.00
11				
12	**Spring Catalog Sales**	=B9+C9		
13				

	A	B	C	D
	B12		=B9+C9	
3	**Sales**			
4		April	May	June
5	Flowers	$8,023.00	$10,450.00	$15,600.00
6	Shrubs	$12,030.00	$14,600.00	$16,433.00
7	Trees	$10,500.00	$12,450.00	$15,670.00
8	Garden Tools	$5,600.00	$7,523.00	$9,750.00
9	Catalog Sales	$10,233.00	$13,850.00	$14,620.00
10	Online Sales	$2,300.00	$3,875.00	$4,130.00
11				
12	**Spring Catalog Sales**	$24,083.00		
14				

TIPS

How do I edit a formula?

To edit a formula, simply click in the cell containing the formula and make any corrections in the Formula bar. You can also double-click in the cell to make edits directly to the formula within the cell. You can use the keyboard arrow keys to move the cursor to the place you want to edit in the data, or simply click the cursor in place. You can press **Backspace** and **Delete** to make changes to the formula and type new values or references as needed. When finished with the edits, press **Enter** or click **Accept** (☑) on the Formula bar.

What happens if I see an error message in my formula?

If you see an error message, such as #DIV/0!, double-check your formula references to ensure that you referenced the correct cells. Also make sure that you did not attempt to divide by zero, which always produces an error. To learn more about fixing formula errors, see the "Audit a Worksheet for Errors" task, later in this chapter.

STOP

Define a Range Name

You can assign distinctive names to the cells and ranges of cells that you work with in a worksheet, making it easier to identify the cell's contents. A *range* is simply a rectangular group of related cells; a range can also consist of a single cell. Naming ranges can also help you when deciphering formulas. A range name, such as Sales_Totals, is much easier to recognize than a generic reference, such as B24:C24.

ASSIGN A RANGE NAME

1 Select the range that you want to name.

2 Click inside the **Name** field on the Formula bar.

● You can also click the **Define Name** ▪ on the Formulas tab and then click **Define** to open the New Name dialog box.

3 Type a name for the range.

4 Press Enter .

Excel assigns the name to the cells.

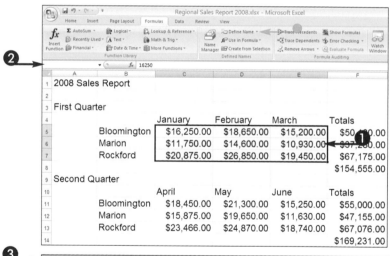

GO TO A RANGE

1 Click the **Name** [▾].

2 Click the range name to which you want to move.

Quarter2	▾					
Quarter1	B	2 C	D	E	F	
Quarter2		Report				
Quarter3						
Quarter4						
3	First Quarter					
4		January	February	March	Totals	
5	Bloomington	$16,250.00	$18,650.00	$15,200.00	$50,100.00	
6	Marion	$11,750.00	$14,600.00	$10,930.00	$37,280.00	
7	Rockford	$20,875.00	$26,850.00	$19,450.00	$67,175.00	
8					$154,555.00	
9	Second Quarter					
10		April	May	June	Totals	
11	Bloomington	$18,450.00	$21,300.00	$15,250.00	$55,000.00	
12	Marion	$15,875.00	$19,650.00	$11,630.00	$47,155.00	
13	Rockford	$23,466.00	$24,870.00	$18,740.00	$67,076.00	
14					$169,231.00	

● Excel immediately activates the cells.

Quarter2	▾	fx	18450			
	A	B	C	D	E	F
1	2008 Sales Report					
2						
3	First Quarter					
4			January	February	March	Totals
5		Bloomington	$16,250.00	$18,650.00	$15,200.00	$50,100.00
6		Marion	$11,750.00	$11,600.00	$10,930.00	$37,280.00
7		Rockford	$20,875.00	$26,850.00	$19,450.00	$67,175.00
8						$154,555.00
9	Second Quarter					
10			April	May	June	Totals
11		Bloomington	$18,450.00	$21,300.00	$15,250.00	$55,000.00
12		Marion	$15,875.00	$19,650.00	$11,630.00	$47,155.00
13		Rockford	$23,400.00	$24,870.00	$18,740.00	$67,076.00
14						$169,231.00

TIPS

Are there any rules for naming ranges?

Yes. Range names must start with a letter or an underscore (_). After that, you can use any character, uppercase or lowercase, or any punctuation or keyboard symbols, with the exception of a hyphen or space. Because neither hyphens nor spaces are allowed in range names, you can substitute them with a period or underscore.

How do I edit a range name?

You can use the Name Manager feature to make changes to your range names. To display the Name Manager, click the **Name Manager** button on the Formulas tab. You can edit existing range names, change the cells referenced by a range, or remove ranges to which you no longer need names assigned in the worksheet.

Reference Ranges in Formulas

You can reference an entire group of cells in a formula by referencing its range name. This can speed up the time it takes to build a formula in a worksheet, and range names are much easier to remember than the default range names that Excel assigns.

Reference Ranges in Formulas

1 Click in the cell to which you want to assign a formula.

2 Type the formula that you want to apply.

Note: See the "Create Formulas" task, earlier in this chapter, to learn more.

3 To insert a range into the formula, click **Use in Formula** on the Formulas tab.

4 Click a range.

Excel automatically inserts the range name.

You can also select the range directly in the worksheet.

5 Continue creating the formula as needed.

6 Press **Enter** or click **Accept** (☑) on the Formula bar to complete the formula.

The formula results appear in the cell.

● You can also click **Use in Formula** on the Formulas tab and click **Paste** to open the Paste Name dialog box, where you can select which range you want to use in the formula.

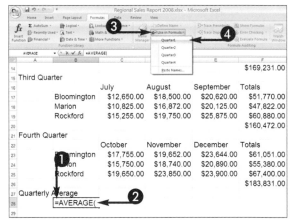

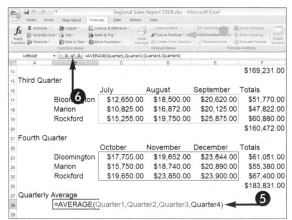

Reference Cells from Other Worksheets

You can reference cells in other worksheets in your Excel formulas. When referencing data from other worksheets, you must specify the worksheet name, followed by an exclamation mark and then by the cell address, such as Sheet2!D12. If the worksheet has a specific name, such as Sales, you must use the name along with an exclamation mark, followed by the cell or range reference (Sales!D12). If the worksheet name includes spaces, enclose the reference in single quote marks, such as 'Sales Totals!D12'.

See Chapter 10 to learn more about naming Excel worksheets.

Reference Cells from Other Worksheets

① Click the cell to which you want to assign a formula.

② Create the formula that you want to apply.

Note: See the "Create Formulas" task, earlier in this chapter, to learn more.

③ When you are ready to insert a cell or range from another worksheet into the formula, type the worksheet name.

④ Type an exclamation mark.

⑤ Type the cell address or range.

You can continue creating the formula as needed.

⑥ When finished, press **Enter** or click **Accept** (☑) on the Formula bar to complete the formula.

● The formula results appear in the cell.

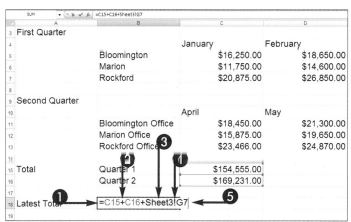

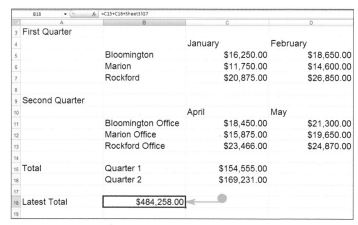

Apply Absolute and Relative Cell References

By default, Excel treats the cells that you include in formulas as relative locations rather than set locations in the worksheet. This is called *relative cell referencing*. For example, when you copy a formula to a new location, the formula automatically adjusts using relative cell addresses. If you want to address a particular cell location no matter where the formula appears, you can assign an *absolute cell reference*. Absolute references are preceded with a dollar sign in the formula, such as =D2+E2.

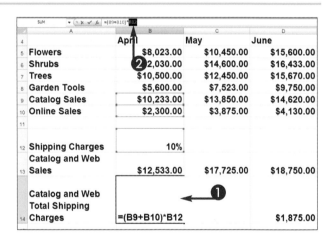

Apply Absolute and Relative Cell References

ASSIGN ABSOLUTE REFERENCES

1 Click in the cell containing the formula that you want to change.

2 Select the cell reference.

3 Press F4 .

Note: You can also type dollar signs to make a reference absolute.

● Excel enters dollar signs ($) before each part of the cell reference, making the cell reference absolute.

Note: You can continue pressing F4 to cycle through mixed, relative, and absolute references.

4 Press Enter or click **Accept** (☑).

Excel assigns the changes to the formula.

ASSIGN RELATIVE REFERENCES

1 Click in the cell containing the formula that you want to change.

2 Select the cell reference.

3 Press F4 to cycle to relative addressing.

Note: *You can press F4 multiple times to cycle through mixed, relative, and absolute references.*

Note: *You can also type dollar signs to make a reference absolute.*

4 Press Enter or click **Accept** (☑).

● Excel assigns the changes to the formula.

	April	May	June
5 Flowers	$8,023.00	$10,450.00	$15,600.00
6 Shrubs	,030.00	$14,600.00	$16,433.00
7 Trees	$10,500.00	$12,450.00	$15,670.00
8 Garden Tools	$5,600.00	$7,523.00	$9,750.00
9 Catalog Sales	$10,233.00	$13,850.00	$14,620.00
10 Online Sales	$2,300.00	$3,875.00	$4,130.00
11			
12 Shipping Charges	10%		
Catalog and Web			
13 Sales	$12,533.00	$17,725.00	$18,750.00
Catalog and Web Total Shipping			
14 Charges	=(B9+B10)*B12		$1,875.00

	April	May	June
5 Flowers	$8,023.00	$10,450.00	$15,600.00
6 Shrubs	$12,000.00	$14,000.00	$10,433.00
7 Trees	$10,500.00	$12,450.00	$15,670.00
8 Garden Tools	$5,600.00	$7,523.00	$9,750.00
9 Catalog Sales	$10,233.00	$13,850.00	$14,620.00
10 Online Sales	$2,300.00	$3,875.00	$4,130.00
11			
12 Shipping Charges	10%		
Catalog and Web			
13 Sales	$12,533.00	$17,725.00	$18,750.00
Catalog and Web Total Shipping			
14 Charges	=(B9+B10)*B12		$1,875.00

When would I use absolute cell references?

You can use absolute referencing to always refer to the same cell in a worksheet. For example, perhaps your worksheet contains several columns of pricing information that refer to one discount rate disclosed in cell G10. When you create a formula based on the discount rate, you want to make sure that the formula always refers to cell G10, even if the formula is moved or copied to another cell. By making cell G10 absolute instead of relative, you can always count on an accurate value for the success of your formula.

When would I use mixed cell references?

You can use mixed referencing to reference the same row or column, but different relative cells within, such as $C6, which keeps the column from changing while the row remains relative. If the mixed reference is C$6, the column is relative but the row is absolute. You can press F4 while writing a formula to cycle through absolute, mixed, and relative cell referencing, or you can type the dollar signs ($) as needed.

Understanding Functions

If you are looking for a speedier way to enter formulas, you can use a wide variety of built-in formulas, called *functions*. Functions are ready-made formulas that perform a series of operations on a specified range of values. Excel offers over 300 functions that you can use to perform mathematical calculations on your worksheet data.

Function Elements

Because functions are formulas, all functions must start with an equal sign (=). Functions are also distinct in that each one has a name. For example, the function that sums data is called the SUM function, while the function for averaging values is called the AVERAGE function. You can type functions directly into your worksheet cells or into the Formula bar. You can also use the Insert Function dialog box to help construct functions. This dialog box offers help in selecting and applying functions to your data.

Constructing Arguments

Functions typically use arguments to indicate the cell addresses that you want the functions to calculate. Arguments are enclosed in parentheses. When applying a function to individual cells in the worksheet, you can use a comma to separate the cell addresses, such as =SUM(A5,B5,C5). When applying a function to a range of cells, you can use a colon to designate the first and last cells in the range, such as =SUM(B5:E12). If your range has a name, you can insert the name, such as =SUM(Sales).

Types of Functions

Excel groups functions into ten categories, and each category can include a variety of functions:

Category	Description
Database & List Management	Includes functions for counting, adding, and filtering database items.
Date & Time	Includes functions for calculating dates, times, and minutes.
Engineering	Offers many kinds of functions for engineering calculations.
Financial	Includes functions for calculating loans, principal, interest, yield, and depreciation.
Information	Includes functions for testing your data.
Logical	Includes functions for logical conjectures, such as if-then statements.
Lookup & Reference	Includes functions that enable you to locate references or specific values in your worksheets.
Mathematical & Trigonometric	Includes a wide variety of functions for calculations of all types.
Statistical	Includes functions for calculating averages, probabilities, rankings, trends, and more.
Text	Includes text-based functions to search and replace data and other text tasks.

Common Functions

The table below lists some of the more popular Excel functions that you might use with your spreadsheet.

Function	Category	Description	Syntax
SUM	Math & Trig	Adds values	=SUM(number1,number2,...)
INT	Math & Trig	Rounds down to the nearest integer	=INT(number)
ROUND	Math & Trig	Rounds a number specified by the number of digits	=ROUND(number,number_digits)
ROUNDDOWN	Math & Trig	Rounds a number down	=ROUNDDOWN(number, number_digits)
COUNT	Statistical	Returns a count of text or numbers in a range	=COUNT(value1,value2,...)
AVERAGE	Statistical	Averages a series of arguments	=AVERAGE(number1,number2,...)
MIN	Statistical	Returns the smallest value in a series	=MIN(number1,number2,...)
MAX	Statistical	Returns the largest value in a series	=MAX(number1,number2,...)
MEDIAN	Statistical	Returns the middle value in a series	=MEDIAN(number1,number2,...)
PMT	Financial	Finds the periodic payment for a fixed loan	=PMT(interest_rate,number_of_periods,present_value,future_value,type)
RATE	Financial	Returns an interest rate	=RATE(number_of_periods, payment,present_value,future_value,type,guess)
TODAY	Date & Time	Returns the current date	=TODAY()
IF	Logical	Returns one of two results that you specify based on whether the value is TRUE or FALSE	=IF(logical_text,value_if_true,value_if_false)
AND	Logical	Returns TRUE if all of the arguments are true, FALSE if any are false	=AND(logical1,logical2,...)
OR	Logical	Returns TRUE if any argument is true, or FALSE if all arguments are false	=OR(logical1,logical2,...)

Apply a Function

You can use functions to speed up your Excel calculations. You can use the Insert Function dialog box to look for a particular function from among Excel's ten function categories.

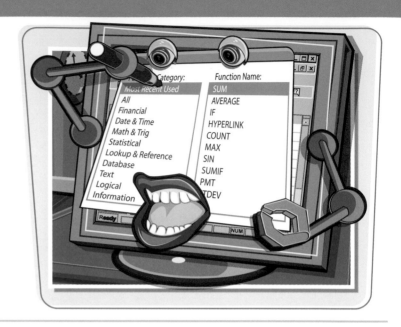

Apply a Function

1 Click in the cell to which you want to assign a function.

2 Click the **Function Wizard** button (fx) on the Formula bar or on the Formulas tab.

● You can also choose from functions listed among the Function Library group on the Formulas tab.

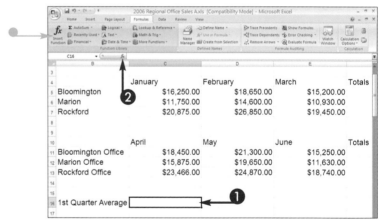

● Excel inserts an equal sign automatically to denote a formula and displays the Insert Function dialog box.

3 Click the **Or select a category** ✓.

4 Click a category.

Excel's built-in functions are grouped into ten categories.

Note: *See the previous task, "Understanding Functions," to learn more about function categories.*

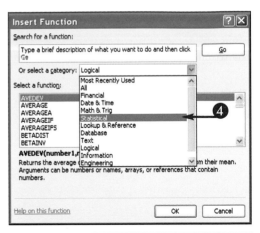

● A list of functions appears here.

5 Click the function that you want to apply.

● A description appears here for the function that you select.

6 Click OK.

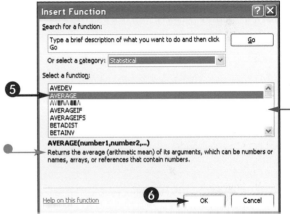

What kind of results can I expect with Excel functions?

Most of the time, the functions that you create will produce number results. However, because functions use different types of arguments, some functions produce different types of results.

Result	Description
Number	Number results can include any integer or decimal number.
Time & Date	When applying time and date functions, you can expect time and date results.
Logical values	Logical arguments produce results such as TRUE, FALSE; YES, NO; 1, 0.
Text	Any text results always appear surrounded by quotation marks.
Arrays	An array is a column or table of cells that are treated as a single value, and array formulas operate on multiple cells.
Cell references	Some function results display references to other cells rather than actual values.
Error values	If a function uses error values as arguments, the results appear as error values as well. Error values are not the same as error messages.

continued

Apply a Function
(continued)

After selecting a function, you can then apply the function to a cell or range of cells in your worksheet. You can use the Function Arguments dialog box to help you construct all of the necessary components of a function. The dialog box can help you to determine what values you need to enter to build the formula.

The Function Arguments dialog box appears.

7 Depending on the function's arguments, select the cells for each argument required by the function.

If you select a cell or range of cells directly in the worksheet, Excel automatically adds the references to the argument.

You can also type a range or cell address into the argument text box.

● The dialog box displays additional information about the function here.

8 If needed, continue adding the necessary cell references to complete all of the function's arguments.

9 When finished constructing the arguments, click **OK**.

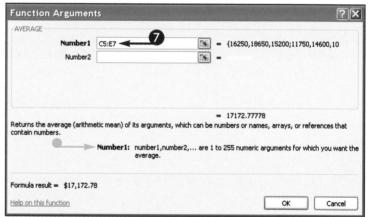

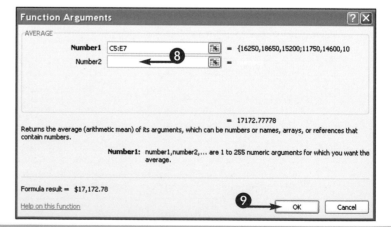

● Excel displays the function results in the cell.

● The function appears in the Formula bar.

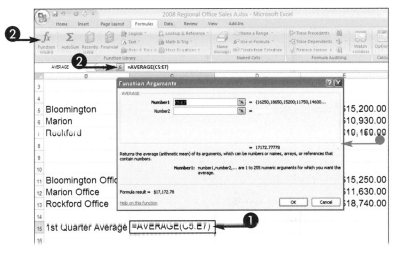

EDIT A FUNCTION

① Click the cell containing the function that you want to edit.

② Click the **Function Wizard** button ( ) on the Formula bar or on the Formulas tab.

● Excel displays the Function Arguments dialog box, where you can make changes to the cell references or values as needed.

How can I find help with a particular function?

If you click the **Help on this function** link in either the Insert Function or Function Arguments dialog box, you can access Excel's Help files to find out more about the function. The function help includes an example of the function being used, and tips about how to use the function.

The Function Arguments dialog box covers the cells that I need to select. How do I move the dialog box out of the way?

You can click the **Collapse** button ( ) at the end of the argument text box to minimize the dialog box. You can then select any cells needed, and click the **Expand** button ( ) to maximize the dialog box again. You can also click and drag the dialog box by its title bar to move it around the screen.

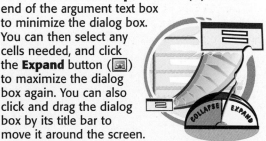

Total Cells with AutoSum

One of the most popular functions available in Excel is the AutoSum function. AutoSum automatically totals the contents of cells. For example, you can quickly total a column of sales figures. AutoSum works by guessing which surrounding cells you want to total, although you can also specify exactly which cells to sum.

① Click in the cell where you want to insert a sum total.

② Click the **Formulas** tab on the Ribbon.

③ Click the **AutoSum** button.

● If you click the **AutoSum** ⬝, you can select another common function to apply, such as Average.

You can also click the **AutoSum** button on the Home tab.

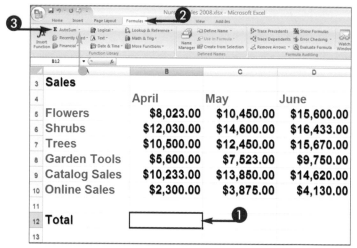

● AutoSum immediately attempts to total the adjacent cells.

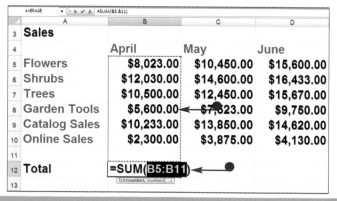

- To sum another range of cells instead of AutoSum's guess, you can select the cells that you want to include in the sum.

④ Press the Enter key or click **Accept** (☑).

	A	B	C	D
	AVERAGE ▼ ⊗ × ✓ ƒx =SUM(B5:B10)			
3	**Sales**			
4	④	April	May	June
5	Flowers	$8,023.00	$10,450.00	$15,600.00
6	Shrubs	$12,030.00	$14,600.00	$16,433.00
7	Trees	$10,500.00	$12,450.00	$15,670.00
8	Garden Tools	$5,600.00	$7,523.00	$9,750.00
9	Catalog Sales	$10,233.00	$13,850.00	$14,620.00
10	Online Sales	$2,300.00	$3,875.00	$4,130.00
11				
12	**Total**	=SUM(B5:B10)		
13		SUM(number1, [number2], ...)		

- Excel totals the selected cells.

	A	B	C	D
	B12 ▼ ⊙ ƒx =SUM(B5:B10)			
3	**Sales**			
4		April	May	June
5	Flowers	$8,023.00	$10,450.00	$15,600.00
6	Shrubs	$12,030.00	$14,600.00	$16,433.00
7	Trees	$10,500.00	$12,450.00	$15,670.00
8	Garden Tools	$5,600.00	$7,523.00	$9,750.00
9	Catalog Sales	$10,233.00	$13,850.00	$14,620.00
10	Online Sales	$2,300.00	$3,875.00	$4,130.00
11				
12	**Total**	$48,686.00		
13				

TIPS

Can I total cells without applying a function?

Yes. Excel's status bar quickly sums cells or displays results from several other popular functions without having to insert a formula or function into a cell. When you select a group of cells that you want to total, Excel immediately adds all of the cell contents and displays a total in the status bar at the bottom of the program window. To sum noncontiguous cells, press and hold Ctrl while clicking the cells.

Can I apply AutoSum to both rows and columns at the same time?

Yes. Simply select both the row and column of data that you want to sum, along with a blank row and column to hold the results. When you apply the AutoSum function, Excel sums the row and column and displays the results in the blank row and column.

Audit a Worksheet for Errors

When dealing with larger worksheets in Excel, it is not always easy to locate the source of a formula error when scrolling through the many cells. To help you with errors that arise, you can use Excel's Formula Auditing tools to examine and correct formula errors. The Error Checking feature looks through your worksheet for errors and helps you find solutions.

Audit a Worksheet for Errors

APPLY ERROR CHECKING

① Click the **Formulas** tab on the Ribbon.

② Click the **Error Checking** ▪.

③ Click **Error Checking**.

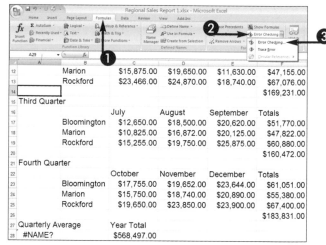

● Excel displays the Error Checking dialog box and highlights the first cell containing an error.

④ To fix the error, click **Edit in Formula Bar**.

● To find help with an error, you can click here to open the Help files.

● To ignore the error, you can click **Ignore Error**.

● You can click **Previous** and **Next** to scroll through all of the errors on the worksheet.

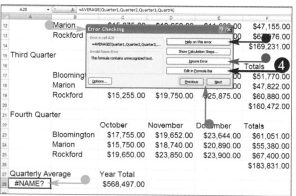

⑤ Make edits to the cell references in the Formula bar.

⑥ Click **Resume**.

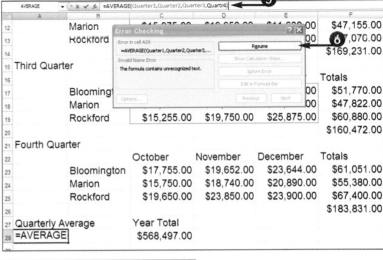

● When the error check is complete, a prompt box appears.

⑦ Click **OK**.

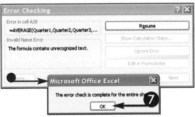

What kinds of error messages does Excel display for formula errors?
The following table explains some of the different types of error values that can appear in cells when an error occurs:

Error Message	Problem	Solution
######	The cell is not wide enough to contain the value	Increase the column width
#DIV/0!	Dividing by zero	Edit the cell reference or value of the denominator
#N/A	Value is not available	Ensure that the formula references the correct value
#NAME?	Does not recognize text in a formula	Ensure that the name referenced is correct
#NULL!	Specifies two areas that do not intersect	Check for an incorrect range operator or correct the intersection problem
#NUM!	Invalid numeric value	Check the function for an unacceptable argument
#REF!	Invalid cell reference	Correct cell references
#VALUE!	Wrong type of argument or operand	Double-check arguments and operands

continued

Auditing tools can trace the path of your formula components and check each cell reference that contributes to the formula. When tracing the relationships between cells, you can display tracer lines to find *precedents*, cells referred to in a formula, or *dependents*, cells that contain the formula results.

Audit a Worksheet for Errors *(continued)*

TRACE PRECEDENTS

① Click in the cell containing the formula results or content that you want to trace.

② Click the **Formulas** tab on the Ribbon.

③ Click the **Trace Precedents** button.

● To trace dependents instead, you can click the **Trace Dependents** button.

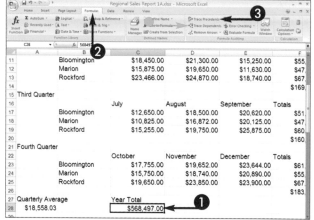

● Excel displays trace lines from the current cell to the cells referenced in the formula.

You can make changes to the cell contents or to the formula to make any corrections.

● In this example, the trace lines show that the wrong total cell is referenced.

● You can click the **Remove Arrows** button to turn off the trace lines.

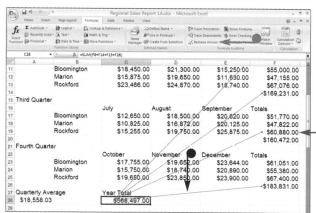

TRACE ERRORS

① Click in the cell containing the error that you want to trace.

② Click the **Formulas** tab on the Ribbon.

③ Click the **Error Checking** .

④ Click **Trace Error**.

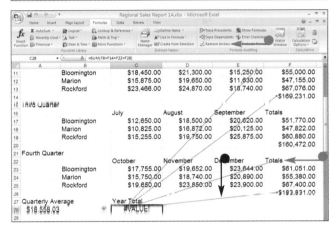

● Excel displays trace lines from the current cell to any cells referenced in the formula.

You can make changes to the cell contents or changes to the formula to correct the error.

● In this example, the text cell is referenced in the formula instead of a numeric value.

● You can click the **Remove Arrows** button to turn off the trace lines.

 TIPS

How do I use the Smart Tag to fix formula errors?
Excel displays a Smart Tag icon (⬦) whenever you encounter an error. You can click the Smart Tag to view a menu of options, including options for correcting the error. For example, you can click the **Help on this error** menu command to find out more about the error message.

What does the Evaluate Formula button do?
You can click the **Evaluate Formula** button (⬚) on the Formula Auditing toolbar to check over your formula or function step by step. When you click the cell containing the formula that you want to evaluate, and click ⬚, Excel opens the Evaluate Formula dialog box, where you can evaluate each portion of the formula to check it for correct references and values.

Add a Watch Window

The longer your worksheet becomes, the more difficult it is to keep important cells and ranges in view as you scroll through your worksheet. You can use a Watch Window to monitor important cell data. A Watch Window displays the cell containing the formula, no matter where you scroll. For example, you may want to see the formula results in a cell at the very top of your worksheet while you make changes to the data referenced in the formula at the bottom of the worksheet.

You can also use the Watch Window to view cells in other worksheets or in a linked workbook.

Add a Watch Window

① Click the **Formulas** tab on the Ribbon.

② Click the **Watch Window** button.

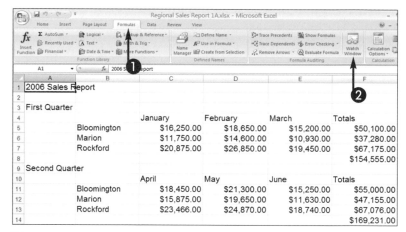

● The Watch Window opens.

③ Click **Add Watch**.

● The Add Watch dialog box appears.

④ Select the cell or range that you want to watch.

● You can also type in the cell reference.

⑤ Click **Add**.

Note: *You can add multiple cells to the Watch Window.*

● Excel adds the cells to the Watch Window, including any values or formulas within the cells.

If you scroll away from the original cells, the Watch Window continues to display the cell contents.

To return to the original cell, you can double-click the cell name.

⑥ Click the **Close** button (■) to close the Watch Window.

TIPS

How do I remove and add cells in the Watch Window?

To remove a cell from the Watch Window, click the cell name, and then click the **Delete Watch** button in the Watch Window. Excel immediately removes the cell from the window. You can add more cells by clicking the **Add Watch** button and selecting the cell that you want to add to the window.

How can I move and resize the Watch Window?

To move the Watch Window, simply click and drag the window's title bar. You can reposition the window anywhere onscreen. You can also dock the window to appear with the toolbars at the top of the Excel program window. To resize the columns within the Watch Window, move the mouse pointer over a column in the Watch Window, and drag to resize the column.

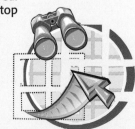

Change Number Formats

You can use number formatting to control the appearance of numerical data in your worksheet. For example, if you have a column of prices, you can apply currency formatting to the data to format the numbers with dollar signs and decimal points. Excel offers several different number categories, or styles, from which to choose.

Change Number Formats

① Select the cell, range, or data that you want to format.

Note: *See Chapter 9 to learn how to select cells; see Chapter 11 to learn about ranges.*

② Click the **Home** tab on the Ribbon.

③ Click the **Number Format** ⏷.

Note: *You can apply number formatting to single cells, ranges, columns, rows, or an entire worksheet.*

④ Click a number format.

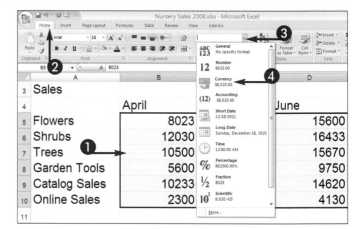

Excel applies the number formatting to the data.

● To quickly apply dollar signs to your data, you can click the **Currency Style** button ($).

● If you click the **Currency Style** ⏷, you can specify a type of currency, such as Euro.

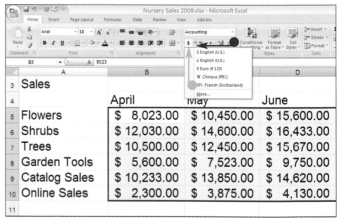

● To quickly apply percent signs to your data, you can click the **Percent Style** button (%).

● You can click the **Number Dialog** button (⬚) to open the Format Cells dialog box to the Number tab to find more formatting options.

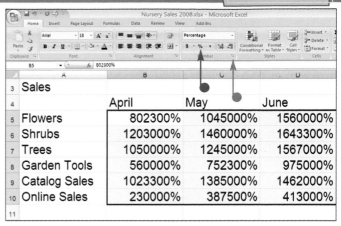

● To quickly apply commas to your number data, you can click the **Comma Style** button (,).

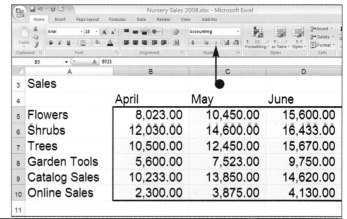

What sort of number formats can I apply to my numeric data?
Each number format style is designed for a specific use. The table below explains each number category:

Style	Description
General	The default category; no specific formatting is applied
Number	General number display with two default decimal places
Currency	Adds dollar signs and decimals to display monetary values
Accounting	Lines up currency symbols and decimal points in a column
Short Date	Used to display short date strings
Long Date	Used to display long date strings
Time	Used to display time values
Percentage	Multiplies cell value by 100 and displays percent sign
Fraction	Displays value as a specified fraction
Scientific	Uses scientific or exponential notation
Text	Treats values as text

Change the Font and Size

You can control the font that you use for your worksheet data, along with the size of the data text. For example, you may want to make the worksheet title larger than the rest of the data, or you may want to resize the font for the entire worksheet to a more legible size to make the data easier to read.

Change the Font and Size

CHANGE THE FONT

① Select the cell or data that you want to format.

Note: See Chapter 9 to learn how to select cells.

② Click the **Home** tab on the Ribbon.

③ Click the **Font** ⊡.

● You can use the scroll arrows or scroll bar to scroll through all of the available fonts.

You can also begin typing a font name to choose a font.

④ Click a font.

● Excel immediately applies the font.

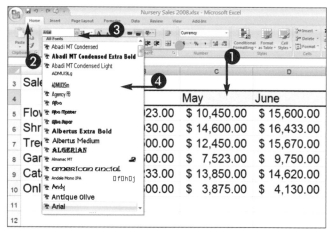

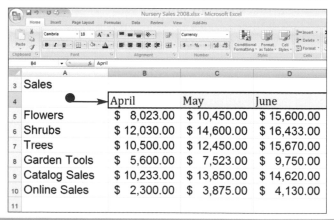

CHANGE THE FONT SIZE

① Select the cell or data that you want to format.

Note: See Chapter 9 to learn how to select cells.

② Click the **Home** tab on the Ribbon.

③ Click the **Font Size** ▣.

④ Click a size.

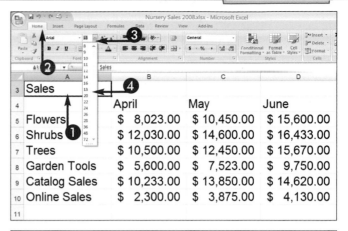

● Excel immediately applies the new size to the selected cell or data.

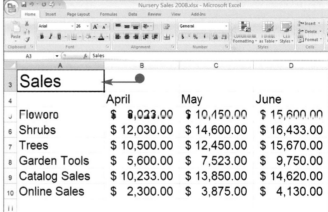

Is there a way to apply multiple formatting options at the same time?

Yes. You can use the Format Cells dialog box to apply a new font, size, or any of the basic formatting, such as bold, italics, and underlining. Follow these steps:

① Click the **Home** tab on the Ribbon.

② Click the **Font Dialog** button (▣) in the corner of the Font group.

The Format Cells dialog box appears and displays the Font tab.

③ You can use the various options within the Font tab to control the font, size, and style of the data.

④ Click **OK** to save your changes.

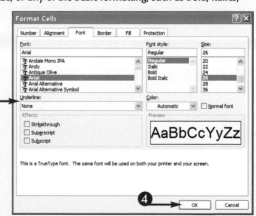

Increase or Decrease Decimals

You can control the number of decimals that appear with numeric data using the Increase Decimal and Decrease Decimal commands. For example, you may want to increase the number of decimals shown in a cell, or reduce the number of decimals in a formula result.

❶ Select the cell or range that you want to format.

Note: See Chapter 9 to learn how to select cells; see Chapter 11 to learn about ranges.

❷ Click the **Home** tab on the Ribbon.

❸ Click a decimal button.

You can click **Increase Decimal** (⊞) to increase the number of decimals.

You can click **Decrease Decimal** (⊞) to decrease the number of decimals.

Excel adjusts the number of decimals that appear in the cell or cells.

● This example removes one decimal.

● You can click ⊞ again to remove another decimal.

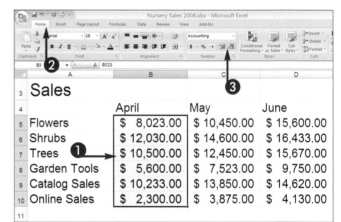

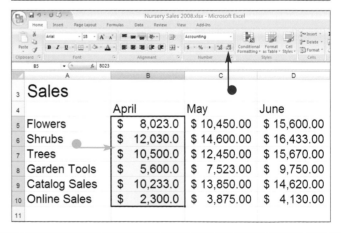

Change Data Color

You can change the color of your data, whether the data is numeric or text. For example, you might choose a brighter color for any cell data to which you want to bring attention, or select a different color for the column headers in your worksheet.

When adding color to worksheets, you should always consider the color's effect on the legibility of your data, both in print and on-screen. You want your worksheet to appear easy to read, not jarring and distracting to the eye.

Change Data Color

① Select the cell, range, or data that you want to format.

Note: See Chapter 9 to learn how to select cells; see Chapter 11 to learn about ranges.

② Click the **Home** tab on the Ribbon.

③ Click the **Font Color** .

● To apply the current color that is shown, simply click the **Font Color** button ().

④ Click a color from the palette.

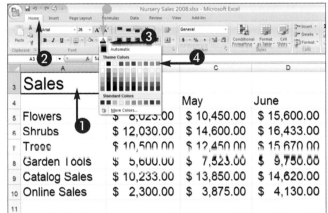

● Excel applies the color to the data.

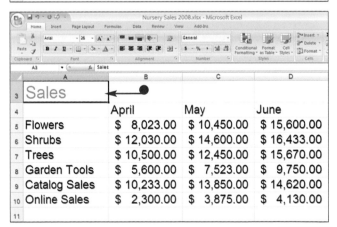

Adjust the Cell Alignment

You can control the alignment of data within your worksheet cells. By default, Excel automatically aligns text data to the left and number data to the right. Data is also aligned vertically to sit at the bottom of the cell. You can change horizontal and vertical alignments to improve the appearance of your worksheet data.

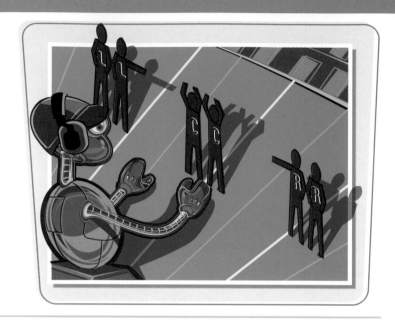

Adjust the Cell Alignment

SET HORIZONTAL ALIGNMENT

1 Select the cells that you want to format.

Note: See Chapter 9 to learn how to select cells.

2 Click the **Home** tab on the Ribbon.

3 Click an alignment button from the Alignment group.

Click the **Align Left** button (▤) to align data to the left.

Click the **Center** button (▤) to center align the data.

Click the **Align Right** button (▤) to align data to the right.

Excel immediately applies the alignment to your cells.

● This example aligns the text data to the right of the cell.

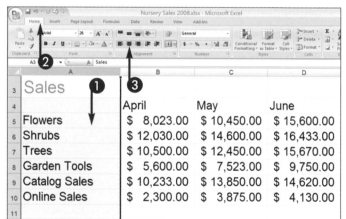

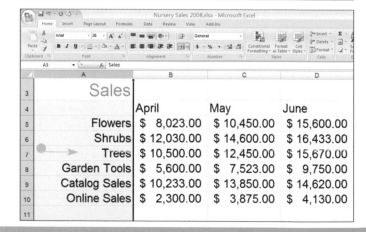

SET VERTICAL ALIGNMENT

① Select the cells that you want to format.

Note: See Chapter 9 to learn how to select cells.

② Click the **Home** tab on the Ribbon.

③ Click an alignment button from the Alignment group.

Click the **Top Align** button (▤) to align data to the top.

Click the **Middle Align** button (▤) to align the data in the middle.

Click the **Bottom Align** button (▤) to align data to the bottom.

Excel immediately applies the alignment to your cells.

● This example aligns the text data to the top of the cell.

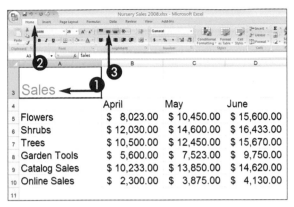

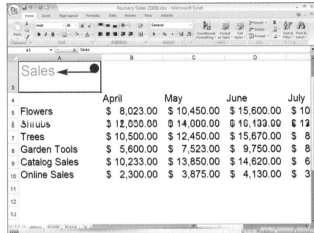

How do I set indents for my cell text?

You can use the Increase Indent and Decrease Indent buttons to add indents to lines of text in your worksheet. To indent text, click the **Increase Indent** button (▤) on the Home tab. To decrease an indent, click the **Decrease Indent** button (▤).

Can I justify my text to create left and right margins in a cell?

Yes. To justify cell text, you must open the Format Cells dialog box and display the **Alignment** tab. To do so, click the **Font Dialog** button (▣) at the bottom of the Alignment group. You can then click the **Horizontal** ☑ and click **Justify** to assign justification to your cell text.

Control Data Orientation

You can use Excel's Orientation command to rotate data in a cell. For example, you might angle column labels to make them easier to distinguish from one another. You can also angle the column labels to format data better on your printed spreadsheet.

① Select the cells that you want to format.

Note: See Chapter 9 to learn how to select cells.

② Click the **Home** tab on the Ribbon.

③ Click the **Orientation** 🔽.

④ Click an orientation.

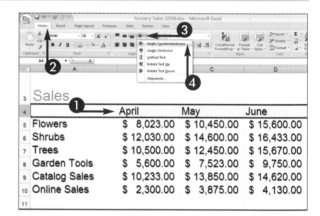

Excel applies the orientation to the cell or cells.

● This example angles the text counterclockwise.

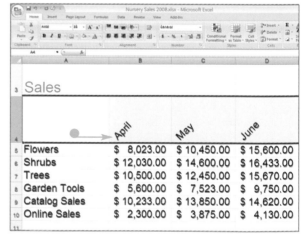

Copy Cell Formatting

You can use the Format Painter feature to copy formatting to other cells in your worksheet. For example, you may have applied a variety of formatting options to a range of cells to create a certain look. When you want to re-create the same look elsewhere in the worksheet, you do not have to repeat the same steps that you applied to assign the original formatting. Instead, you can paint the formatting to the other cells in one action.

Copy Cell Formatting

① Select the cell or range containing the formatting that you want to copy.

Note: *See Chapter 9 to learn how to select cells.*

② Click the **Home** tab on the Ribbon.

③ Click the **Format Painter** button ( ).

The ⬚ changes to ⬚⬚.

④ Click and drag over the cells to which you want to copy the formatting.

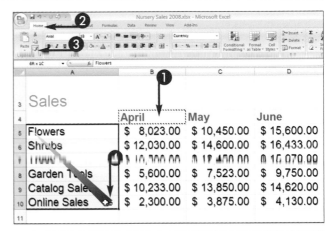

● Excel immediately copies the formatting to the new cells.

Note: *To copy the same formatting multiple times, double-click the **Format Painter** button ( ).*

Note: *You can press* Esc *to cancel the Format Painter at any time.*

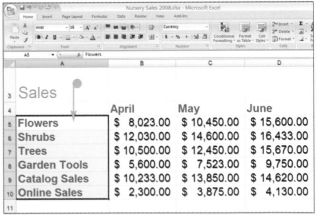

Add Borders

You can add borders to your worksheet cells to help define the contents or more clearly separate the data from surrounding cells. By default, Excel displays a grid format to help you enter data, but the borders defining the grid do not print.

You can add borders to all four sides of a cell, or choose to add borders to just one or two sides. Any borders that you add to the worksheet print along with the worksheet data.

Add Borders

ADD QUICK BORDERS

1. Select the cells that you want to format.

Note: See Chapter 9 to learn how to select cells.

2. Click the **Home** tab on the Ribbon.

3. Click the **Borders** ▾.

● To apply the current border selection shown, simply click the **Borders** button (▦).

4. Click a border style.

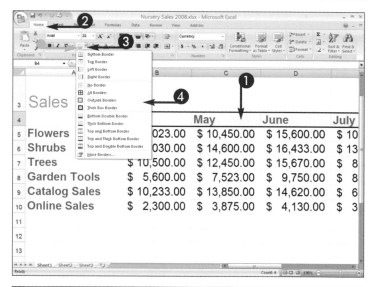

● Excel immediately assigns the borders to the cell or cells.

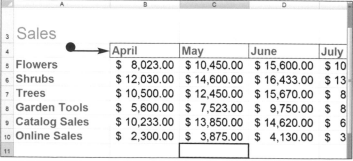

CREATE CUSTOM BORDERS

1. Select the cells that you want to format.

Note: *See Chapter 9 to learn how to select cells.*

2. Click the **Home** tab on the Ribbon.

3. Click the **Borders** ▾.

4. Click **More Borders**.

   The Format Cells dialog box appears with the Border tab displayed.

5. Click a border type to assign.

   You can click multiple border buttons to create a custom border.

● To set a particular line style to the border, click a style.

● Assign a color to the border lines here.

● Click here to assign a preset style

6. Click **OK**.

● Excel assigns the border.

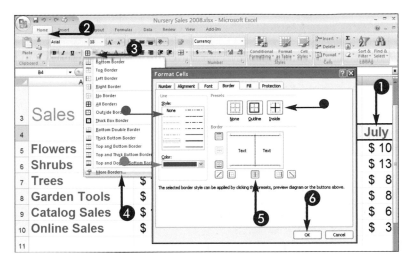

	A	B	C	D	
3	Sales				
4		April	May	June	July
5	Flowers	$ 8,023.00	$ 10,160.00	$ 15,600.00	$ 10
6	Shrubs	$ 12,030.00	$ 14,600.00	$ 16,433.00	$ 13
7	Trees	$ 10,500.00	$ 12,450.00	$ 15,670.00	$ 8
8	Garden Tools	$ 5,600.00	$ 7,523.00	$ 9,750.00	$ 8
9	Catalog Sales	$ 10,233.00	$ 13,850.00	$ 14,620.00	$ 6
10	Online Sales	$ 2,300.00	$ 3,875.00	$ 4,130.00	$ 3
11					

TIPS

Can I turn the worksheet gridlines on or off?

Yes. By default, Excel displays gridlines to help you differentiate between cells as you build your worksheets. You can turn gridlines off to view how your data will look when printed. Click the **Page Layout** tab on the Ribbon. Under the Sheet Options group, click the **View** check box for gridlines (☐ changes to ☑). Excel immediately turns off the gridlines display on-screen. Optionally, you can also turn the gridlines on or off for printing if you select or deselect the **Print** option on the Ribbon. Excel does not print gridlines unless you specify them.

How do I add color inside my worksheet cells?

You can click the **Fill Color** ▾ on the Home tab to display a palette of fill colors. When you select a color, the cell's background changes to the color that you choose. Be careful not to pick a color that makes reading your cell data difficult.

Format Data with Styles

You can use Excel's Styles to apply preset formatting designs to your worksheet data. You can apply table styles to a group of worksheet data, or you can apply cell styles to individual cells or ranges of cells. When you apply a table style, Excel converts the data into a table.

Format Data with Styles

FORMAT AS A TABLE

1. Select the cells that you want to format.

Note: See Chapter 9 to learn how to select cells.

2. Click the **Home** tab on the Ribbon.

3. Click the **Format as Table** button.

4. Click a table style.

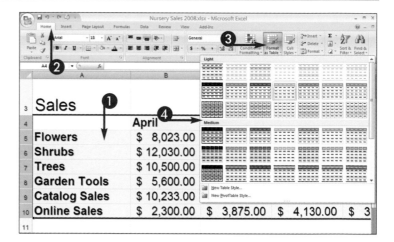

● The Format As Table dialog box appears.

5. Verify the selected cells.

6. Click **OK**.

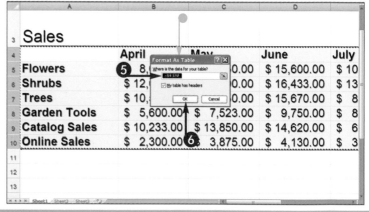

● Excel applies the formatting style.

APPLY A CELL STYLE

1 Select the cell or cells that you want to format.

Note: See Chapter 9 to learn how to select cells.

2 Click the **Home** tab on the Ribbon.

3 Click the **Cell Styles** button.

4 Click a style.

● Excel applies the formatting to the selected cell.

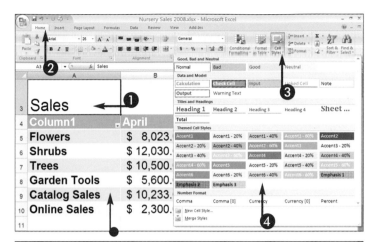

Can I add a background to my spreadsheet?

Yes. You can add a background picture to any sheet. To do so, click the **Page Layout** tab on the Ribbon and click the **Background** button. This opens the Sheet Background dialog box, in which you can navigate to the picture that you want to use. Be very careful when applying background images to your worksheet, and ensure that the image does not distract from the legibility of your cell data.

How do I apply a theme?

You can use themes to create a similar appearance among all of the Office documents that you create. Themes are shared through Word, PowerPoint, and Excel. To apply a theme to your spreadsheet, simply click the **Page Layout** tab on the Ribbon, click the **Themes** button, and then select a theme from the list. You can use the Colors, Fonts, and Effects tools to fine-tune a theme.

Assign Conditional Formatting

You can use Excel's conditional formatting feature to assign certain formatting only when the value of a cell meets the required condition. For example, your worksheet may track weekly sales and compare them to last year's sales during the same week. You can set up conditional formatting to alert you if a sales figure falls below last year's level, and make the cell data stand out among the other cells.

You can use color scales and data bars as additional visual guides to help you distinguish which cells meet your conditional rules.

Assign Conditional Formatting

APPLY A CONDITIONAL RULE

① Select the cell or range to which you want to apply conditional formatting.

② Click the **Home** tab on the Ribbon.

③ Click the **Conditional Formatting** button.

④ Click **Highlight Cells Rules**.

⑤ Click the type of rule that you want to create.

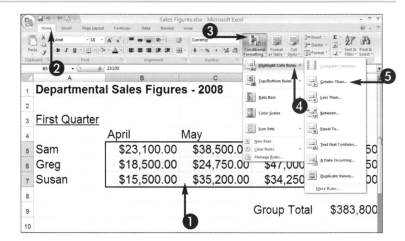

● A rule dialog box appears.

⑥ Specify the values that you want to assign for the condition.

⑦ Click **OK**.

● If the cell value changes to meet the condition, Excel applies the conditional formatting.

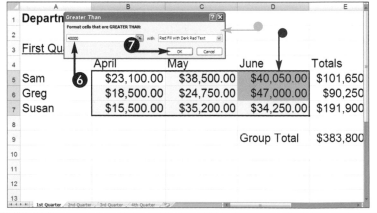

APPLY A COLOR SCALE

1. Select the cell or range that contains the conditional formatting.

2. Click the **Home** tab on the Ribbon.

3. Click the **Conditional Formatting** button.

4. Click **Color Scales**.

5. Click a color scale to apply.

● You can apply color bars instead by clicking **Data Bars**.

● Excel applies the color scale to the conditional formatting.

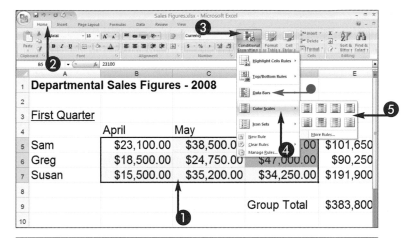

How do I create a new rule for conditional formatting?

You can open the New Formatting Rule dialog box to set a new rule and formatting for the condition that you set. Click the **Conditional Formatting** button on the Home tab, and then click **New Rule** to open the dialog box. Use the dialog box to define the condition of the rule, as well as what formatting you want to apply when the condition is met.

How do I remove conditional formatting from a cell?

To remove conditional formatting, you can use the Conditional Formatting Rules Manager dialog box. Select the data, click the **Conditional Formatting** button on the Home tab, and then click **Manage Rules**. Next, click the rule that you want to remove, and click **Delete Rule**.

Create a Chart

In Excel 2007, charting is simpler than ever before. You can quickly turn your spreadsheet data into easy-to-read charts and customize the chart style to suit your needs. You can choose from a wide variety of chart types, and Excel makes it easy to determine exactly which type of chart works best for your data. After you create a chart, you can use the Chart Tools on the Ribbon to fine-tune the chart to best display and explain the data.

Create a Chart

1 Select the range of data that you want to chart.

Note: See Chapter 9 to learn how to select cells; see Chapter 11 to learn about ranges.

You can include any headings and labels, but do not include subtotals or totals.

2 Click the **Insert** tab on the Ribbon.

3 Click a chart type from the Charts group.

4 Click a chart style.

● Excel immediately creates a chart, places it on the worksheet, and displays three chart tabs (Design, Layout, Format) for working with the chart.

Note: You may need to move your chart. See the next task to learn how.

● You can click the **Design** tab to find tools for controlling different design elements in the chart, such as the legend, chart style, and chart type.

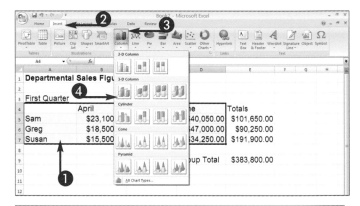

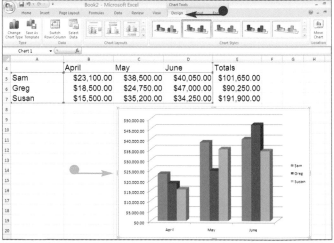

● You can click the **Layout** tab to find tools for controlling how the chart elements are positioned on the chart.

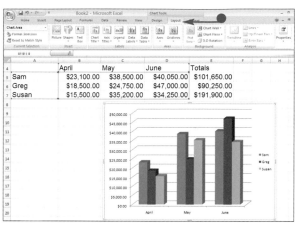

	April	May	June	Totals
Sam	$23,100.00	$38,500.00	$40,050.00	$101,650.00
Greg	$18,500.00	$24,750.00	$47,000.00	$90,250.00
Susan	$15,500.00	$35,200.00	$34,250.00	$191,900.00

● You can click the **Format** tab to find tools for formatting various chart elements, including chart text and shapes.

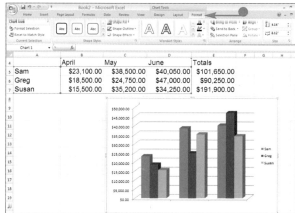

	April	May	June	Totals
Sam	$23,100.00	$38,500.00	$40,050.00	$101,650.00
Greg	$18,500.00	$24,750.00	$47,000.00	$90,250.00
Susan	$15,500.00	$35,200.00	$34,250.00	$191,900.00

TIPS

Can I select noncontiguous data to include in a chart?

Yes. The data that you select for a chart do not have to be adjacent to each other. To select noncontiguous cells and ranges, select the first range and then press and hold Ctrl while selecting additional ranges that you want to include.

How do I create an organizational chart in Excel?

You can add an organizational chart to track the hierarchy of an organization or method. When you insert an organizational chart, Excel creates four shapes to which you can add your own text. You can add additional shapes and branches to the chart as needed. To create an organizational chart, click the **Insert** tab on the Ribbon, and then click the **SmartArt** button. To learn more about using this feature, see Chapter 3.

Move and Resize Charts

You can move and resize an embedded chart on your worksheet. For example, you may want to reposition the chart at the bottom of the worksheet, or resize it to make the chart easier to read.

Move and Resize Charts

MOVE A CHART

① Click an empty area of the chart.

● Excel selects the chart and surrounds it with handles.

② Move the mouse over the edge of the chart.

The ⌖ changes to ⌖.

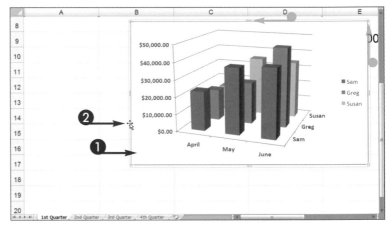

③ Click and drag the chart to a new location on the worksheet.

● A dimmed, gray border represents the chart as you move it on the worksheet.

④ Release the mouse button.

Excel moves the chart.

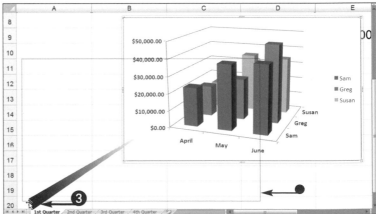

RESIZE A CHART

1 Click an empty area of the chart.

● Excel selects the chart and surrounds it with handles.

2 Move the mouse over a handle.

The ⬡ changes to ⬡.

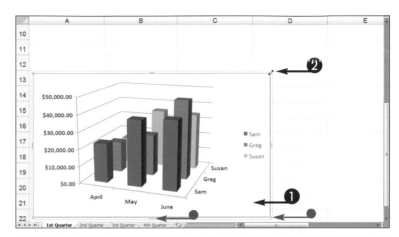

3 Click and drag a handle to resize the chart.

● A dotted border represents the chart as you resize it on the worksheet.

4 Release the mouse button.

Excel resizes the chart.

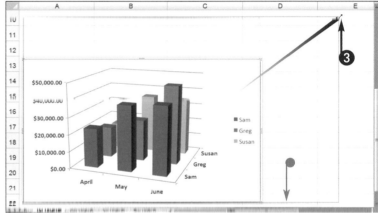

TIPS

How can I move a chart to its own worksheet?

Select the chart, and then click the **Design** tab on the Ribbon. Click the **Move Chart** button at the end of the tab. This opens the Move Chart dialog box. Click the **New Sheet** option and click **OK**. Excel adds a new worksheet to the workbook and places the chart on the worksheet.

How do I delete a chart that I no longer want?

To remove an embedded chart, simply select the chart and press Delete. Excel immediately removes the chart from the worksheet. If your chart appears on its own worksheet, you can right-click the worksheet name and click **Delete**. When Excel asks you to confirm the deletion, click **Delete**.

Change the Chart Type

You can change the chart type at any time to present your data in a different way. For example, you might want to change a bar chart to a line chart.

① Click an empty area of the chart to select the chart.

② Click the **Design** tab on the Ribbon.

③ Click the **Change Chart Type** button.

The Change Chart Type dialog box appears.

④ Click a new chart type.

⑤ Click a chart style.

⑥ Click **OK**.

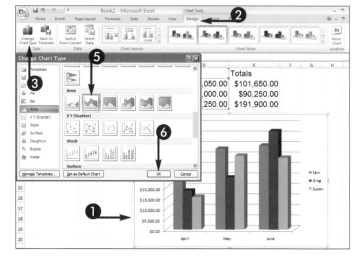

● Excel changes the chart to the chart type that you selected.

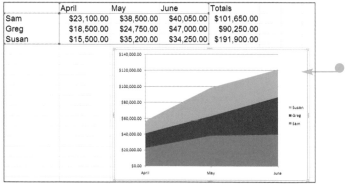

Change the Chart Style

You can change the chart style to change the appearance of a chart. For example, you might prefer a brighter color scheme for the chart. You can choose from a wide variety of styles to find just the look you want.

Change the Chart Style

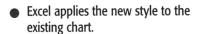

① Click an empty area of the chart to select the chart.

② Click the **Design** tab on the Ribbon.

③ Click a new chart style from the Chart Styles group.

● Click the **More** button (⊟) to view the full palette of styles.

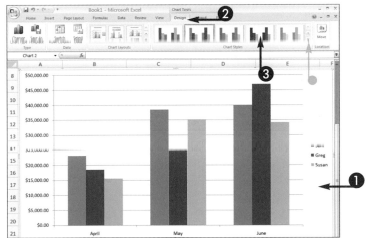

● Excel applies the new style to the existing chart.

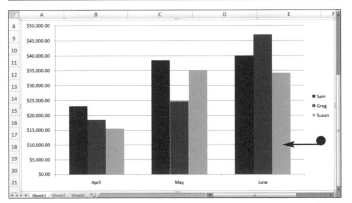

Change the Chart Layout

You can change the chart layout to change how chart elements are positioned. For example, you may prefer to show a legend on the top of the chart rather than on the side. You can use Excel's layout options to further customize your chart's appearance.

① Click an empty area of the chart to select the chart.

② Click the **Design** tab on the Ribbon.

③ Click a new layout from the Chart Layouts group.

● You can click the **More** button (⬚) to view the full palette of layouts.

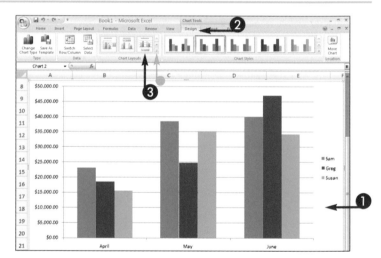

● Excel applies the new layout to the existing chart.

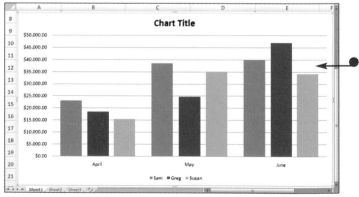

Add Axis Titles

You can add x- and y-axis titles on your chart to identify your chart data. You can add axis titles in a variety of positions on the axes. If your chart has existing titles, you can change them to more descriptive titles, or if your titles are too long, you can shorten the title text.

Axes are used to show the scale of all of the values in a chart. The x-axis is the horizontal value display in a chart, and the y-axis is the vertical value display.

Add Axis Titles

① Click the **Layout** tab on the Ribbon.

② Click the **Axis Titles** button.

③ Click the axis type that you want to add.

④ Click an axis option.

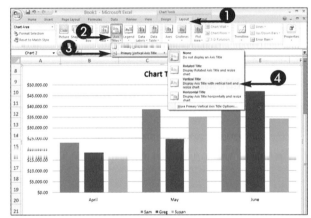

● Excel adds the new title to the chart.

⑤ Replace the placeholder text with your own title text.

You can click anywhere outside the selected object to deselect the object.

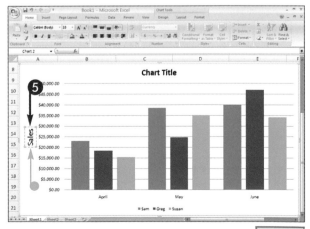

Format Chart Objects

You can change the formatting for any of the elements, called *objects* in Excel, that are contained within a chart. For example, you can change the background color or pattern for the plot area, or change the color of a data series on the chart.

Depending on which object you select, you can open the Format dialog box and display settings that are specific to that type of chart object. In this task, you learn how to change the data series and data labels. You can apply these same techniques to format other chart objects.

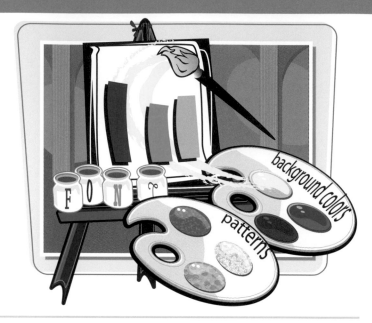

FORMAT THE DATA SERIES OBJECTS

1 Click the data series object that you want to edit.

● Excel automatically selects all of the corresponding objects in the series.

2 Click the **Format** tab on the Ribbon.

3 Click the **Format Selection** button.

The Format Data Series dialog box appears.

4 Click the type of formatting that you want to change.

In this example, the Marker Fill options appear.

5 Change any settings that you want in order to format the object differently.

6 Click **Close** to apply the changes.

● Excel changes the format option that you selected.

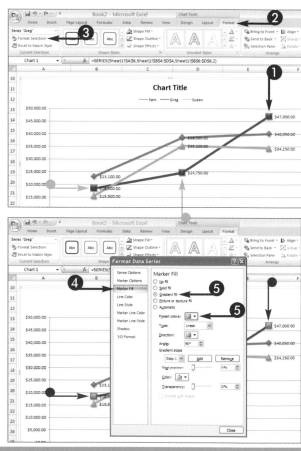

FORMAT THE DATA LABELS

1 Click the data series object that you want to edit.

● Excel automatically selects all of the corresponding objects in the series.

2 Click the **Format** tab on the Ribbon.

3 Click the **Format Selection** button.

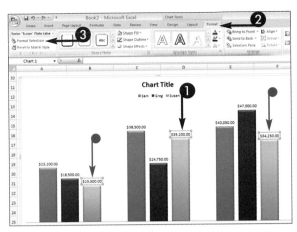

The Format Data Labels dialog box appears.

4 Click the type of formatting that you want to change.

In this example, the Label options appear.

5 Change any settings that you want in order to format the object differently.

6 Click **Close** to apply the changes.

● Excel changes the data label format option that you selected.

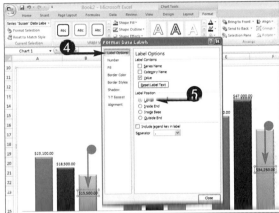

 TIPS

How do I change the font for my chart text?

The quickest way to change the font is to first select the chart element that contains text, and then right-click the element to display the mini toolbar. You can then activate any of the formatting controls, including the **Font** ▾.

How do I print my chart?

To print only the chart, first select the chart on the worksheet, click the **Office** button, and then click **Print**. The Print dialog box appears. Ensure that the **Selected Chart** option is selected (○ changes to ◉), and then click **OK** to print the chart. If the chart is on its own worksheet, you can just click the **Print** button (🖨) on the Quick Access toolbar to print the worksheet.

Add Gridlines

You can add objects to your charts, such as gridlines, using the tools on the Layout tab on the Ribbon. The Layout tab is one of three special tabs that appear when you select a chart on a worksheet. The tab lists chart objects that you can turn on or off in your chart.

Although this task shows how to add gridlines to enhance the plotting of units on a chart, you can use this same technique to add other objects to your chart with the Layout tab tools. Keep in mind that you can add gridlines to all charts except pie charts.

Add Gridlines

① Click an empty area in the chart that you want to edit.

② Click the **Layout** tab on the Ribbon.

③ Click the **Gridlines** button.

④ Click the type of gridlines that you want to add.

Select **Primary Horizontal Gridlines** to add horizontal gridlines.

Select **Primary Vertical Gridlines** to add vertical gridlines.

⑤ Click a gridline option.

Excel adds the gridlines to the chart.

● This example adds horizontal gridlines.

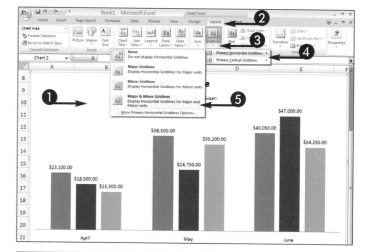

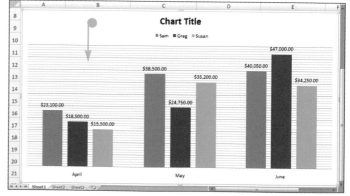

Change the Chart Data

Whenever you change data that is referenced in your chart, Excel automatically updates the chart data. For example, if you change a value, the chart updates to reflect the new value. If you need to add more data to the chart, you can easily update the source cells.

Change the Chart Data

1 Select the chart that you want to edit.

2 Click the **Design** tab on the Ribbon.

3 Click the **Select Data** button.

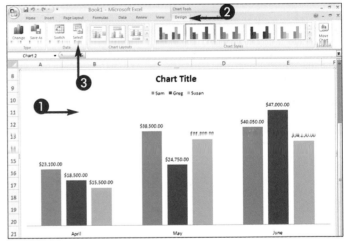

● Excel highlights the source data in the worksheet with a dashed border and displays the Select Data Source dialog box.

Note: You may need to move the dialog box to view the data.

4 Edit the data range here, or click and drag the corner handle of the source range to add or subtract cells.

● You can edit the series or axis labels using these options.

5 Click **OK**.

Excel updates the chart.

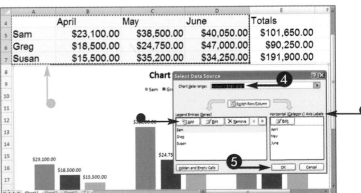

PART
IV

Part IV: PowerPoint

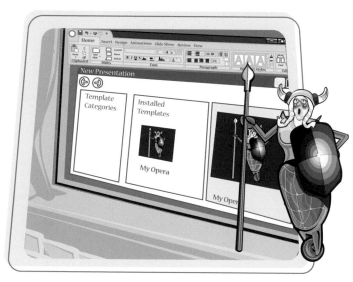

PowerPoint is a presentation program you can use to convey all kinds of messages to an audience. You can use PowerPoint to create slide shows to present ideas to clients, explain a concept or procedure to employees, or teach a class about a new subject. In this part, you learn how to create slide shows, add text and artwork, and package your show on a CD-ROM. You also learn how to add special effects to make your slide show lively and engaging to watch.

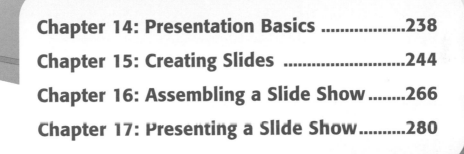

Create a Presentation with a Template

You can use PowerPoint's templates to help you create a new presentation. PowerPoint installs with a wide variety of templates featuring different types of designs and color schemes. For example, you might use the Financial Overview template to create a slide show about your company's financial status.

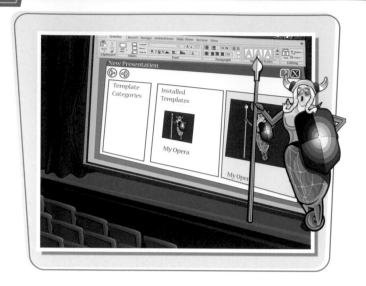

Create a Presentation with a Template

1. Click the **Office** button.

2. Click **New**.

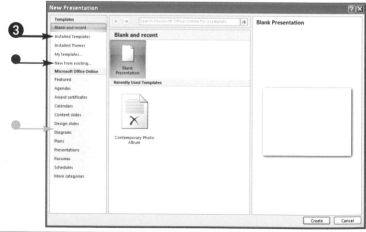

The New Presentation dialog box appears.

3. Click **Installed Templates**.

● You can click a category to view available templates on the Microsoft Office Online Web site.

● You can click here to create a new template based on the current presentation.

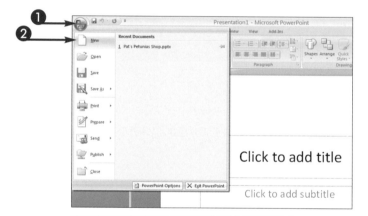

④ Click a template.

● PowerPoint displays a sample of the template design.

⑤ Click **Create**.

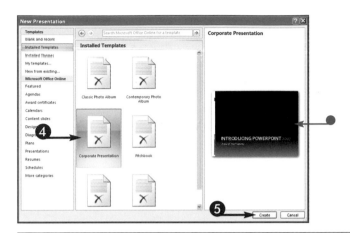

● PowerPoint creates the presentation and displays it in Slide view.

You can add your own text to each slide.

Note: *See Chapter 15 to learn how to add slide text.*

Where can I find more presentation templates?
You can download additional presentation templates from the Microsoft Office Web site. To view available templates, open the New Presentation dialog box and click the Microsoft Office Online template category that you want to view, such as **Presentations** or **Agendas**. Click the template that you want, and then click the **Download** button to start downloading the file.

How do I navigate between slides in a new presentation?
Click the **Outline** tab to view the new presentation in outline form. This allows you to build the slide show by typing text into the Outline pane. You can also type text directly onto a slide. Click the **Slides** tab to view individual slides in the presentation. You can click a slide to view the larger slide in the work area and add your own presentation content.

Build a Blank Presentation

You can create a blank presentation, containing just one slide, and add your own slide show elements and formatting. This technique allows you the freedom to create your own color schemes and design touches. You can use PowerPoint's layouts to quickly assign a layout to any blank slide.

By default, PowerPoint opens a blank slide for you whenever you start the program. You can use the slide as the first slide in your presentation and add more slides as you go along. See Chapter 15 to learn more about working with slides.

Build a Blank Presentation

1 Click the **Office** button.

2 Click **New**.

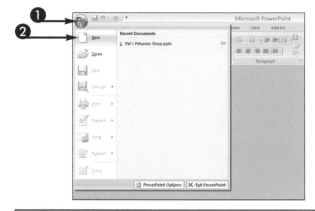

The New Presentation dialog box appears.

3 Click **Blank Presentation**.

4 Click **Create**.

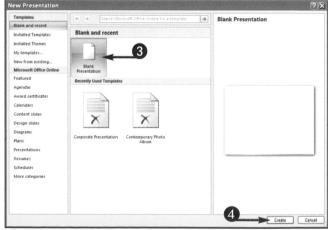

PowerPoint opens a new, blank slide.

● To change the slide layout, you can click **Layout** and choose another layout.

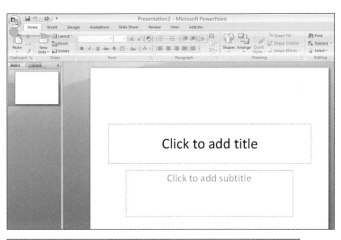

● To fill in slide text, you can click a text box and type your own text.

● You can add notes about each slide in the Notes box.

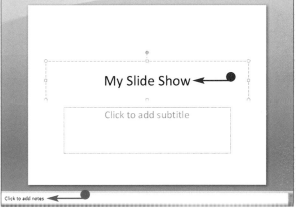

 TIPS

How do I add a design theme to my blank presentation?

To add a theme to your blank presentation, simply click the **Design** tab on the Ribbon, and then choose a theme from the Themes group. PowerPoint themes include a preset color scheme and font scheme for the presentation. When you select a theme, it is applied only to the current slide. If you have already created several slides for the presentation, you can assign the theme to the whole slide show by right-clicking over the theme on the Ribbon and clicking **Apply to All Slides**.

How do I save a slide show as a template?

You can turn any presentation you create into a template file that you can reuse to make new slide shows. Simply click the **Office** button, and then click **Save As** to open the Save As dialog box. Navigate to the folder or drive to which you want to save the template, and then click the **Save as type** ☑ and click **PowerPoint Template (*.potx)**. Type a name for the file in the **File name** text box and click **Save**. PowerPoint saves the presentation as a template file that you can reuse to create new presentations.

Change PowerPoint Views

You can use PowerPoint's views to change how your presentation appears on-screen. The PowerPoint view modes can help you with the various presentation elements that you want to edit. By default, PowerPoint displays your presentation in Normal view, which displays a single slide. You can switch to Outline view to see your presentation in an outline format, or Slide Sorter view to see all of the slides at the same time.

Change PowerPoint Views

USE OUTLINE VIEW

① Click the **Outline** tab.

PowerPoint displays the presentation in an outline format.

● You can click the outline text to edit it.

● You can click a slide icon to view the slide.

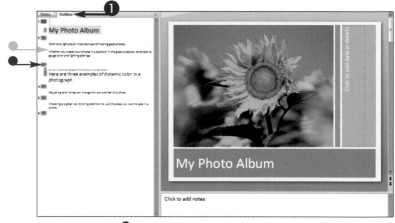

USE SLIDES VIEW

① Click the **Slides** tab.

● PowerPoint displays the current slide in the presentation.

● To view a particular slide, you can click the slide in the Slides tab.

● To close the tabs pane entirely and free up on-screen workspace, you can click ⊠.

Note: *To redisplay the tabs pane, you can click the View tab on the Ribbon, then click the **Normal** button.*

USE SLIDE SORTER VIEW

1 Click the **Slide Sorter View** button (▦).

● PowerPoint displays all of the slides in the presentation.

Note: To learn more about using Slide Sorter view to prepare a presentation, see Chapter 16.

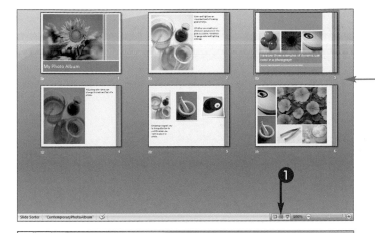

USE NORMAL VIEW

1 Click the **Normal View** button (▣).

● PowerPoint returns to the default view, displaying the current slide in the presentation.

● You can also click the **Slide Show View** button (▱) to view your presentation as a slide show.

Note: To learn more about running a presentation with Slide Show view, see Chapter 17.

How do I zoom my view of a slide?

To zoom your magnification of a slide, you can drag the **Zoom** bar on the Status bar at the bottom of the PowerPoint window. You can also click the **View** tab on the Ribbon, and then click the **Zoom** button to select a zoom percentage. You can click the **Fit slide to current window** button (▦) on the Status bar to return the view to the default view of the slide.

Can I resize the PowerPoint pane areas?

Yes. You can resize any of the panes shown in the PowerPoint program window, including the task pane and the tabs pane. Simply move the mouse ⍚ over the pane's border, and then click and drag to resize the pane's width.

Add and Edit Slide Text

When you apply one of PowerPoint's text layouts to a slide, the text box appears with placeholder text. You can replace the placeholder text with your own text.

ADD SLIDE TEXT

1 Click the text box to which you want to add text.

Note: *It is easiest to add slide text in Normal view. See Chapter 14 to learn more about PowerPoint's views.*

PowerPoint hides the placeholder text and displays a cursor.

2 Type the slide text that you want to add.

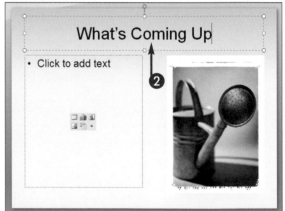

EDIT SLIDE TEXT

1 Click in the text box where you want to edit.

PowerPoint selects the object and adds a cursor to the text box.

What's Coming Up

Here's what's coming up this fall:

- We'll soon be featuring the newest line of Edgar Worthington's award-winning gardening tools. In fact, we're the only garden shop in the area to carry his tools!

1

2 Make any changes that you want to the slide text.

You can use the keyboard arrow keys to move the cursor in the text, or you can click where you want to make a change.

What's Coming Up

Here's what's coming up this fall:

- We'll soon be featuring the newest line of Edgar Worthington's award-winning gardening tools. In fact, we're the only garden shop in the area to carry his quality tools!

2

How do I add slide text in Outline view?

You can use PowerPoint's Outline view to see your entire presentation in an outline format. When viewing a slide in Normal view, the Slides and Outline tabs appear in the left pane. To add text to slides in Outline view, follow these steps:

1 Click the **Outline** tab.

2 Click the slide that you want to edit.

3 Type the text that you want to add or change.

PowerPoint immediately changes the text on the slide.

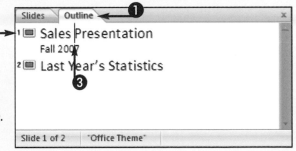

Change the Font and Size

When you assign slide layouts and designs, they use a default font and size for the text. You can change the font and size to change the appearance of your slide text. For example, you might want to increase the size of a slide's title text, or change the font of the body text to make the words more legible on a background color.

Change the Font and Size

CHANGE THE FONT

① Click the text or text box that you want to edit.

To select a text box without selecting text within, click the text box border.

② Click the **Home** tab on the Ribbon.

③ Click the **Font** ⏷.

④ Click a font.

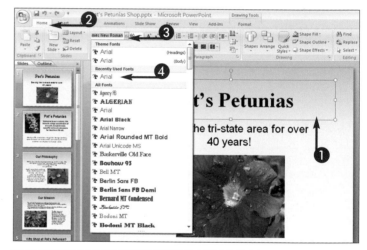

● PowerPoint immediately applies the new font to the text box.

CHANGE THE SIZE

① Click the text that you want to edit.

To select a text box without selecting text within, click the text box border.

② Click the **Home** tab on the Ribbon.

③ Click the **Font Size** ⊡.

④ Click a size.

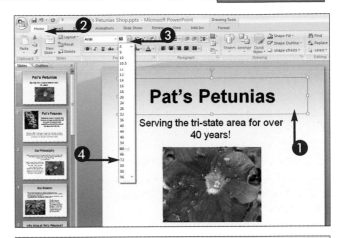

● PowerPoint immediately applies the new font size to the text in the text box.

● To quickly increase or decrease the font size, you can click the **Increase Font Size** and **Decrease Font Size** buttons (⟨A⟩ and ⟨A⟩) in the Font command group on the Home tab.

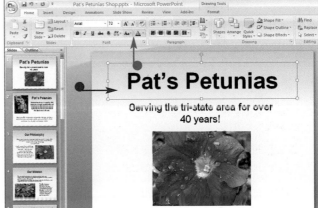

TIP

Is there another way to change both the font and size at the same time?

Yes. You can use the Font dialog box to make all kinds of changes to the font, size, font style, text color, and more. Follow these steps:

① Select the text that you want to edit and click the **Home** tab on the Ribbon.

② Click the **Font Dialog** button (⊡).

The Font dialog box appears.

③ Make changes to the font, size, style, color, or effects.

④ Click **OK**.

PowerPoint applies your changes to the selected text.

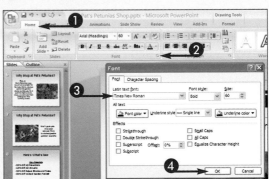

Change the Text Color

You can change the color of your slide text to create a different look for a slide. For example, you may need to change the text color to make the text more legible against the slide background.

CHOOSE A COORDINATING COLOR

① Click the text box that you want to edit.

To select a text box without selecting text within, click the text box border.

② Click the **Home** tab on the Ribbon.

③ Click the **Font Color** button ⏷.

● PowerPoint displays coordinating theme colors designed to go with the current slide design.

④ Click a color.

● PowerPoint applies the color to the text in the selected text box.

You can also add color formatting to text within the text box, such as a single word or phrase.

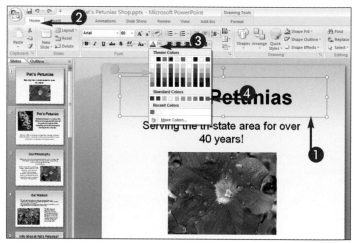

OPEN THE COLORS DIALOG BOX

① Click the text box that you want to edit.

You can also add color formatting to text within the text box, such as a single word or phrase.

② Click the **Home** tab on the Ribbon.

③ Click the **Font Color** button ▾.

④ Click **More Colors**.

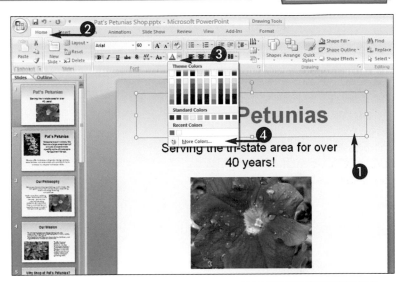

The Colors dialog box appears.

⑤ Click the **Standard** tab.

⑥ Click a color.

⑦ Click **OK**.

PowerPoint applies the color to the text in the selected text box.

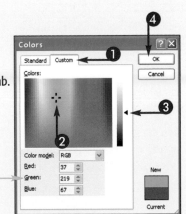

How do I set a custom color?

You can use the Colors dialog box to create your own custom color to use with the slide text or other slide elements. To set a custom color, follow these steps:

① Open the Colors dialog box, as shown in this task, and click the **Custom** tab.

② Click the color that you want to customize.

③ Drag the intensity arrow to adjust the color intensity.

● You can also adjust the color channel settings.

④ Click OK.

PowerPoint assigns the custom color.

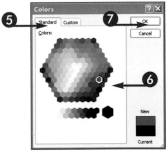

Change the Text Style

You can quickly change the appearance of text by changing the text style. You can choose from four different font styles: bold, italic, underline, and shadow.

Change the Text Style

1 Select the text box or text that you want to edit.

2 Click the **Home** tab on the Ribbon.

3 Click a style button.

Click the **Bold** button (**B**) to make the text bold.

Click the **Italic** button (**I**) to italicize the text.

Click the **Underline** button (**U**) to underline the text.

Click the **Shadow** button (**S**) to add a shadow effect to the text.

PowerPoint assigns the formatting.

● In this example, the subheading text is now bold.

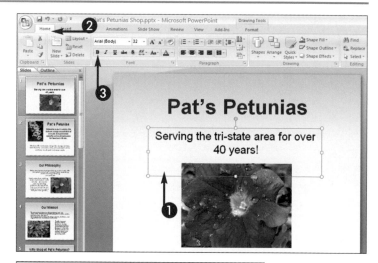

You can change the horizontal positioning of text in a text box by assigning a different alignment command. By default, PowerPoint usually centers the text in text objects, with the exception of bulleted text, which uses left alignment.

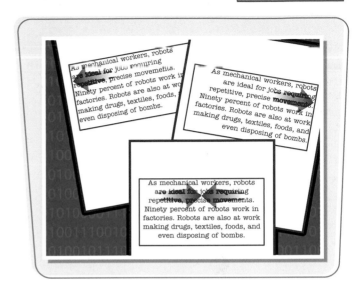

Change the Text Alignment

1 Select the text or text box that you want to edit.

2 Click the **Home** tab on the Ribbon.

3 Click an alignment button.

Click the **Align Left** button (≣) to align the text to the left side of the text box.

Click the **Center** button (≣) to align the text in the center of the text box.

Click the **Align Right** button (≣) to align the text to the right side of the text box.

PowerPoint assigns the formatting.

● In this example, the text is now left aligned.

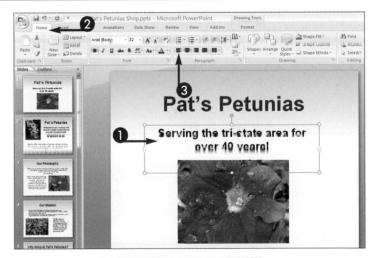

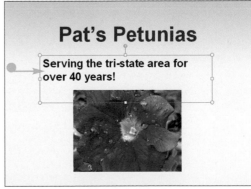

Set Line Spacing

You can change the line spacing to create more or less space between lines of text. For example, you might want to increase line spacing so the text fills up more space in the text box, or to make the text easier to read.

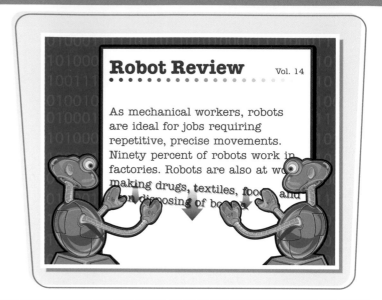

① Select the text box or text that you want to edit.

To select a text box without selecting text within, click the text box border.

② Click the **Home** tab on the Ribbon.

③ Click the **Line Spacing** button ▪.

④ Click a line spacing amount.

⦿ You can click the **Character Spacing** button (▦) to set character spacing for horizontal placement of characters in a line of text.

PowerPoint applies the line spacing.

⬤ This example applies 1.5 spacing.

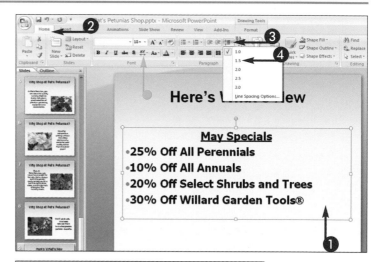

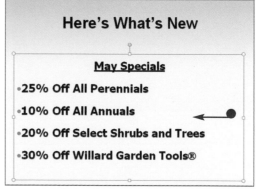

Assign a Theme

PowerPoint installs with a variety of designs, called themes, which allow you to give every slide in your presentation the same look and feel. Themes include preset fonts, colors, and backgrounds. When you assign a theme, PowerPoint applies the new theme to the entire presentation.

① Click the **Design** tab on the Ribbon.

② Click a theme from the Themes box.

● You can scroll through the available themes.

● You can click the **More** button (⊡) to view the full palette of themes.

● PowerPoint applies the theme to all of the slides in the presentation.

● You can use these controls to customize various aspects of the theme, such as color and font.

● You can also find more themes online. Click the **More** button (⊡) in the corner of the Themes box and then click **Search Office Online**.

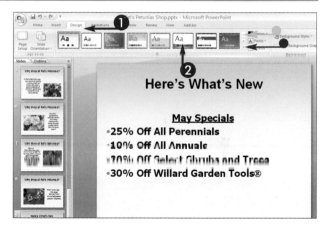

Change the Slide Layout

You can change a slide's layout at any time. For example, you may want to change a slide to include a bulleted text box or use one of PowerPoint's many content layouts.

If you assign a new slide layout to a slide with existing text, you may need to make a few adjustments to the text position and size to fit the new layout. For best results, you should assign a new layout before adding content to your slides.

Change the Slide Layout

① Display the slide that you want to change.

② Click the **Home** tab on the Ribbon.

③ Click the **Layout** button.

④ Click a layout.

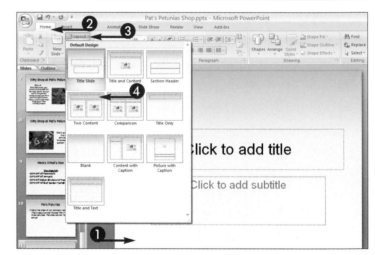

● PowerPoint immediately assigns the layout to the slide.

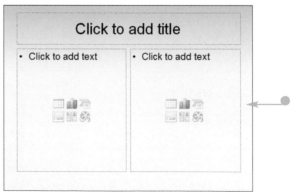

You can add new text boxes to a slide when you need to customize a layout. Text boxes are simply receptacles for text in a slide. With new text boxes, you can control the placement and size of the text object.

Add a New Text Object

① Click the **Insert** tab on the Ribbon.

② Click the **Text Box** button.

③ Click and drag where you want to place a text box on the slide.

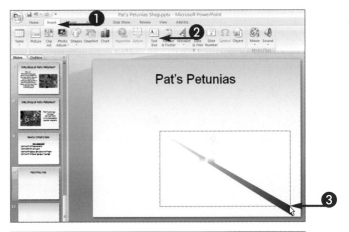

④ Type the text that you want to insert.

● PowerPoint immediately displays the Home tab, where you can use the formatting buttons to change the font, size, alignment, and more.

You can click anywhere outside the text box to deselect the text object.

Note: *To delete a slide object that you no longer need, select the object and press* Delete .

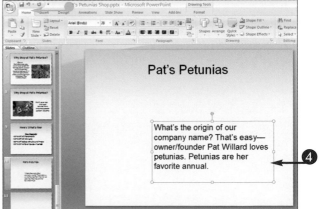

Add Clip Art to a Slide

You can add artwork to a slide by inserting clip art images. Clip art is premade art. Office installs with a clip art collection that includes many illustrations for a variety of topics. You can add clip art to a placeholder object or insert a new clip art object.

Add Clip Art to a Slide

① Click the Clip Art icon.

● If you are adding a new clip art object, click the **Clip Art** button on the Insert tab.

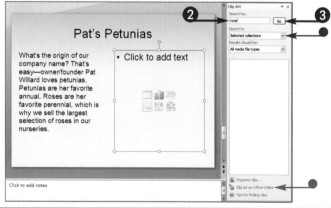

The Clip Art task pane opens.

② Type a keyword or phrase for the type of clip art that you want to insert.

● To search in a particular collection, click the **Search in** ☑ and click a collection.

● You can also search for clip art on the Office Web site by clicking this link.

③ Click **Go**.

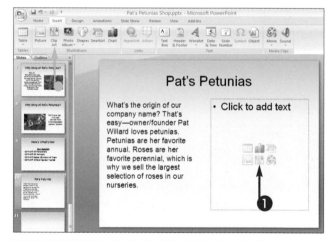

The Clip Art task pane displays any matches for the keyword or phrase that you typed.

④ To add a clip art image, click the image.

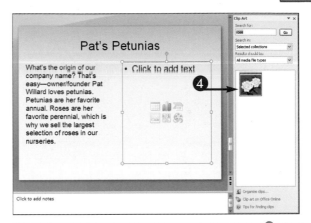

● The clip art is inserted and the Picture Tools appear on the Format tab.

You can resize or move the clip art.

Note: *See the "Move a Slide Object" or "Resize a Slide Object" tasks later in this chapter to learn more.*

To deselect the clip art, click anywhere else in the work area.

● You can click the **Close** button (⊠) to close the pane.

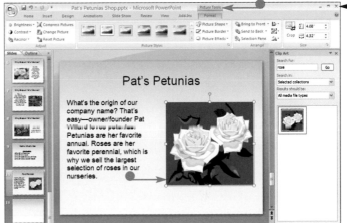

How do I insert a photo or image file instead of clip art?
To insert a photograph or other image file onto a slide, follow these steps:

① Click the Picture button on the Insert tab of the Ribbon, or if using a content layout, click the Insert Picture icon (🖾) in the placeholder box.

The Insert Picture dialog box appears.

② Navigate to the file that you want to insert and select it.

③ Click Insert.

PowerPoint inserts the file.

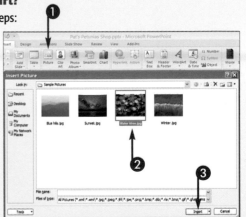

Add a Chart to a Slide

If you also use Excel 2007 on your computer, you can add a chart to a PowerPoint slide to turn numeric data into a visual element that your audience can quickly interpret and understand. You can create a chart in PowerPoint using an Excel worksheet. You can type your own chart data and choose the type of chart that you want to display.

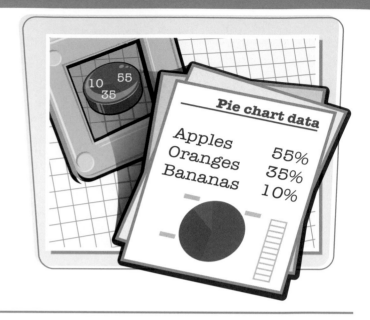

Add a Chart to a Slide

① Click the **Chart** icon (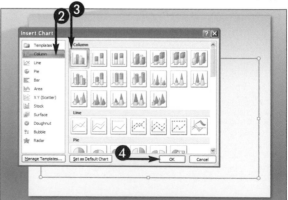).

● If you are adding a new chart object, click the **Chart** button on the **Insert** tab.

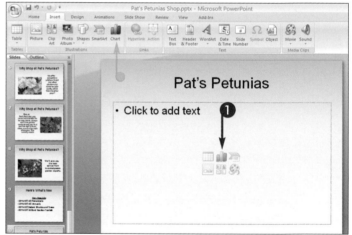

The Create Chart dialog box appears.

② Click a chart category.

③ Click a chart type.

④ Click **OK**.

- PowerPoint immediately displays a sample of the chart type on the slide.

- The Excel program window opens.

⑤ Replace the placeholder data with the chart data that you want to illustrate.

You can press **Tab** to move from cell to cell.

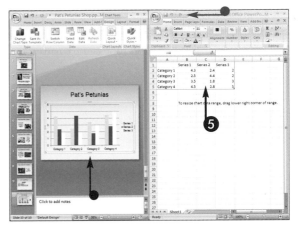

⑥ When finished entering chart data, click anywhere in the chart area to update the data.

- To edit the chart at any time, click the **Edit Data** button.

- Click the **Quick Styles** button to change the chart style.

- Click the **Close** button (☒) to close the Excel window.

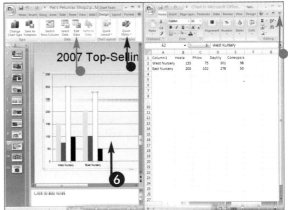

 TIPS

Can I insert an existing Excel chart into my PowerPoint slide?

Yes. You can use the Copy and Paste commands to copy an Excel chart and insert it into a PowerPoint slide. You can also link and embed an Excel chart. To learn more about copying and pasting data between Office programs, see Chapter 2.

How do I make changes to my chart formatting?

When you click a chart, the Ribbon shows a collection of tabs called Chart Tools that you can use to make changes to the chart. Click the **Design** tab to find options for changing the chart layout and style. Click the **Layout** tab to find tools for changing individual elements on the chart, such as the axis or legend. Click the **Format** tab to find tools for changing fill colors and shape styles. To remove a chart entirely, select the chart and press **Delete**.

Add a Table to a Slide

You can add tables to your slides to organize data in an orderly fashion. Tables use a column-and-row format to present information. For example, you might use a table to display a list of products or classes.

Add a Table to a Slide

1 Click the icon for the table you want to edit.

● If you are adding a new table object, click the **Table** button on the **Insert** tab.

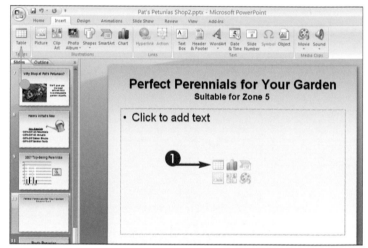

The Insert Table dialog box appears.

2 Type the number of columns that you want to appear in the table.

3 Type the number of rows that you want to appear in the table.

4 Click **OK**.

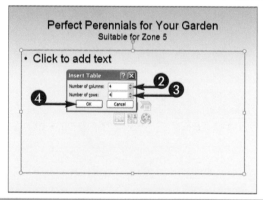

● PowerPoint inserts the table into the slide and displays the Table Tools tabs on the Ribbon.

● You can click to change the table style.

5 Click inside the first table cell and type your data.

You can press `Tab` to move from one table cell to the next.

6 Continue typing additional table cell data to fill the table.

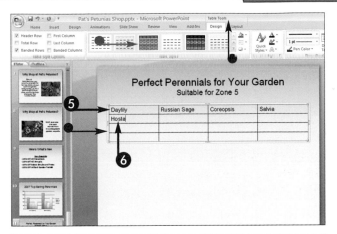

● You can use the tools on the Layout tab to merge table cells, split table cells, change alignment, add borders, and more.

● You can resize columns or rows by clicking and dragging the borders.

7 When you finish typing table data, click anywhere outside of the table area to deselect the table.

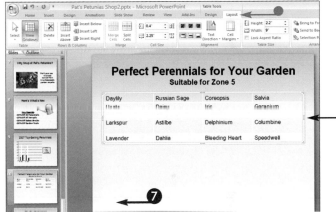

How do I add a column or a row to my table?

To add a column or a row to a table, follow these steps:

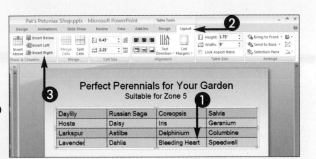

1 Select the row below, or the column to the right of, where you want to insert a new row or column. You can also click in a cell next to where you want to insert a new column or row.

2 Click the **Layout** tab on the Ribbon.

3 Click an **Insert** button, such as **Insert Below** or **Insert Left**.

PowerPoint immediately inserts a new row or column.

Move a Slide Object

You can move any slide element to reposition it in the slide. For example, you can move a text box to make room for a clip art box, or move a title to make the text fit better on a slide.

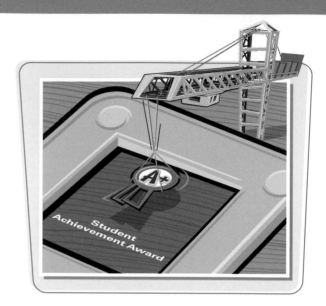

1 Click the slide object that you want to move.

The ⌖ changes to ✛ .

2 Drag the object to a new location on the slide.

● PowerPoint immediately repositions the object.

Note: *You can also resize slide elements. See the next task, "Resize a Slide Object," to learn more.*

Resize a Slide Object

You can resize any slide element to make it larger or smaller on the slide. For example, you can resize a text box to make room for more text, or resize a clip art box to make the artwork larger.

Resize a Slide Object

① Click the slide object that you want to resize.

● PowerPoint surrounds the object box with handles.

② Click and drag a handle.

The ⍚ changes to +.

Drag a corner handle to resize the object's height and width.

Drag a side handle to resize the object only along the one side.

● PowerPoint immediately resizes the object.

Note: You can also move slide elements. See the previous task, "Move a Slide Object," to learn more.

Create a Custom Layout with the Slide Master

PowerPoint layouts determine the positioning of objects on a slide, such as text boxes, clip art, and charts. You can choose from a variety of preset layouts that install with PowerPoint, or you can create your own custom layouts to reuse. When you create a custom layout, you control how many placeholder objects appear on the slide, as well as their size and placement. You can use Slide Master view to create custom layouts.

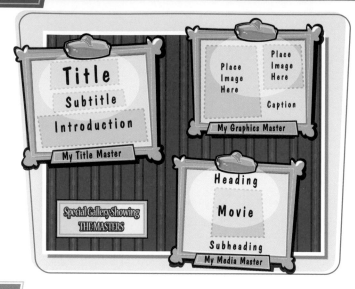

Create a Custom Layout with the Slide Master

① Click the **View** tab on the Ribbon.

② Click **Slide Master**.

● PowerPoint displays the Slide Master view and opens the Slide Master pane.

③ Click a location below where you want the new layout to appear.

④ Click the **Insert Layout** button on the Slide Master tab.

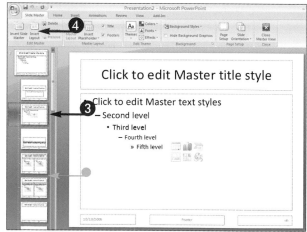

PowerPoint inserts a new layout that you can customize to suit your needs.

● You can delete objects by selecting the placeholder and clicking the **Delete** button or pressing Delete .

⑤ Click the **Insert Placeholder** button.

⑥ Click a slide object type.

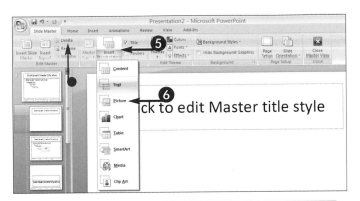

⑦ Click and drag to change the object's size and placement.

You can add more elements.

● To change text formatting, click the **Home** tab to display the formatting tools.

When you create the layout and save it as a template file, PowerPoint adds it to the list of available layouts.

Note: See Chapter 2 to learn how to save Office files.

⑧ Click **Close Master View** to close Slide Master view.

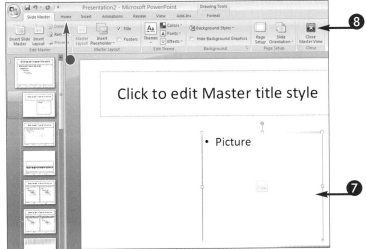

What are the default placeholders?

By default, every new layout that you create in Slide Master view starts with a title placeholder, along with three footer placeholders for date/time, footer, and slide numbers. You can keep the existing placeholders, or remove them entirely and add your own custom slide objects. You can quickly remove the default placeholders by clicking the **Title** and **Footers** check boxes (☑ changes to ☐) on the Slide Master tab on the Ribbon.

How do I assign a background to my custom layout?

To add a custom background to the layout, simply choose a theme from the **Themes** palette on the Slide Master tab, or set a new background style by clicking the **Background Styles** button and selecting a new style.

Insert and Delete Slides

You can add more slides to a presentation, or you can remove slides that you no longer want. PowerPoint makes it easy to insert new slides and delete existing slides by using buttons on the Ribbon's Home tab. You can add and remove slides on the Slides tab in Normal view, or you can switch to Slide Sorter view and manage your presentation's slides.

Insert and Delete Slides

INSERT A SLIDE IN SLIDE SORTER VIEW

① In Slide Sorter view, click the slide that appears before where you want to insert a new slide.

Note: See Chapter 14 to learn how to work with PowerPoint views.

② Click the **New Slide** button on the Ribbon's Home tab.

③ Click a slide design.

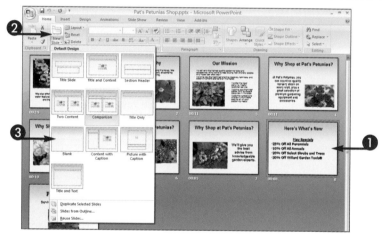

● PowerPoint adds a new slide.

● You can click the **Normal View** button (⊡) to switch to Normal view to add a layout and content to the new slide.

Note: See Chapter 15 to learn how to work with slide content.

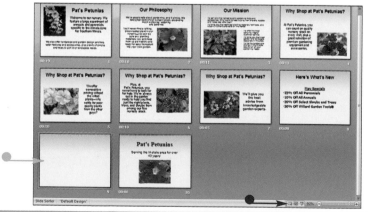

DELETE A SLIDE IN SLIDE SORTER VIEW

① In Slide Sorter view, click the slide that you want to remove from the presentation.

② Click the **Delete** button on the Home tab or press `Delete`.

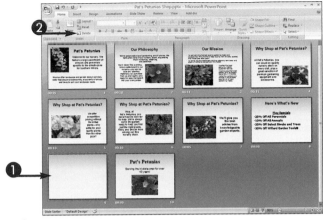

● PowerPoint immediately deletes the slide.

● If you accidentally delete the wrong slide, click the **Undo** button () to undo the mistake.

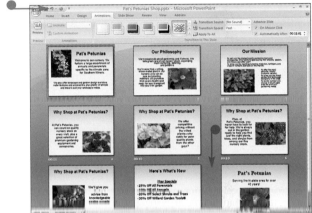

TIPS

How do I add and remove slides in Normal view?

In Normal view, you can quickly add slides using the Slides tab. Simply click where you want to insert a new slide in the Slides tab, and then click the **Add Slide** button on the Ribbon's Home tab. Select a slide layout from the menu; PowerPoint immediately adds the new slide to the presentation. See Chapter 15 to learn more about slide layouts. To remove a slide in the Slides tab, click the slide and click the **Delete** button or press `Delete`.

Can I add slides from another presentation?

Yes. Click where you want the new slides to appear in Slide Sorter view, click the **Add Slide** button on the Home or Insert tab, and then click **Slides from Outline**. Use the Insert Outline dialog box to navigate to the folder containing the presentation, and select the file that you want to insert. You may need to change the Files of Type setting to **All** to view other PowerPoint presentation files in the dialog box.

Reorganize Slides

You can reorganize the order of your slides to make changes to the presentation. For example, you may want to move a slide to appear later in the presentation, or swap the placement of two side-by-side slides. PowerPoint makes it easy to change the slide order in Slide Sorter view or by using the Slides tab in Normal view.

Reorganize Slides

MOVE SLIDES IN SLIDE SORTER VIEW

① In Slide Sorter view, click the slide that you want to move.

Note: See Chapter 14 to learn how to work with PowerPoint views.

The ⇧ changes to ⇧.

② Drag the slide to a new location in the presentation.

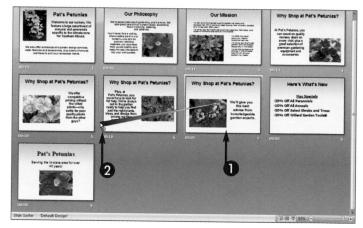

● PowerPoint moves the slide.

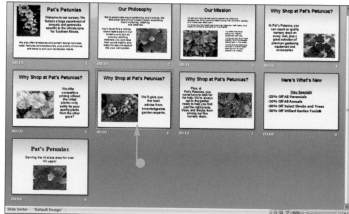

MOVE SLIDES IN NORMAL VIEW

① In Normal view, click the slide that you want to move on the Slides tab.

Note: *See Chapter 14 to learn how to work with PowerPoint views.*

The ⌖ changes to ⌖.

② Drag the slide to a new location on the tab.

● PowerPoint moves the slide.

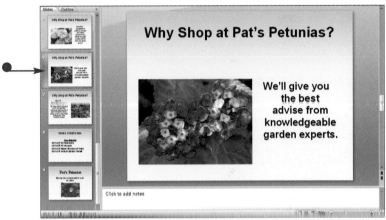

How do I hide a slide in my presentation?

If you want to hide a particular slide before giving your presentation, you can activate the Hide Slide feature. Click the slide that you want to hide in Slide Sorter view, and then click the **Slide Show** tab on the Ribbon. Click the **Hide Slide** button on the Slide Show tab. PowerPoint hides the slide during the actual presentation, but keeps the slide displayed in Slide Sorter view. To unhide the slide again, repeat the steps. You can always tell when a slide is hidden if the Hide Slide button appears activated when you select the slide in Slide Sorter view.

Can I move multiple slides at once to reorganize my presentation?

Yes. To move multiple slides at the same time, press and hold Ctrl as you click each slide, and then drag the slides to a new location. This technique works both in Slide Sorter view, and when using the Slides tab in Normal view.

Define Slide Transitions

You can add transition effects to your slides to control how one slide segues to the next. Transition effects include fades, dissolves, and wipes. You can control the speed of the transition to appear fast or slow. You can also specify how PowerPoint advances the slides, either manually or automatically.

Use good judgment when assigning transitions. If you use too many different types of transitions, you may end up distracting from your presentation.

Define Slide Transitions

1 In Slide Sorter view, click the slide that you want to edit.

Note: You can also use Normal view to assign transitions; however, you may find it easier to assign effects to your entire presentation in Slide Sorter view. See Chapter 14 to learn about PowerPoint views.

2 Click the **Animations** tab on the Ribbon.

● You can scroll through the available transition effects.

● You can click the **More** button (⬛) to view all of the transition effects.

● You can move the mouse pointer over a transition to learn more about the effect.

3 Click a transition.

● PowerPoint immediately displays a preview of the transition effect.

● PowerPoint adds an animation icon below the slide.

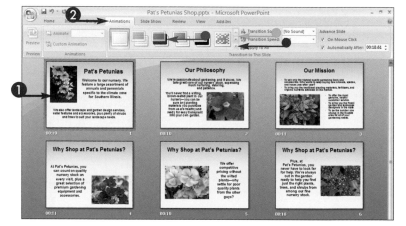

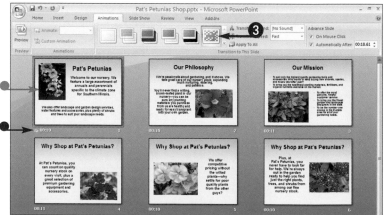

④ Click the **Transition Speed** ▾.

⑤ Click a speed setting for the transition.

● PowerPoint immediately displays a preview of the transition effect.

● You can click **Apply to All** to apply the same transition to the entire slide show.

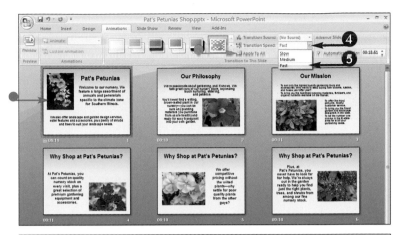

⑥ Under the Advance Slide options, click an advance option (☐ changes to ☑).

To use a mouse click to move to the next slide, click the **On Mouse Click** option (☐ changes to ☑).

To move to the next slide automatically, click the **Automatically After** option (☐ changes to ☑) and set a time.

Note: See Chapter 17 to learn how to run the slide show.

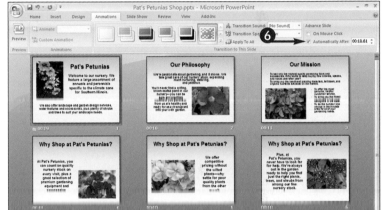

How do I remove a transition effect?

To remove a transition effect, first select the slide containing the transition that you want to remove in Slide Sorter view. Click the **Animations** tab, and then click the **No Transition** option in the Transitions list box. PowerPoint removes the previous transition that you assigned to the slide and returns the slide to the default state.

What does the sound option do?

You can assign sounds as transition effects with your slides. For example, you might assign the Applause sound effect for the first or last slide in a presentation. To assign a sound transition, click the **Transition Sound** ▾ on the Animations tab and select a sound. PowerPoint immediately previews the sound with the slide transition.

Add Animation Effects

You can use PowerPoint's animation effects to add even more visual interest to your slide show presentations. You can add a simple animation effect — such as a fade, wipe, or fly in — to any slide element, including text boxes, clip art, and other objects. You can also assign a custom animation. PowerPoint's custom animation schemes include a variety of preset animations, such as spinning, zooming, and scrolling credits.

You should avoid assigning too many animation effects or you may overwhelm the audience. For best results, limit the effects to slides in which they make the most impact.

Add Animation Effects

ADD A SIMPLE ANIMATION EFFECT

① In Normal view, click the slide element that you want to edit.

Note: *See Chapter 14 to learn how to work with PowerPoint views.*

You can assign an animation to any object on a slide, including text boxes, shapes, and pictures.

② Click the **Animations** tab on the Ribbon.

③ Click the **Animate** 🔽.

④ Click an animation effect.

● PowerPoint immediately assigns the effect and previews the effect on the slide.

● You can click the **Preview** button to preview the effect again.

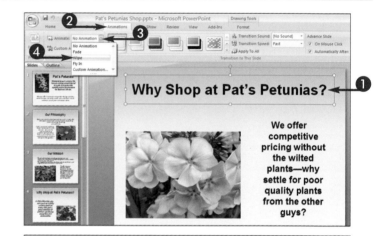

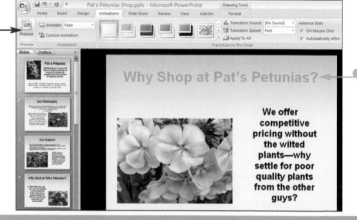

ADD A CUSTOM EFFECT

1 In Normal view, click the slide element that you want to animate.

You can assign an animation to any object on a slide, including text boxes, shapes, and pictures.

2 Click the **Animations** tab on the Ribbon.

3 Click **Custom Animation**.

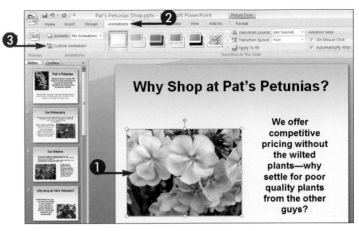

The Custom Animation task pane opens.

4 Click **Add Effect**.

5 Click an effect category.

6 Click an animation.

PowerPoint immediately assigns the animation and previews the effect.

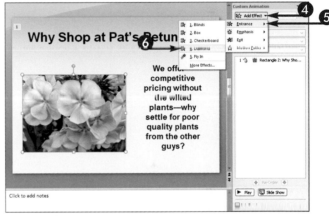

 TIPS

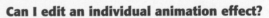

How do I remove an animation effect?

To remove a simple animation effect, first select the slide element containing the effect that you want to remove. Click the **Animations** tab, click the **Animate** , and then click the **No Animation** option. PowerPoint removes the effect. If you assigned custom effects, click the **Custom Animations** button to display the Custom Animation task pane, click the effect that you want to remove in the list box, and then click the **Remove** button.

Can I edit an individual animation effect?

Yes. If you use the Custom Animation task pane to add an animation effect, you can customize how the effect appears in the slide. For example, if you assign a wipe effect, you can specify a direction for the wipe effect to appear for the element, and control the speed of the wipe effect. You can also use the Custom Animation task pane to specify whether the animation starts automatically or with a mouse click.

Insert a Media Clip

You can insert media clips onto your PowerPoint slides to play during a slide show presentation. For example, when creating a presentation showcasing the latest company product, you might place a video clip of the department head discussing the new item, or insert a voice clip from the designer describing the product's features. You can also insert music clips from audio CDs to play as background sound in a show.

Insert a Media Clip

① In Normal view, display the slide to which you want to add a media clip.

② Click the **Insert** tab.

③ Click **Movie** or **Sound**.

If you click the **Movie** or **Sound** ▾, you can select a source for the clip.

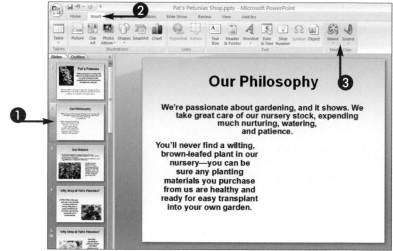

The Insert Movie or Insert Sound dialog box appears.

④ Navigate to the folder or drive containing the media clip that you want to use.

⑤ Click the filename.

⑥ Click **OK**.

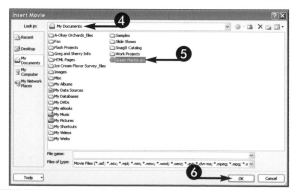

- PowerPoint displays a dialog box, prompting you to specify how you want the clip to play.

7 Click an option.

- Click **Automatically** to make the clip play automatically.

- Click **When Clicked** to play the clip only when it is clicked.

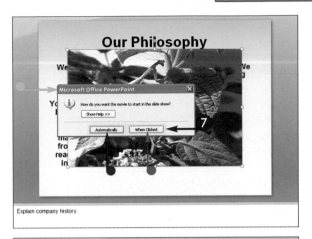

PowerPoint inserts the clip into the slide.

- If you insert an audio clip, the audio icon appears and you can double-click the icon to play the clip.

- If you insert a media clip, you can right-click over the clip and then click **Preview** to play the clip.

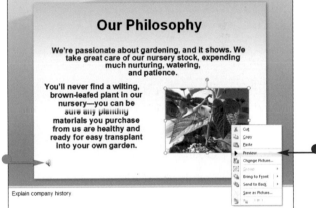

TIP

Can I add an action button to a slide?

Yes. You can turn any shape you draw on a slide into an action button that, when clicked, jumps to a designated slide, opens a program, or runs a macro. To turn a shape into an action button, follow these steps:

1 Click the shape that you want to edit.

2 Click the **Insert** tab on the Ribbon.

3 Click the **Action** button.

The Action Settings dialog box appears.

4 Use the Mouse Click tab settings to control which action you want to assign to the button when the user clicks it with the mouse.

5 Click **OK**.

PowerPoint assigns the action to the button.

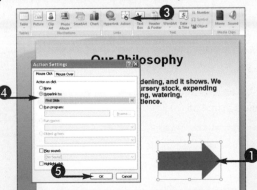

Record Narration

If your presentation needs some narration, you can use PowerPoint's Record Narration feature to record a narration track to go along with the show. If your computer has a microphone, you can record a narration, and save it along with the file.

Record Narration

① Click the **Slide Show** tab on the Ribbon.

② Click **Record Narration**.

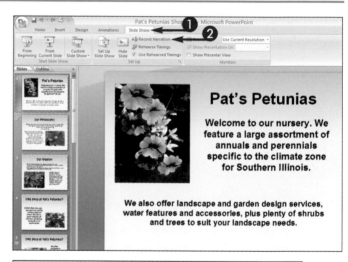

The Record Narration dialog box appears.

● To set your microphone level, click **Set Microphone Level** to run a check.

● To check the sound quality, click **Change Quality** to change the format.

③ Click **OK**.

PowerPoint starts the show, and you can begin talking into the computer's microphone to record your narration.

Note: When you finish recording, an audio icon appears at the bottom of each slide to which you have assigned narration.

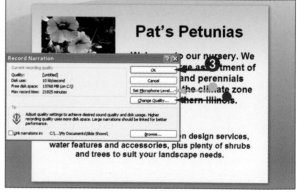

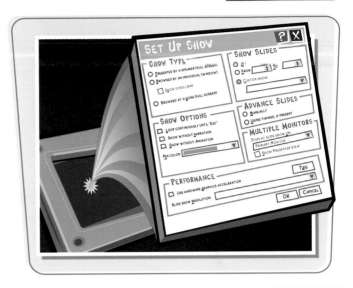

You can set up how you want a slide show to run using the Set Up Show feature. For example, you can specify whether you want the show to loop continuously, advance manually, or advance with preset timings.

Set Up a Slide Show

① Click the **Slide Show** tab on the Ribbon.

② Click **Set Up Slide Show**.

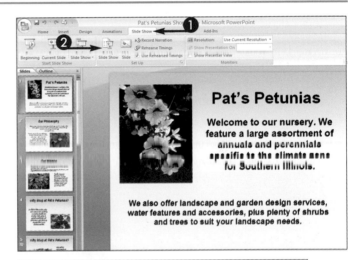

The Set Up Show dialog box appears.

③ Set any options that you want to assign to the show.

● The Show type settings specify how the slide show is presented.

● The Show options settings control looping, narration, and animation.

● The Show slides settings specify which slides appear in the show.

● The Advance slides settings specify how each slide advances.

④ Click **OK**.

PowerPoint assigns the new settings.

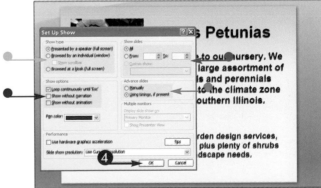

Create a Photo
Album Presentation

You can quickly turn any
collection of digital photos
on your computer into a slide
show in PowerPoint. You can
then share the presentation
with others, or e-mail the file
to family and friends.

Create a Photo Album Presentation

① Click the **Insert** tab on the Ribbon.

② Click **Photo Album**.

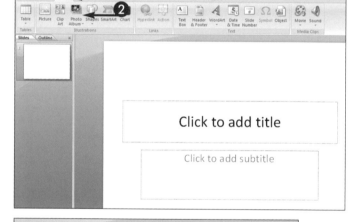

The Photo Album dialog box appears.

③ Click the **File/Disk** button.

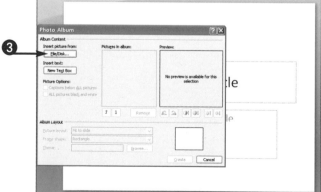

The Insert New Pictures dialog box appears.

④ Navigate to the folder or drive containing the digital pictures that you want to use.

⑤ Click the pictures that you want to use.

● To use multiple pictures, you can press and hold **Ctrl** while clicking the pictures that you want to use.

⑥ Click **Insert**.

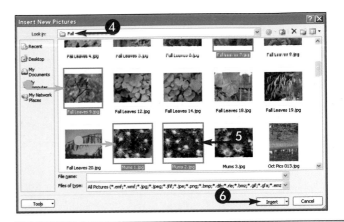

● You can change the picture order using these buttons.

● To remove a picture, you can click **Remove**.

● You can use the tool buttons to change the picture orientation, contrast, and brightness levels.

⑦ Click **Create**.

PowerPoint creates the slide show as a new presentation file.

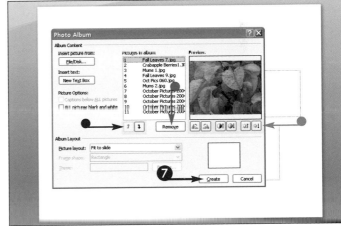

How do I add captions to my photos?

You can add text to a photo slide show in two ways. Either you can add captions to appear below the images and add your own text, or you can add individual text slides after each photo and then add your own text. You can find both options as part of the Album Content settings in the Photo Album dialog box. To add captions, click the **Captions below ALL pictures** check box (☐ changes to ☑). To add text box slides instead, click the **New Text Box** button. You can type text for your captions or text slides after you close the Photo Album dialog box.

How do I fit multiple pictures onto a single slide?

You can use the Picture layout setting in the Photo Album dialog box to control how many pictures appear on a slide. By default, PowerPoint displays a single picture as an entire slide. You can choose to display up to four pictures on a slide. You can also add text boxes to a picture to insert a caption below the photos. When you choose an option other than a single picture, you can control the shape of the image and add a background theme to the slide page.

Rehearse a Slide Show

You can time exactly how long each slide displays during a presentation using PowerPoint's Rehearse Timings feature. When rehearsing a presentation, you should rehearse what you want to say during each slide, as well as allow the audience time to read the entire content of each slide. After you record the timings, PowerPoint saves them.

Rehearse a Slide Show

① Click the **Slide Sorter** button (▦).

② Click the **Rehearse Timings** button on the Slide Show tab.

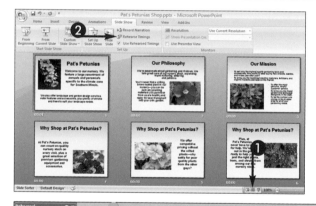

● PowerPoint switches to Slide Show mode, displays the first slide and the Rehearsal toolbar, and starts a timer.

③ Rehearse what you want to say while the slide displays.

● If you need to pause the rehearsal, you can click the **Pause** button (▯▯).

 If you need to restart the timing, you can click ▯▯ again.

④ When you finish with the first slide, click the **Next** button (▣).

PowerPoint displays the next slide.

⑤ Repeat Steps **3** and **4** for each slide in your presentation.

● When the slide show is complete, a dialog box appears, displaying the total time for the slide show.

⑥ Click **Yes**.

● PowerPoint saves the timings and displays them below each slide.

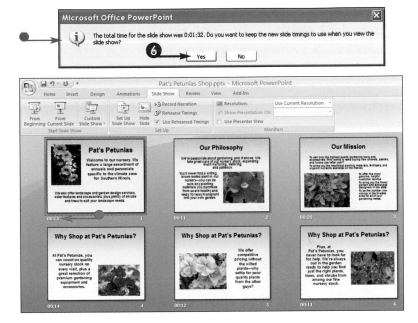

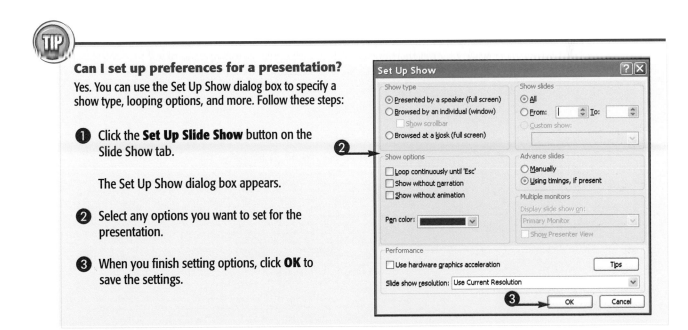

Can I set up preferences for a presentation?

Yes. You can use the Set Up Show dialog box to specify a show type, looping options, and more. Follow these steps:

❶ Click the **Set Up Slide Show** button on the Slide Show tab.

The Set Up Show dialog box appears.

❷ Select any options you want to set for the presentation.

❸ When you finish setting options, click **OK** to save the settings.

You can view a presentation using PowerPoint's Slide Show view. Slide Show view displays full-screen images of your slides. You can advance each slide manually, or instruct PowerPoint to advance the slides for you.

Run a Slide Show

1 Click the **Slide Show** button (🖵).

Note: *To learn more about PowerPoint views, see Chapter 14.*

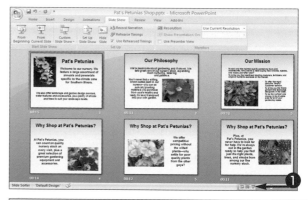

PowerPoint switches to Slide Show mode and displays the first slide.

● When you move the mouse near the bottom-left corner, a small slide-show control bar appears.

2 Click anywhere in the slide to advance to the next slide, or click the **Next** button.

● To return to a previous slide, you can click the **Previous** button.

Pat's Petunias

Welcome to our nursery. We feature a large assortment of annuals and perennials specific to the climate zone for Southern Illinois.

We also offer landscape and garden design services, water features and accessories, plus plenty of shrubs and trees to suit your landscape needs.

- To view a menu of slide-show commands, click here.

- You can pause the show by activating the **Pause** command.

- You can end the show early by activating the **End Show** command.

Note: You can end a slide show at any time by pressing `Esc`.

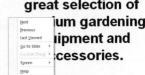

Why Shop at Pat's Petunias?

At Pat's Petunias, you can count on quality nursery stock on every visit, plus a great selection of ...ium gardening ...ipment and ...cessories.

③ When the slide show is complete, click anywhere on-screen.

PowerPoint closes the presentation.

③

TIP

Can I draw on my slides as I present the show?

Yes. You can use PowerPoint's pointer options to draw directly on the screen using the mouse. You can choose from several pen tools and colors. Follow these steps:

① During the slide show, click the **Pen** button.

② Click a pen style.

- You can click here to choose a pen color.

③ Draw where you want to mark on the slide.

To erase your markings, press `E` and drag across the markings.

At the end of the slide show, PowerPoint asks if you want to save any of your markings.

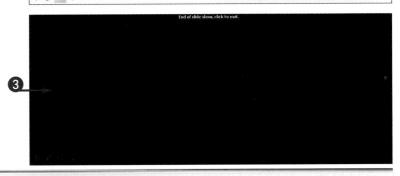

Create
Speaker Notes

You can create speaker notes for your presentation. Speaker notes, also called notes pages, are notations that you add to a slide and that you can print out and use to help you give a presentation. You can also use speaker notes as handouts for your presentation. When creating notes pages, PowerPoint includes any note text that you add, as well as a small picture of the actual slide.

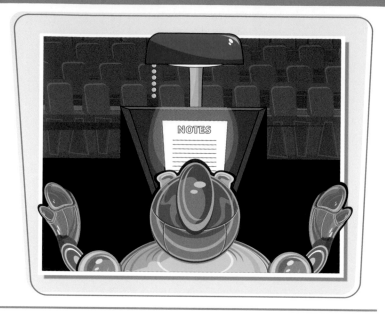

Create Speaker Notes

① In Normal view, click the slide to which you want to add notes.

Note: *To learn more about PowerPoint views, see Chapter 14.*

② Click in the Notes pane, and type any notes that you want to include.

You can repeat Step **2** for other slides to which you want to add notes.

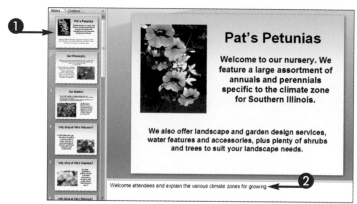

③ Click the **View** tab.

④ Click **Notes Page**.

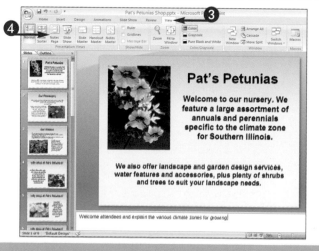

The Notes Page view opens and displays the first page in your slide show.

● You can use the scroll bars to scroll through the notes.

● You can drag the Zoom slider to magnify your view of the notes.

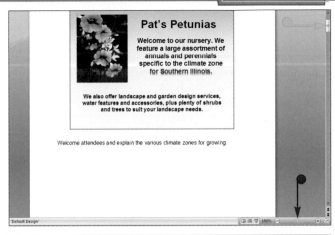

● You can edit and format your notes text.

● You can click **Normal** to return to Normal view.

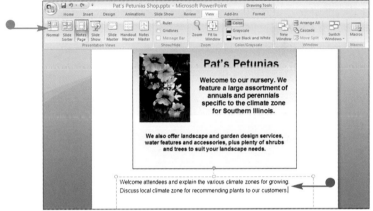

How do I print my notes?

To print your speaker notes, follow these steps:

❶ Click the **Office** button.

❷ Click **Print**.

The Print dialog box appears.

❸ Click the **Print what** ☑ and click **Notes Pages**.

❹ Click **OK**.

PowerPoint prints the notes.

You can also print out your presentation as single slides or as handouts, which print multiple slides on a printed page. To learn more about printing Office files, see Chapter 2.

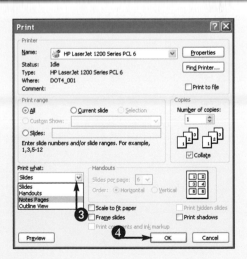

Package Your Presentation on a CD

PowerPoint can help you save your slide show to a CD to take with you for presentations on the go. With the Package for CD feature, PowerPoint bundles the presentation along with all of the necessary clip art, multimedia elements, and other items needed to run your show.

Package Your Presentation on a CD

1 Click the **Office** button.

2 Click **Publish**.

3 Click **Package for CD**.

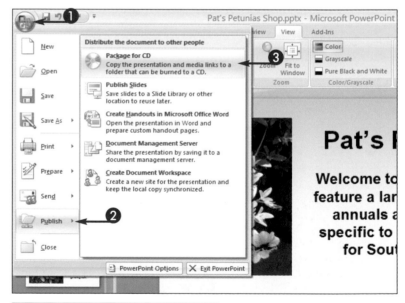

The Package for CD dialog box appears.

4 Type a name for the CD.

5 Click **Copy to CD**.

● PowerPoint copies the presentation files.

Depending on the size of the presentation, the copying process can take a few minutes.

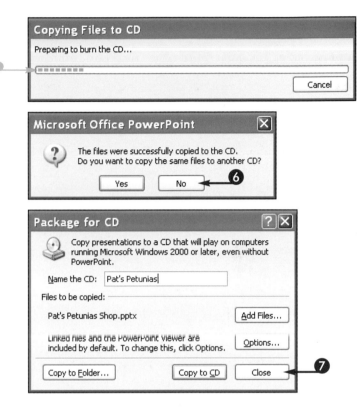

Copying Files to CD

Preparing to burn the CD...

[========]   Cancel

When the copying process is complete, a dialog box appears.

6 Click **No**.

If you want to continue packing additional copies of the presentation, you can click **Yes**.

7 Click **Close**.

The Package for CD dialog box closes.

Microsoft Office PowerPoint   ☒

? The files were successfully copied to the CD.
Do you want to copy the same files to another CD?

Yes   No ◀—— **6**

Package for CD   ?☒

Copy presentations to a CD that will play on computers running Microsoft Windows 2000 or later, even without PowerPoint.

Name the CD: Pat's Petunias|

Files to be copied:

Pat's Petunias Shop.pptx   Add Files...

Linked files and the PowerPoint Viewer are included by default. To change this, click Options.   Options...

Copy to Folder...   Copy to CD   Close ◀—— **7**

TIPS

What if I want to give the presentation to someone who does not have PowerPoint?

The Package for CD feature automatically includes a PowerPoint Viewer with the file in case the recipient does not have PowerPoint installed on his computer. The PowerPoint Viewer allows users to view slide shows without all of the extra PowerPoint tools and features found in the full program.

How do I view information about a presentation file?

By default, when you save a presentation, PowerPoint stores information about the author as well as the date the file is created. To view the information, click the **Office** button, click **Finish**, and then click **Properties**. This opens the Document Information panel, which you can use to add more information, such as company name, subject, comments, and more. To view more information, click the **Property Views and Options** button and then click **Advanced** to open the File Properties dialog box to view additional properties.

Part V: Access

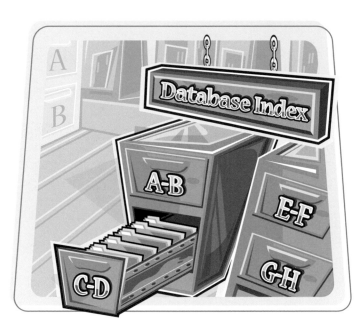

Access is a robust database program you can use to store and manage large quantities of data. You can use Access to manage anything from a home inventory to a giant warehouse of products. Access can help you organize your information into tables, speed up data entry with forms, and perform powerful analysis using filters and queries. In this part, you learn how to build and maintain a database file, add tables, create forms, and analyze your data using filters, sort, and queries.

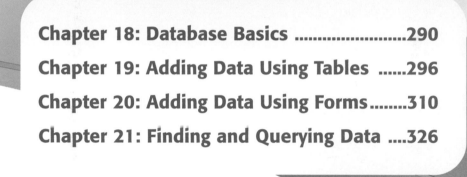

Understanding Database Basics

Access is a popular database program that you can use to catalog and manage large amounts of data. You can use Access to manage anything, from a simple table of data to large, multifaceted lists of information. If you are new to Access, you should take a moment and familiarize yourself with the basic terms that are associated with the program.

Defining Databases

Simply defined, a *database* is a collection of information. You use databases every day whether you are aware of it or not. Common databases include telephone directories or television program schedules. Your own database examples might include a list of contacts that contains addresses and phone numbers. Other examples of real-world databases include product inventories, client invoices, and employee payroll lists.

Tables

The heart of any Access database is a table. A table is a list of information organized into columns and rows. In the example of a client contact database, the table might list the names, addresses, phone numbers, company name, title, and e-mail addresses of your clients. You can have numerous tables in your Access database. For example, you might have one table listing client information and another table listing your company's products.

Records and Fields

Every entry that you make in an Access table is called a *record*. Records always appear as rows in a database. You can organize the information for each record in a separate column, which is called a *field*. For example, in a client contact list, you might include fields for first name, last name, company name, title, address, city, zip code, phone number, and e-mail address. Field names appear at the top of the table.

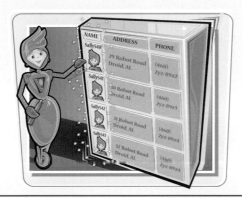

Forms

You can enter your database records directly into an Access table, or you can simplify the process by using a *form*. Access forms present your table fields in an easy-to-read, fill-in-the-blank format. Forms allow you to enter records one at a time. Forms are a great way to speed up data entry, particularly if other users are adding information to your database list.

Reports and Queries

As soon as you create an Access database, you can begin to manipulate data. You can use the report feature to summarize data in your tables and generate printouts of pertinent information, such as your top ten salespeople and your top-selling products. You can use queries to sort and filter your data. For example, you can choose to view only a few of your table fields and filter them to match certain criteria.

Planning a Database

The first step to building an Access database is to decide what sort of data you want to store and manage. Think about what sort of actions you want to perform on your data, and how you want to organize it. How many tables of data do you need? What types of fields do you need for your records? What sort of reports and queries do you hope to create? You might also take time to sketch out on paper how you want to group the information into tables and how the tables will relate to each other. Taking time to plan the database in advance can save you time when you build the file.

Create a Blank Database

You can start a new, blank database and populate it with data. When you create a new database file, Access prompts you to assign a name to the file. Every time you launch Access, the Getting Started screen, or Welcome screen, appears with options for creating a new database or for opening an existing file

To learn how to add data to a database, see Chapter 19.

Create a Blank Database

① Launch Access and click the **Blank Database** option in the Getting Started window.

● To open an existing database file that you have already created, click the filename or click **More** to navigate to the file.

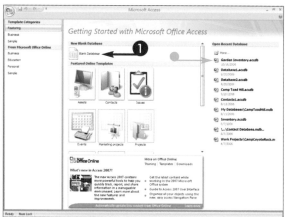

② Type a name for the database.

Access automatically assigns the .accdb extension to all database files. This extension stands for Access Database.

● You can click the **Browse** button (📁) to navigate to the folder or drive where you want to store the new file.

③ Click **Create**.

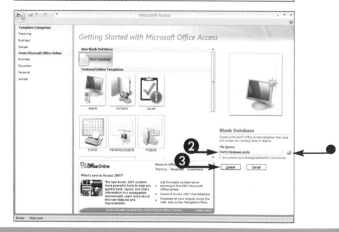

● Access creates a new, blank database and opens a new table ready for data.

You can now create your own tables, enter records, and more.

Note: *See Chapter 19 to learn how to populate a database with data.*

● The Navigation pane displays database objects that you create, such as tables and forms.

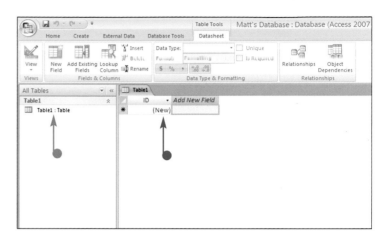

● If Access is already open, you can start a new, blank database by clicking the **Office** button, and then clicking **New**.

The Getting Started screen opens, and you can follow Steps **2** and **3** to create a new file.

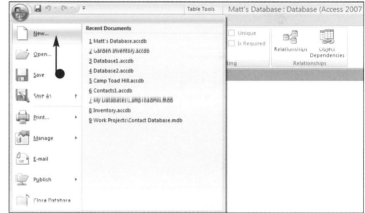

What happened to the database window?

In previous versions of Access, the database window listed all of the objects associated with your database, such as tables, forms, queries, and reports. In Access 2007, the Navigation pane replaces the database window. You can use the pane to open various objects. By default, the pane appears on the left side of the program window. You can collapse the pane to increase the onscreen workspace. Simply click the **Shutter Bar Open/Close** button (◄) in the top-right corner of the pane to collapse the pane. Click the button again to expand the pane.

How many databases can I open in Access?

Unlike other Office programs, you can only work with one database file at a time in Access. When you open a new or existing database, Access closes the currently open database file.

Create a Database Based on a Template

You can build a new database based on any of the Access online templates. When you create a new database using a template, the database includes pre-built tables and forms that you can use to simply fill in your own data. You can control the structure of your database by determining which preset tables and fields are included in the file.

Create a Database Based on a Template

① Launch Access and click the template category that you want to search in the Getting Started window.

● You can also download templates from the Office Web site by clicking a template category in this list.

● Access lists recently opened database files here. To open a database file, you can click the filename or click **More** to navigate to the file.

② Click a template.

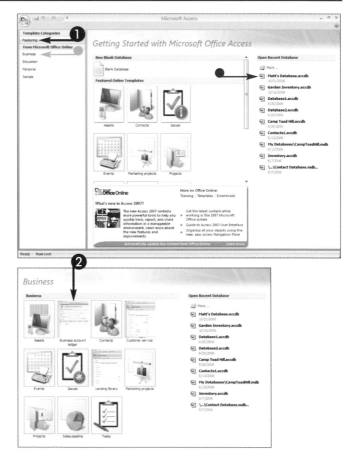

3 Type a name for the database.

Access automatically assigns the .accdb extension to all database files.

4 Click **Download**.

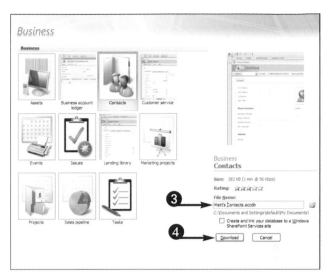

● Access downloads the template and creates a new, blank database, opening a new table ready for data.

You can now create your own tables, enter records, and more.

Note: *See Chapter 19 to learn how to populate a database with data.*

● You can maximize the Navigation pane by clicking the **Shutter Bar Open/Close** button (⏵⏵). The Navigation pane displays database objects that you create, such as tables and forms.

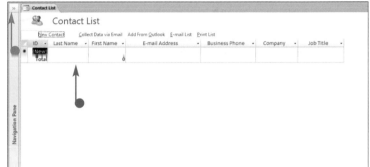

How do I know which fields to keep in or remove from my table?

To best determine which fields you need in your database, you should take time to do a little preplanning. Decide what kinds of information you want to track in your database and what sorts of reports and queries you want to generate to view your data. The Database Wizard lists suggested fields most users find necessary for the database along with optional fields. For best results, use the suggested fields. You can always remove fields that you do not use at a later time.

What kinds of templates can I find to use for a database?

Microsoft offers all kinds of templates in a variety of categories. For example, the Business category includes templates for creating contact lists, assets, marketing projects, and events. The Education category includes templates for creating student and faculty database lists. You can also log onto the Website weekly to find new featured templates you can download.

Create a New Table

You can start building a database by entering data into a table. Access stores all data in tables, and you can have multiple tables in a single database. Tables consist of columns and rows that intersect to form *cells* for holding data. Each row is considered a *record* in a table. You can use columns to hold *fields*, which are the individual units of information contained within a record.

To learn more about starting a database file, see Chapter 18.

Create a New Table

1 Click the **Create** tab on the Ribbon.

2 Click the **Table** button.

***Note:** See Chapter 18 to learn how to create a database file.*

● To enter data into an existing table, you can double-click the table name in the Navigation pane.

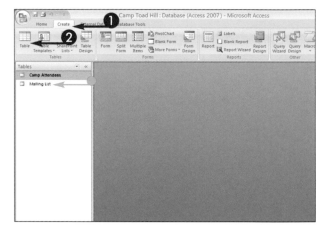

Access opens a new table in Datasheet view.

***Note:** See the "Change Table Views" task to learn more about Datasheet view.*

3 To create a field name, double-click the column header.

4 Type a name for the field.

5 Press Enter .

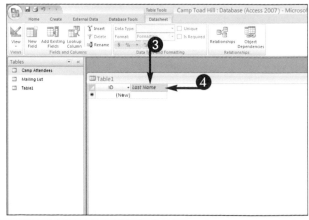

6 Repeat Steps **3** to **5** to create more fields for the table.

● You can resize a column by dragging the column border left or right.

● You can use the scroll bars to view different portions of the table.

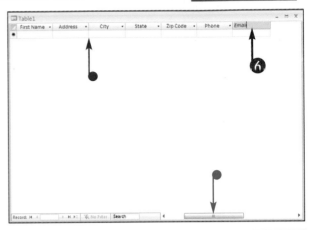

7 To enter the first record, click inside the first field of the first row and type the data.

8 Press Tab .

9 Type the next field's data.

Repeat Steps **8** and **9** to complete the record.

When you reach the last field, you can press Enter to start a new record.

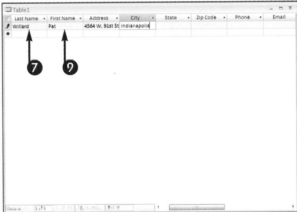

How do I navigate a table?

You can click in a cell to make the cell active, or you can use the keyboard keys to navigate around a table. You can press Tab to move from cell to cell, or you can press the keyboard arrow keys. To move backward to a previous cell, press Shift + Tab .

Is there an easy way to repeat an entry for a cell?

Yes. You can press Ctrl + '' to copy the contents of the cell directly above the active cell. For example, if you are copying the same state name in the State field, you can press Ctrl + '' and Access immediately fills in the same text for you. This shortcut only works in Datasheet view, not in Form view. See the "Change Table Views" task to learn more about Access views.

continued

When creating a new table, you can give the table a unique name. After you save the table, you can reopen it to add more data or make changes to the existing data. All table objects that you create appear listed in the Navigation pane.

Create a New Table *(continued)*

10 Continue filling the table with data.

11 When finished, click the **Close** button (⊠).

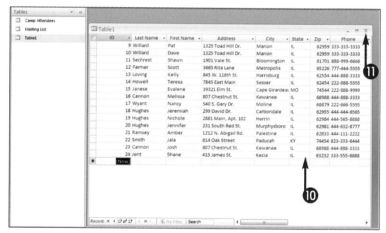

● Access prompts you to save the table changes.

12 Click **Yes**.

● The Save As dialog box appears.

⑬ Type a name for the table.

⑭ Click **OK**.

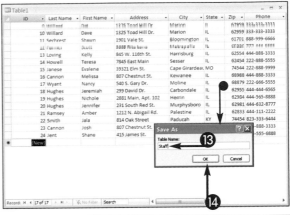

● Access lists the table among the database objects in the Navigation pane.

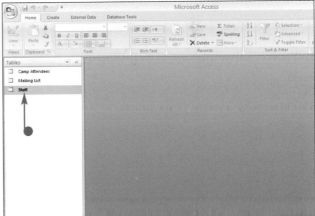

TIPS

What is a primary key?

A *primary key* uniquely identifies each record in a table. For many tables, the primary key is a numbering field that stores a unique number for each record as it is entered into the database. You can also designate another field as a primary key. To do so, switch the table to Design view, select the field that you want to set as the primary key, and click the **Primary key** button on the **Design** tab.

How do I edit a record?

To edit a record, reopen the table in Datasheet view and make changes to the data. When you close the table, Access prompts you to save your changes.

Create a Table with a Table Template

You can use an Access table template to help you create and customize a table for your database. You can choose from a variety of table types. After you create the table, you can insert your own data.

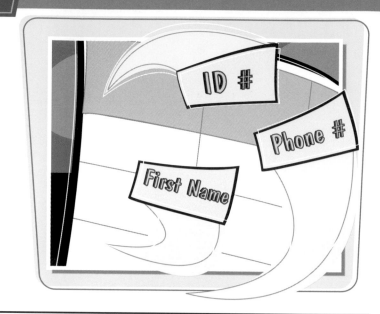

Create a Table with a Table Template

1 Click the **Create** tab on the Ribbon.

2 Click the **Table Templates** button.

Note: *See Chapter 18 to learn how to create a database file.*

3 Click a template.

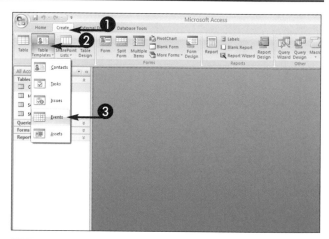

Access opens a new table in Datasheet view.

Note: *See the "Change Table Views" task to learn more about Datasheet view.*

4 To enter the first record, click inside the first field of the first row and type the data.

5 Press Tab .

6 Type the next field's data.

7 Repeat Steps **4** to **6** to complete the record.

When you reach the last field, you can press Enter to start a new record.

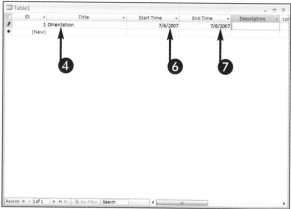

8 When finished, click the **Close** button (☒).

Access prompts you to save the table changes.

9 Click **Yes**.

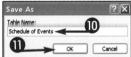

The Save As dialog box appears.

⑩ Type a name for the table.

⑪ Click **OK**.

Access saves the table and lists it in the Navigation pane.

Can I rename the table fields?

Yes. You can rename fields in any table by double-clicking the field label and typing a new name. When you finish, press Enter . To add new fields, see the "Add a Field" task later in this chapter. To delete a field, see the "Delete a Field" task.

How do I remove a table that I no longer want?

Before attempting to remove a table, ensure that it does not contain any important data that you need. To delete the table, select it in the Navigation pane and press Delete . Access asks you to confirm the deletion before permanently removing the table, along with any data that it contains.

Change Table Views

You can view your table data using two different view modes: Datasheet view and Design view. In Datasheet view, the table appears as an ordinary grid of intersecting columns and rows where you can enter data. In Design view, you can view the skeletal structure of your fields and their properties. You can use Design view to modify the design of the table.

Change Table Views

SWITCH TO DESIGN VIEW

① Click the **Home** tab on the Ribbon.

② Click the **View** button.

③ Click **Design View**.

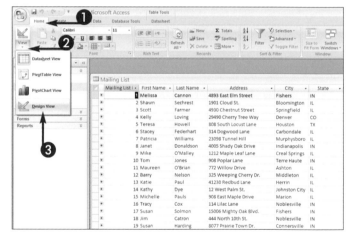

● Access displays the design of the table and shows the field properties.

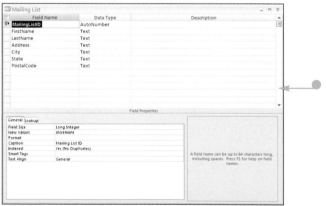

SWITCH TO DATASHEET VIEW

① Click the **Home** tab on the Ribbon.

② Click the **View** button.

③ Click **Datasheet View**.

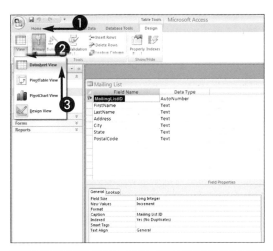

● Access displays the default Datasheet view of the table.

What sort of modifications can I make in Design view?

You can add fields by typing new field names in the Field Name column. You can also change the field names or change the type of data that is allowed within a field, such as text or number data only. The Field Properties sheet at the bottom of Design view allows you to change the design of the field itself, specifying how many characters the field can contain, whether or not fields can be left blank in the record, and other properties.

What do the PivotTable and PivotChart views do?

If you create a PivotTable, you can use PivotTable view to summarize and analyze data by viewing different fields. You can use the PivotChart feature to create a graphical version of a PivotTable, and use the PivotChart view to see various graphical representations of the data. See the Access Help files to learn more about the PivotTable and PivotChart features.

Add a Field

You can add fields to your table to include more information in your records. For example, you may need to add a separate field to a Contacts table for mobile phone numbers.

① Open the table to which you want to add a field in Datasheet view.

Note: See the previous task, "Change Table Views," to learn more about the Access views.

② Click the **Datasheet** tab on the Ribbon.

③ Click where you want to insert a new field.

Note: Access adds a new field to the right of the existing field you select.

④ Click the **New Field** button.

The Field Templates pane opens.

● You can scroll through the list of available fields.

⑤ Click and drag the field name that you want to add to the table.

● Access adds the new field.

● You can click the **Close** button (⊠) to close the pane.

● To add a blank field, simply click the **Insert** button on the Datasheet tab.

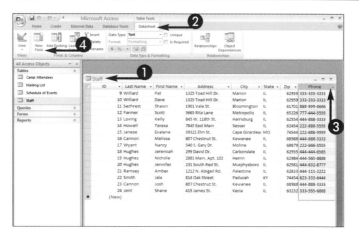

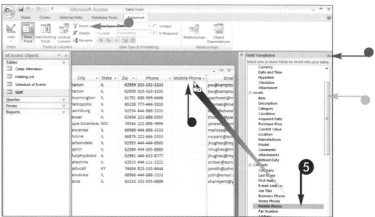

You can delete a field that
you no longer need in a table.
When you remove a field, Access
permanently removes any data
contained within the field for
every record in the table.

Delete a Field

① Open the table that you want to edit in
Datasheet view.

Note: See the "Change Table Views" task, earlier in this
chapter, to learn more about the Access views.

② Click the field that you want to remove.

③ Click the **Delete** button.

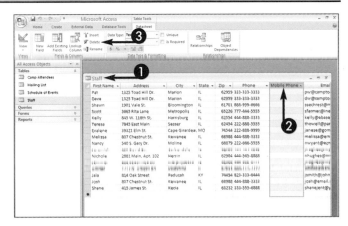

● Access displays a prompt box.

④ Click **Yes**.

Access removes the field and any
record content for the field from the
table.

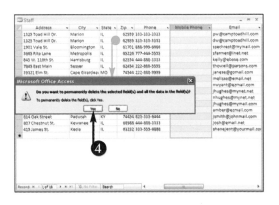

Hide a Field

You can hide a field in your table by hiding the entire column of data. You might hide a field to focus on other fields for a printout or to prevent another user on your computer from seeing the field.

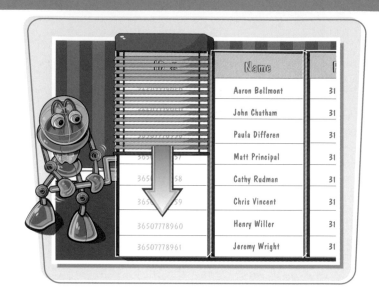

① Click the field column header that you want to hide.

Access selects the entire column.

② Right-click the field name.

③ Click **Hide Columns**.

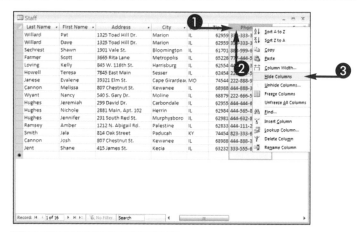

Access hides the column.

● To view the column again, you can right-click the field next to the hidden field, click **Unhide Columns**, select the column that you want to display again, and click **OK**.

Note: Because Access does not mark hidden fields, you need to remember if you have previously hidden fields or activate the **Unhide Columns** command when in doubt.

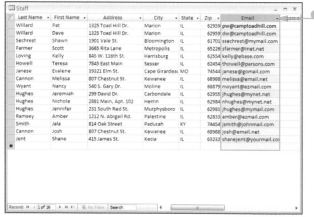

Move a Field

You can move a field in your table to rearrange how you view and enter record data. For example, you may want to move a field to appear before another field to suit the way you type your record data.

Move a Field

1 Click the field column header that you want to move.

Access selects the entire column.

2 Drag the column to a new position in the table.

The ⌖ changes to ⌖.

● A bold vertical line marks the new location of the column as you drag.

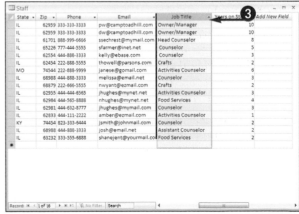

3 Release the mouse button.

Access moves the field to the new location.

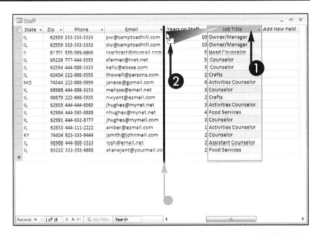

Add a Record

You can add new records to your database table whenever you want. Any new records that you add appear at the end of the table.

Add a Record

① Click the **New** button on the Home tab.

● You can also click the **New** button (▶) on the navigation bar to add a new record.

● Access immediately adds a new record at the bottom of the table.

You can fill in the record's fields as needed.

Note: *See the "Create a Table" task, earlier in this chapter, to learn how to enter record data.*

● As your table grows longer, you can use the navigation buttons to move between records.

Delete a Record

You can remove a record from your database if it holds data that you no longer need. Removing old records can reduce the overall file size of your database and make it easier to manage. When you delete a record, all of the data within its fields is permanently removed.

Delete a Record

① Click the record that you want to delete.

② Click the **Home** tab on the Ribbon.

③ Click the **Delete** button.

You can also right-click the record, and then click **Delete Record**.

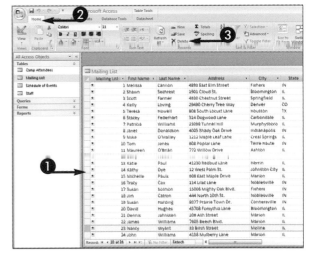

● Access displays a warning box about the deletion.

④ Click **Yes**.

● Access permanently removes the record from the table.

Create a Form Using a Wizard

You can use the Access Form Wizard to help you create and customize a form for entering records into your database. The wizard guides you through each of the necessary steps for creating a form. You can choose exactly which fields the form contains.

Create a Form Using a Wizard

1. Click the **Create** tab on the Ribbon.
2. Click the **More Forms** button.
3. Click **Form Wizard**.

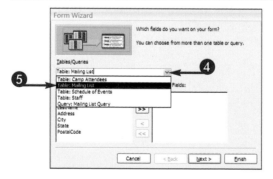

The Form Wizard opens.

4. Click the **Tables/Queries** ☑.
5. Click a table containing the fields on which you want to base the form.

    Depending on the database template that you used to create the file, you may see one or several tables from which to choose.

6 Click a field that you want to include in the form.

7 Click the **Add** button (>).

● To add all of the sample fields, click the **Add All** button (>>).

● Access adds the field to the form.

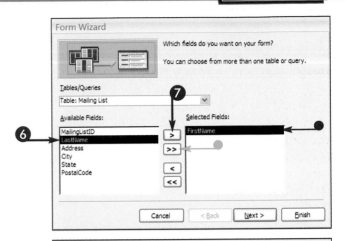

8 Repeat Steps **6** and **7** to add more fields to the form.

● To remove a field from the list, click it and then click the **Subtract** button (<).

9 Click **Next**.

Can I select fields from different tables for my form?

Yes. If you have more than one table in your database, you can choose fields from the different tables to use in a single form. Simply select a table from the **Tables/Queries** drop-down list in Step **4**, and choose a different table.

Is there a way that I can create a blank form?

Yes. You can click the **Blank Form** button on the **Create** tab to open a blank form and a field list containing all of the fields from all of the tables in the database. You can populate the form with as many fields as you need. You can also create a new form based on the fields in a selected table. See the next task, "Create a Quick Form," for more information.

continued

When creating a form, you can choose a layout and a design style, and assign a unique name to the form. After you create a new form with the wizard, you can begin entering records using the form.

Create a Form Using a Wizard *(continued)*

⑩ Click a layout option for the form
(○ changes to ◉).

⑪ Click **Next**.

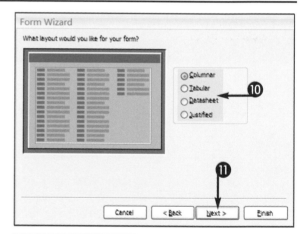

⑫ Click a style for the form.

⑬ Click **Next**.

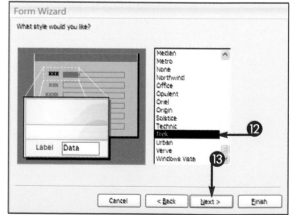

14 Type a name for the form.

● You can click this option to view the form immediately (◯ changes to ◉).

15 Click **Finish**.

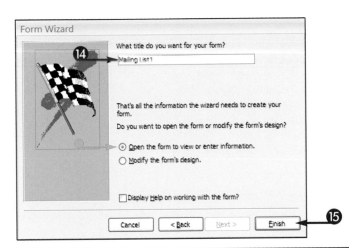

14

Form Wizard

What title do you want for your form?

Mailing List1

That's all the information the wizard needs to create your form.

Do you want to open the form or modify the form's design?

◉ Open the form to view or enter information.

◯ Modify the form's design.

☐ Display Help on working with the form?

Cancel | < Back | Next > | Finish

15

● Access creates the new form.

Access adds the form name to the list of form objects in the database window.

Note: *See the "Add a Record" task to learn how to use a form to add data to your database.*

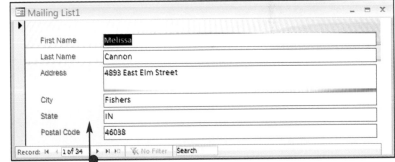

Mailing List1

First Name	Melissa
Last Name	Cannon
Address	4893 East Elm Street
City	Fishers
State	IN
Postal Code	46038

Record: 14 ‹ 1 of 34 › ›I ›I ¤ No Filter Search

TIP

What kinds of layouts are available for my form?

You can choose from four different layouts. The table below describes the appearance of each layout format.

Format	Appearance
Columnar	Sets up your form fields in a column
Tabular	Presents your fields much like a table
Datasheet	Makes the form look just like a datasheet
Justified	Presents your fields so that they line up with both the left and right sides of the form

You can create an instant form based on any table in your database and use it to enter data into the database. Access inserts fields into the form for each field in the selected table.

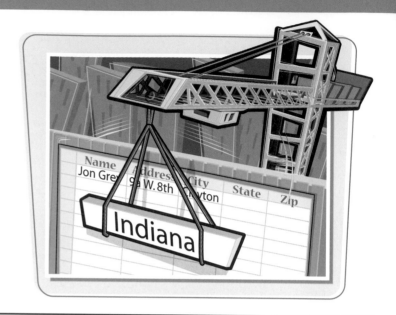

Create a Quick Form

① Click the table on which you want to base a form.

② Click the **Create** tab on the Ribbon.

③ Click the **Form** button.

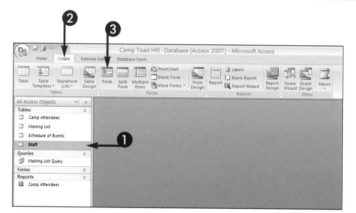

● Access creates the form.

● You can use the Formatting and Arrange tabs to make changes to the form.

④ Click the **Close** button (⊠) to close the form.

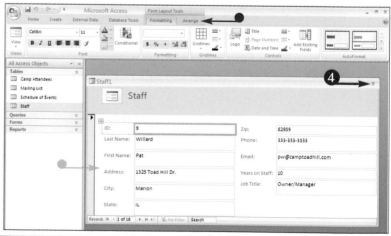

● Access prompts you to save your changes.

⑤ Click **Yes**.

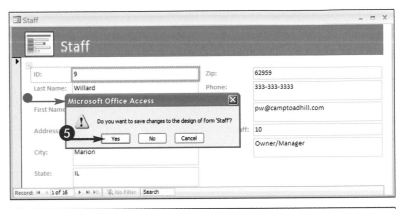

● The Save As dialog box appears.

⑥ Type a name for the form.

⑦ Click **OK**.

Access saves the form.

TIPS

How do I access my forms?

The Navigation pane keeps a list of all of the database objects in your file. To change the view of the list, click the drop-down arrow (▾) at the top of the pane. Click the **All Access Objects** option to see all of the tables, forms, queries, and reports that are stored in your database. To view only forms, click the **Forms** option in the drop-down menu.

How do I delete a form that I no longer need?

To remove a form, display the forms on the Navigation pane and click the one that you want to delete. You can then press Delete or click the **Delete** button on the Home tab. Access asks you to confirm the deletion. When you click **Yes**, Access permanently removes the form.

Add a Record

You can use forms to quickly add records to your Access databases. Forms present your record fields in an easy-to-read format. The form window presents each field in your table as a box that you can use to enter data.

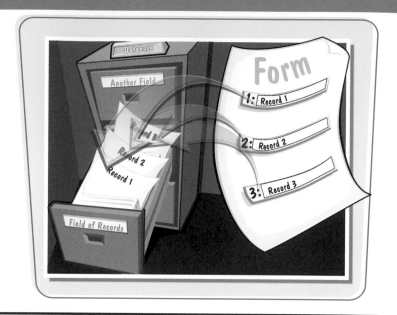

Add a Record

① Display the Forms objects in the database window.

● If the Forms objects are not shown, you can click here (⊡) and click **Forms**.

② Double-click the form that you want to use.

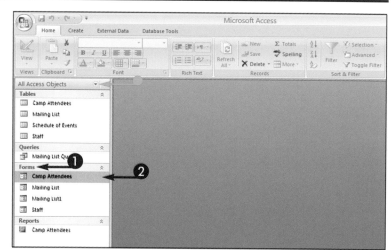

● Access opens the form.

③ Click the **New Record** button (⊡) on the Navigation bar.

④ Click inside the first field and type the data.

⑤ Press Tab .

Access moves to the next field in the form.

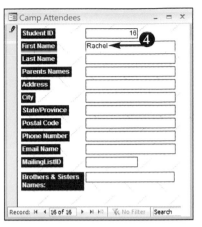

⑥ Repeat Steps **4** and **5** to fill in data for all the form fields in the record.

⑦ In the last field, press Enter or click the **Next Record** button (▶).

Access displays another blank record, ready for data.

Note: See the task, "Navigate Records," to learn how to move among records using a form.

● To close the form window, you can click the **Close** button (✕).

Are there other ways to insert a new record?

Yes. You can click the **New** button on the Home tab of the Ribbon to open a new, blank record in your form. The Home tab features a group of tools that you can use to work with records in your form. You can also click the **New Record** button (▶*) on the form window's navigation bar.

How do I edit a record?

You can reopen the form, navigate to the record that you want to change, and make your edits directly to the form data. When you save your changes, Access automatically updates the data in your table. To learn how to display a particular record in a form, see the next task, "Navigate Records."

Navigate Records

You can navigate your table records using a form. The Form window includes a navigation bar for viewing different records in your database. You may find it easier to read a record using a form rather than reading it from a large table containing other records.

Navigate Records

1 Open the form that you want to view.

Note: See the "Create a Form Using a Wizard" task, earlier in this chapter, to learn how to build a form.

● The Record Number box displays the number of the current record that you are viewing.

2 Click the **Previous Record** (◀) or **Next Record** (▶) buttons to move back or forward by one record.

● Access displays the previous or next record in the database.

● You can click the **First Record** (◀) or **Last Record** (▶) buttons to navigate to the beginning or end of the table.

● You can click the **New Record** button (▶*) to start a new, blank record.

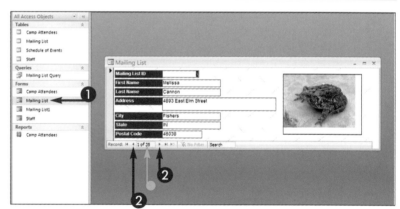

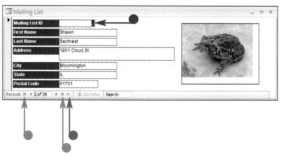

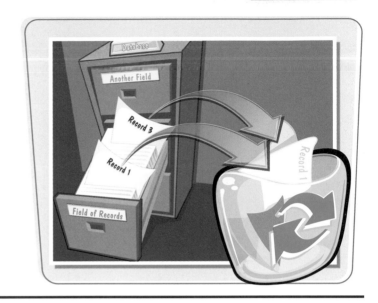

You can remove records that you no longer need by using a form. Removing old records can reduce the overall file size of your database and make it easier to manage. When you delete a record, all of the data within its fields is permanently removed.

Delete a Record

① In the form window, navigate to the record that you want to delete.

● You can use the navigation bar to display different records in your table.

② Click the **Home** tab on the Ribbon.

③ Click the **Delete** button.

④ Click **Delete Record**.

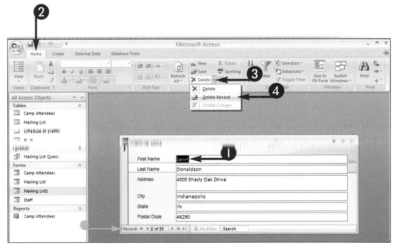

● Access displays a warning box about the deletion.

⑤ Click **Yes**.

Access permanently removes the record.

Change Form Views

You can customize your form using Design view and Layout view. In Design view, each object appears as a separate, editable element in the form. For example, you can edit both the field box that contains the data as well as the field label that identifies the data. In Layout view, you can rearrange the form controls and adjust their sizes directly on the form. You can use the View button to toggle between views.

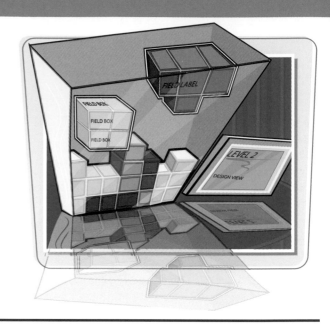

Change Form Views

① Open your form and click the **View** button on the Home tab.

② Click **Design View**.

● Access displays the form's design.

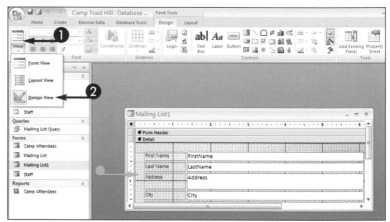

③ Click the **View** button.

④ Click **Layout View**.

● Access displays the form as it originally appears, but each element is editable.

To return to Form view, you can click the **View** button and then click **Form View**.

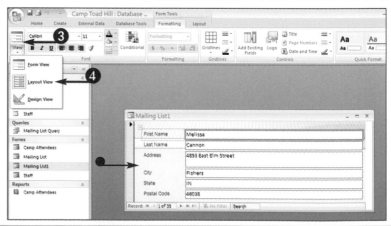

You can move a field to another location on your form. When you select a field for editing, the field label is also selected, making it easy to move both the field and the label at the same time.

Although you can move a field in Design view or in Layout view, you might find it easier to make changes to your form in Layout view. This is because Layout view is more intuitive to use.

Move a Field

1 Open the form that you want to edit in Layout view.

Note: See the previous task, "Change Form Views," to learn how to switch to Layout view.

2 Click the field that you want to move.

To move both the field and the associated label, press and hold **Shift** and then click both items.

3 Move the mouse pointer over the top of the field.

The ☞ changes to ✛.

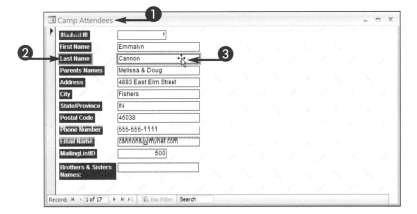

4 Drag the field to a new location on the form.

Access repositions the field.

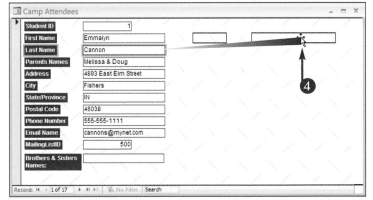

Delete a Field

You can delete a field that you no longer need in a form. When you remove a field, you need to remove both the data box and the field label. Removing a form field does not remove the field from the table upon which the form is originally based.

Delete a Field

① Open the form that you want to edit in Layout view.

Note: *See the "Change Form Views" task, earlier in this chapter, to learn how to switch to Layout view.*

② Click the field that you want to delete.

To move both the field and the associated label, press and hold Shift while clicking both items.

③ Press Delete or click the **Delete** button on the Home tab.

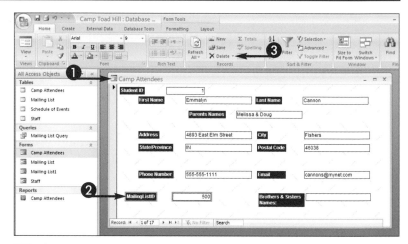

● Access removes the field and label from the form.

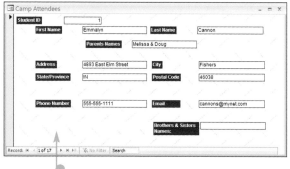

Add a Field

You can add new fields to your form by selecting from a list of available table fields. After you add a field, you can place it where you want in the form.

See the "Move a Field" task, earlier in this chapter, to learn how to reposition fields in Layout view.

Add a Field

1 Open the form that you want to edit in Layout view.

Note: See the "Change Form Views" task, earlier in this chapter, to learn how to switch to Layout view.

2 Click the **Add Existing Fields** button on the Formatting tab.

The Field List pane appears.

3 Drag the field that you want to add from the Field List pane, and drop it onto the form.

The ⌖ changes to ⌖.

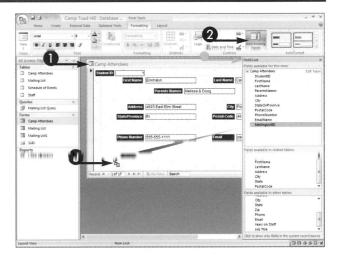

● Access adds the field to the form.

You can reposition the field, if needed.

Note: See the "Move a Field" task, earlier in this chapter, to learn how to move a field in Layout view.

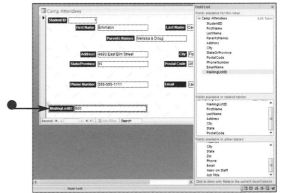

Change the Field Formatting

You can add formatting to your fields and field labels by using the formatting buttons on the Formatting tab on the Ribbon. For example, you can change the font, size, style, alignment, or color of the text. The Formatting tab appears only when you view the form in Layout view.

Change the Field Formatting

1 Open the form that you want to edit in Layout view.

Note: See the "Change Form Views" task to learn how to switch to Layout view.

2 Click the field or label that you want to edit.

3 Click the **Formatting** tab on the Ribbon.

4 Click the formatting that you want to apply, such as a fill color.

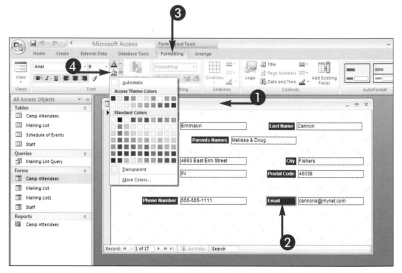

Access applies the formatting to the field.

● This example assigns another color to the field label.

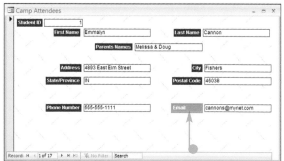

You can change the
design of a form to give
it a different appearance.
You can use the Quick
Format feature to choose
another design theme.
This feature includes a
variety of preset designs,
fonts, and colors that you
can apply to the form.

Apply a Quick Format

1 Open the form that you want to edit in
Layout view.

*Note: See the "Change Form Views" task to learn how to
switch to Layout view.*

2 Click the **Formatting** tab on the
Ribbon.

3 Click the **More** button (⬚) in the
AutoFormat group.

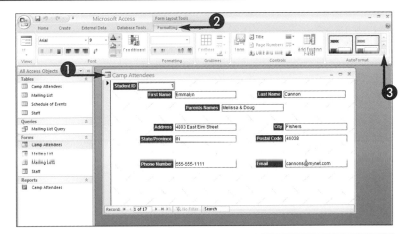

The full palette of formats appears.

4 Click a new style.

● Access applies the new format to the
form.

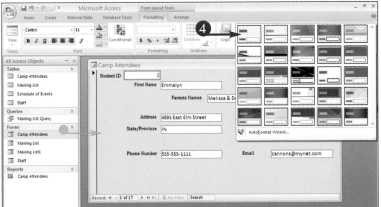

Sort Records

One of the easiest ways to manipulate your database data is to perform a sort. Sorting allows you to put your database records in a logical order to match any criteria that you specify. For example, with a contacts database, you might want to sort the records alphabetically or based on the zip code. You can sort in ascending order or descending order.

You can either sort records in a table, or you can use a form to sort records. See Chapter 19 to learn more about Access tables. See Chapter 20 to more learn about forms.

Sort Records

SORT A TABLE

① Open the table that you want to sort.

② Click the column header for the field that you want to sort.

③ Click the **Home** tab on the Ribbon.

④ Click a sort button.

Click **Ascending** (⊞) to sort the records in ascending order.

Click **Descending** (⊞) to sort the records in descending order.

Access sorts the table records based on the field that you choose.

● This example sorts the records alphabetically by state in ascending order.

● In the prompt box that appears when you close the table, you can click **Yes** to make the sort permanent, or **No** to leave the original order intact.

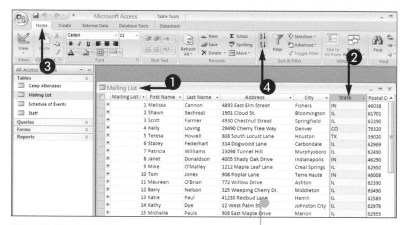

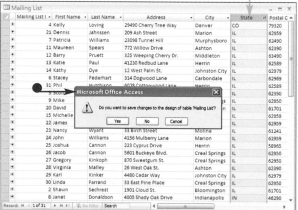

SORT USING A FORM

① Open the form that you want to use.

② Click in the field that you want to sort.

③ Click the **Home** tab on the Ribbon.

④ Click a sort button.

Click **Ascending** (⊞) to sort the records in ascending order.

Click **Descending** (⊞) to sort the records in descending order.

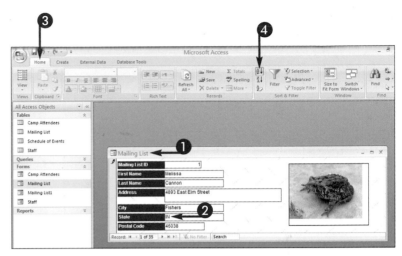

● Access sorts the records in ascending order.

● You can use the navigation buttons to view the sorted records.

Note: See Chapter 20 to learn how to navigate records in Form view.

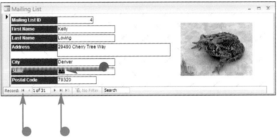

What happens if I have empty records and perform a sort?

If you perform a sort on a field without any data for some of your records, those records are included in the sort. Any empty fields are sorted first when you perform an ascending sort, or last with a descending sort.

SORT DATA

How do I remove a sort order?

With the sorted table open, click the **Clear All Sorts** button (⊞) in the Sort & Filter group on the Home tab. This removes the sort order and returns the table to its original order. You can also use this technique to remove a sort from a query or report.

Clear All Sorts

Filter Records

You can use the filter feature to view only specific records that meet your criteria. For example, you may want to view all of the clients buying a particular product, or anyone in a contacts database that has a birthday in June. You can use an Access filter to temporarily filter out all of the records except those that you want to view.

You can apply a simple filter on one field in your database using the Selection tool, or you can filter several fields using the Filter by Form command.

Filter Records

APPLY A SIMPLE FILTER

① Open the form to which you want to apply a filter, and click the field that contains the criteria that you want to filter.

② Click the **Home** tab on the Ribbon.

③ Click the **Selection** button.

④ Click a criterion.

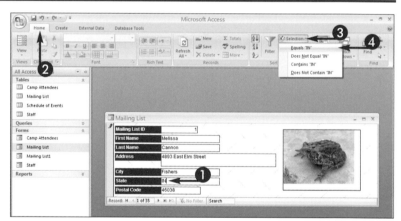

Access filters the records.

● In this example, Access finds eight records matching the filter criterion.

● You can use the navigation buttons to view the filtered records.

Note: See Chapter 20 to learn how to navigate records in Form view.

● To undo a filter, click the **Toggle Filter** button.

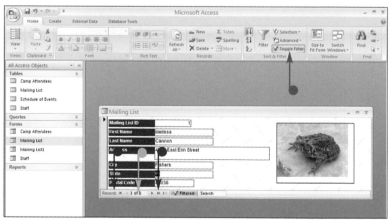

FILTER BY FORM

1. Open the form to which you want to apply a filter, and click the field that contains the criteria that you want to filter.

2. Click the **Home** tab on the Ribbon.

3. Click the **Advanced** button.

4. Click **Filter By Form**.

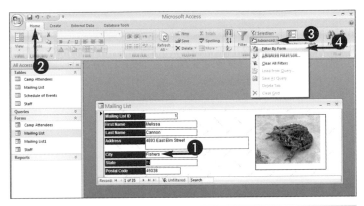

● A blank form appears.

5. Click the ☑ for the field that you want to filter, and click a criterion.

● You can set additional filter criteria for other fields using the tabs at the bottom of the form.

6. Click the **Toggle Filter** button.

Access filters the records.

To return the database to its original order, you can click the **Toggle Filter** button again.

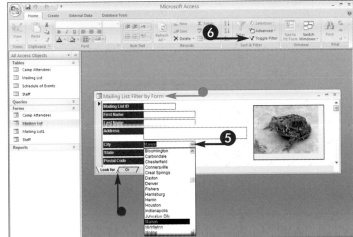

Can I filter by exclusion?

Yes. You can filter out records that do not contain the search criteria that you specify. To do so, first click in the field that you want to filter in the form, click the **Selection** button on the Home tab, and then click an exclusion option. Access filters out any records that do not contain the data found in the field that you selected.

What can I do with an Advanced filter?

You can filter by multiple fields, so that you can designate multiple criteria for a filter. Click the **Advanced** button on the Home tab, and then click **Advanced Filter/Sort** to open the feature. Start by choosing a primary field for the filter and specifying the criteria, and then enter secondary fields as needed. When you are ready to filter the records, click the **Toggle Filter** button.

Perform a Simple Query

You can use a selection query to extract information that you want to view in a database. Queries are especially useful when you want to glean data from two or more tables. Queries are similar to filters, but offer you greater control over the records that you want to view. You can use the Query Wizard to help you select which fields you want to include in the analysis.

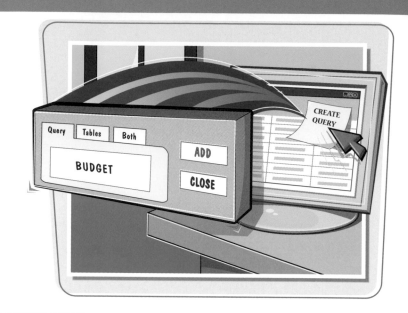

Perform a Simple Query

CREATE A QUERY WITH THE WIZARD

1 Click the **Create** tab on the Ribbon.

2 Click the **Query Wizard** button.

Note: You need at least one table to perform a selection query. See Chapter 19 to learn how to add tables to your database.

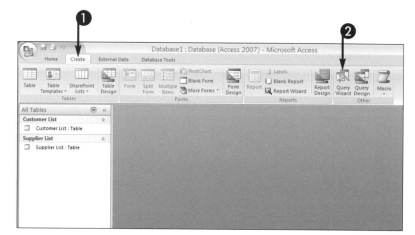

The New Query dialog box appears.

3 Click **Simple Query Wizard**.

4 Click **OK**.

The Simple Query Wizard opens.

⑤ Click the **Tables/Queries** ▾.

⑥ Click a table containing the fields on which you want to base the query.

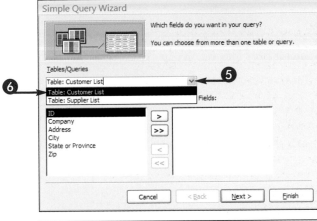

⑦ Double-click each field that you want to include in the query.

● To add all of the sample fields, click the **Add All** button (>>).

● Access adds the fields to the list.

You can repeat Steps **5** and **6** to choose another table from which to add fields.

Note: *When using fields from two or more tables, the tables must have a prior relationship.*

⑧ Click **Next**.

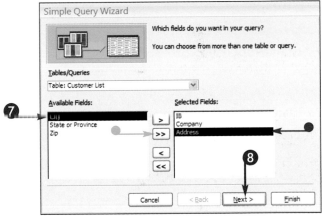

What types of relationships exist between tables?

You can use relationships between tables to bring related information together for analysis. If you create your database using a template, Access has already defined some table relationships for you. For example, one table might include customer names and addresses, while another table might contain orders placed by your customers. By defining a relationship between the two tables, you can create queries to find all customers ordering the same product. You can click **Database Tools** and then click **Relationships** to define relationships between your tables.

Are there other types of queries that I can create?

Yes. When you display the New Query dialog box, you can choose from several other query types to create a query. For example, the Crosstab Query Wizard helps you to group related information for a summary.

continued ➤

Perform a Simple Query *(continued)*

During the process of creating a new query, the wizard asks you to give the query a unique name. All queries that you create are saved in the Queries objects in the Navigation pane. You can open a query in Design view to add criteria to the query.

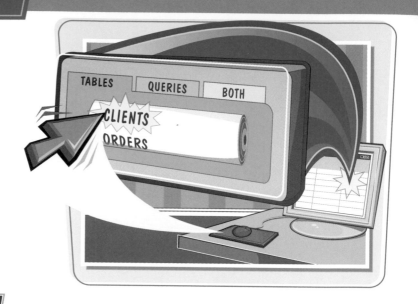

Perform a Simple Query *(continued)*

⑨ Type a name for the query.

● You can click this option to open the query after finishing the wizard (○ changes to ◉).

⑩ Click **Finish**.

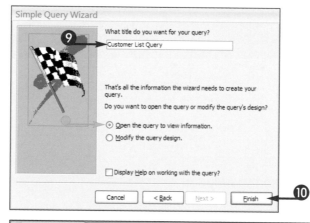

● A query datasheet appears, listing the fields.

ID	Company	Address	City	State or Prov	Zip
6	Baldwin Museu	10 Main Street	New York	NY	12345
7	Blue Yonder Ai	52 1st St.	Boston	MA	1234
8	Coho Winery	3122 75th Aven	Seattle	WA	98100
9	Contoso Pharm	1 Contoso Blvd	London		NS1 EW2
10	Fourth Coffee	28 Edwin St.	London		W1J 8QB
11	Consolidated N	899 80th St.	Seattle	WA	98100
12	Graphic Design	151 Strand	London		WC2 R1A
13	Litware, Inc.	3 Macrofilm Pk	Portland	OR	97200
14	Tailspin Toys	22 Wicklow St.	London		WC1 0AC
15	Woodgrove Ba	37 Lothbury	London		E2R 7ED
*	(New)				

ADD CRITERIA TO A QUERY

① With the query open, switch to Design view.

Note: See Chapter 19 to learn how to switch views.

② Click in the **Criteria** field and type the data that you want to view.

● This example lists a city name as the criterion.

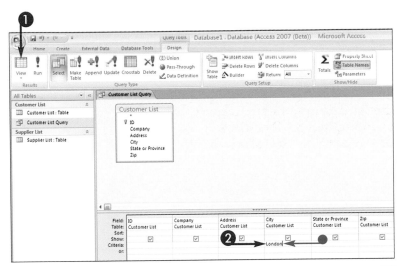

③ Switch back to Datasheet view to see the results.

The table now shows only the records matching the criteria.

● This example lists records in which London is listed as the city name.

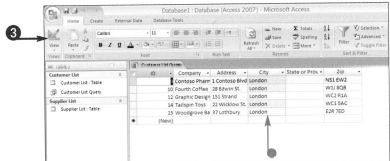

How do I add another table to my query?

Switch to Design view, click the **Design** tab on the Ribbon, and then click the **Show Table** button. This opens the Show Table dialog box where you can add another table to the query and choose from among the available fields to customize the query.

Can I sort or filter my query?

Yes. You can use the sorting and filtering features to further define your query results. To learn how to sort data, see the "Sort Records" task, earlier in this chapter. To learn how to apply a filter, see the "Filter Records" task, also earlier in this chapter.

Create a Report

You can use the Report tool to turn any table, form, or query into a professional report document. The Report Wizard guides you through all of the steps necessary to turn your database data into an easy-to-read printout.

Create a Report

① Click the **Create** tab on the Ribbon.

② Click the **Report Wizard** button.

The Report Wizard opens.

③ Click the **Tables/Queries** ☑.

④ Click a table containing the fields on which you want to base the report.

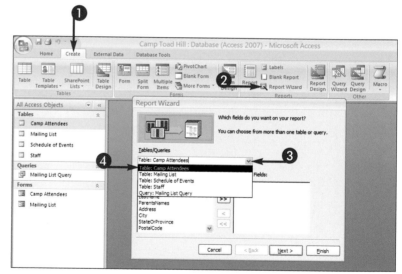

⑤ Double-click each field that you want to include in the report.

● To add all of the sample fields, click the **Add All** button (>>).

⑥ Click **Next**.

The next wizard screen asks how you want to group related data in the report.

7 Double-click the field that you want to use to group the data.

● A sample of the grouping appears here.

8 Click **Next**.

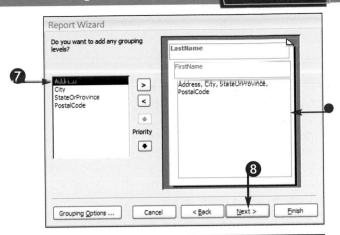

The next wizard screen asks you how you want to set the sort order.

9 Click the first ⌄ and click a sort field.

You can add more sort fields as needed.

10 Click **Next**.

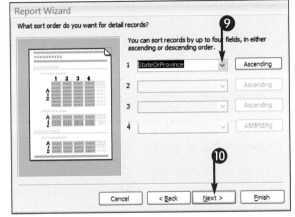

TIPS

Can I choose different fields from different tables to create a report?

Yes. First choose fields from one table, and then follow Steps **3** and **4** in this task to select another table containing fields that you want to use in the report. You can choose fields from more than one table or query for your Access report.

How do I remove a field that I do not want in the report?

With the first Report Wizard screen open, you can click a field that you previously placed in the Selected Fields list box and click the **Subtract** button (<) to remove the field. To remove all of the fields and start over again with the list, click the **Subtract All** button (<<).

continued

Create a Report
(continued)

As the Report Wizard guides you through the steps for building a report, you are asked to decide upon a sort order and a layout for the report's appearance. After you create the report, you can print it.

Create a Report *(continued)*

The next wizard screen asks you to select a layout for the report.

⑪ Click a layout option (⚪ changes to ⦿).

● You can set the page orientation for a report using these options.

⑫ Click **Next**.

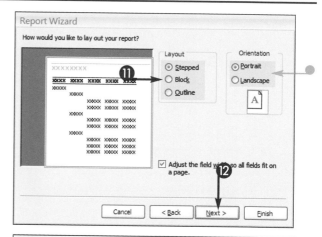

⑬ Click a style for the report.

⑭ Click **Next**.

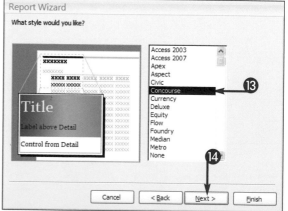

⑮ Type a name for the report.

⑯ Click **Finish**.

● Access creates the report and displays the report in Print Preview mode.

● If Print Preview mode is not displayed, you can click the **Print Preview** button (🔍) at the bottom right corner of the program window.

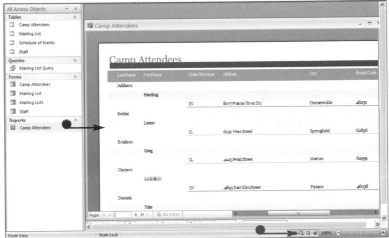

TIPS

How do I print a report?
To print a report from Print Preview, click the **Print** button on the Print Preview tab on the Ribbon. You can also click the **Office** button and then click **Print** to open the Print dialog box and assign any printing options before printing the report.

How can I customize a report in Access?
You can further customize a report using Design view. You can change the formatting of fields, move fields around, and more. To learn more about switching to Design view and using the formatting tools, see Chapter 20.

PART

VI

Part VI: Outlook

Outlook is a personal information manager for the computer desktop. You can use Outlook to manage your calendar, keep track of a contacts list, organize lists of things to do, and more. You can perform a wide variety of everyday tasks from the Outlook window, including sending and receiving e-mail messages, scheduling appointments, and organizing an address book of contacts. In this part, you learn how to put Outlook to work for you using each of the major components to manage everyday tasks.

View Outlook Components

You can use Outlook to manage everyday tasks and e-mail correspondence. Outlook works much like a personal organizer and contains components for certain tasks, such as a Mail folder for e-mail tasks and a Calendar folder for scheduling appointments.

Outlook features five main components: Mail, Calendar, Contacts, Tasks, and Notes. You can switch between components, depending on the task that you want to perform.

View Outlook Components

USE THE NAVIGATION PANE

1 Click the button in the Navigation pane for the component that you want to open.

● You can use the new To-Do Bar to see your daily items at a glance.

Note: *To learn more about the To-Do Bar, see the "Customize the To-Do Bar" task, later in this chapter.*

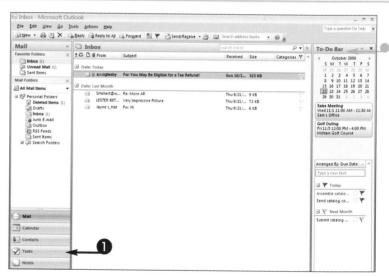

Outlook displays the component.

● This example displays the Tasks component.

● To change the way you view a component, you can click the **View** menu, click **Current View**, and then click a view.

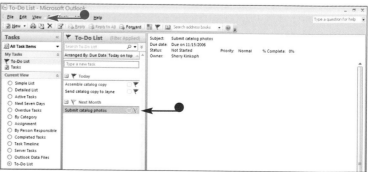

USE THE GO MENU

① Click **Go**.

② Click an Outlook component.

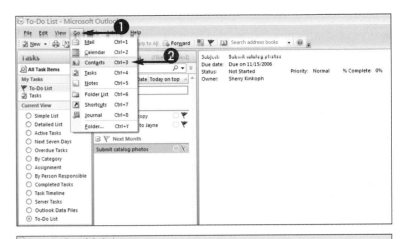

Outlook displays the component.

● This example displays the Contacts component.

Depending on the component, Outlook offers different ways to view the information using the View menu.

Can I customize which component opens by default when I start Outlook?

Yes. By default, Outlook opens the Inbox for your Mail tasks as soon as you start the program. To start with another component instead, follow these steps:

① Click **Tools**.

② Click **Options**.

③ In the Options dialog box, click the **Other** tab.

④ Click **Advanced Options**.

⑤ In the Advanced Options dialog box, click **Browse**.

⑥ In the Select Folder dialog box, click the component that you want to set as the default component, such as **Calendar**.

⑦ Click **OK**.

⑧ Click **OK**.

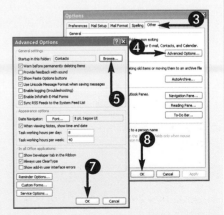

Schedule an Appointment

You can use Outlook's Calendar component to keep track of your schedule. You can add notations on the calendar to remind you of appointments and other important events. When adding new appointments to the Calendar, you fill out appointment details, such as the name of the person with whom you are meeting, and the start and end times of the appointment.

Schedule an Appointment

1 Open the Calendar component.

Note: See the previous task, "View Outlook Components," to learn how to open a component.

2 Navigate to the date for which you want to set an appointment, and click the date.

3 Click **Day** or **Week** view.

4 Double-click the time slot for the appointment that you want to set.

Outlook opens the Appointment window, displaying the Appointment tab.

5 Type a subject for the appointment.

● Outlook adds the subject to the window's title.

6 Type a location for the appointment.

7 Click the **End time** ▼ and set an end time for the appointment.

● If you did not select the correct time slot in Step **4**, you can click the **Start time** ▼ and click a start time.

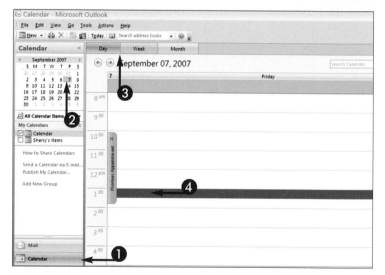

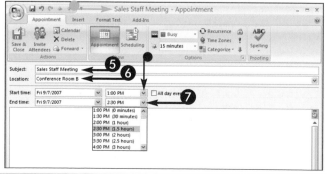

Outlook automatically sets a reminder about the appointment.

● You can click the **Categorize** button to change the reminder setting.

● You can type any notes about the appointment here.

⑧ Click the **Save & Close** button.

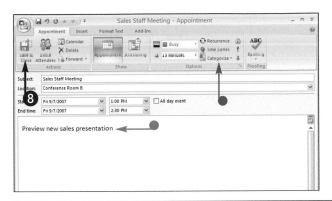

● Outlook displays the appointment in the Calendar.

To view the appointment details again or to make changes, you can double-click the appointment to reopen the Appointment window.

● The days on which you have any appointments scheduled appear bold in the Date Navigator.

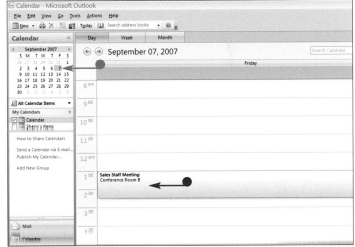

How do I receive a reminder before an appointment?

If you set a Reminder option (⬜) for an appointment, Outlook displays a prompt box at the designated time to remind you about the appointment. The Outlook program window must be running for the reminder audio beep to sound and the reminder prompt box to appear. You can leave Outlook open, but keep the program window minimized on your taskbar to work with other programs.

What does the Categorize option do?

You can click the **Categorize** button and assign color categories to your appointments. You can use color categories to help organize appointments in your calendar. For example, you might categorize all work-related appointments as blue and all non-work appointments as red.

Schedule a Recurring Appointment

If your schedule includes many of the same appointments over and over again, such as weekly sales or department meetings, you can set the appointment as a recurring appointment. Outlook adds the appointment to each week or month as you require.

You can use this same technique to set recurring meetings and events on your Outlook Tasks.

Schedule a Recurring Appointment

1 Open the Calendar component and the Appointment window for the appointment that you want to schedule in a recurring pattern.

Note: See the previous task, "Schedule an Appointment," to learn how to open an Appointment window.

2 Click the **Recurrence** button on the Appointment tab.

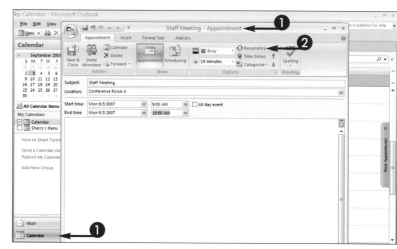

The Appointment Recurrence dialog box appears.

3 Select the Recurrence pattern that you want to set.

● You can also set a range of the recurrence if the appointments continue only for a set number of weeks or months.

4 Click **OK**.

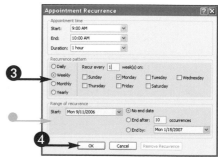

● Outlook marks the appointment as a recurring appointment.

5 Click the **Save & Close** button.

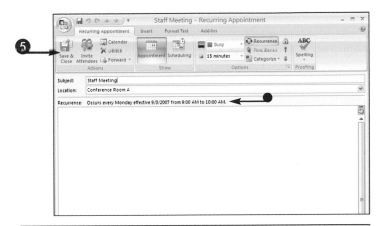

Outlook displays the appointment in the Calendar.

● Recurring appointments show a tiny recurrence icon () in the lower-right corner of the appointment on the Calendar.

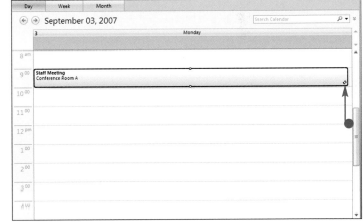

 TIPS

How do I delete an appointment from the Calendar?
To remove an appointment, right-click the appointment on the Calendar and click **Delete**. You can also press Delete. Outlook immediately deletes the appointment from your schedule.

Is there an easy way to set an appointment with one of my contacts?
Yes. You can quickly create an appointment with anyone in your Contacts list. In the Contacts component, right-click the contact with whom you want to schedule an appointment. Next, click **Create**, and then click **New Meeting Request with Contact**. This opens the Message window, where you can set up details concerning the appointment — such as the date and time — and e-mail the request.

Schedule an Event

If you need to track an activity that lasts the entire day or spans several days, such as an anniversary or a conference, you can schedule the date as an event. Events appear as banners at the top of the scheduled date.

① Click **Actions**.

② Click **New All Day Event**.

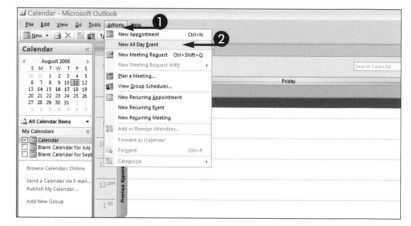

Outlook displays the Event window, which looks the same as the Appointment window.

③ Type a subject for the event.

● Outlook adds the subject to the window's title.

④ Type a location for the event, if applicable.

⑤ Use the Start time and End time options to set a date and time frame for the event.

● You can click ⊡ to display a pop-up calendar of dates.

You can also add a reminder or add notes about the event.

Note: *To learn how to set appointments, see the "Schedule an Appointment" task, earlier in this chapter. To learn more about using notes, see the "Add a Note" task, later in this chapter.*

⑥ Click the **Save & Close** button.

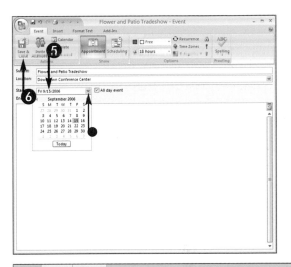

● Outlook displays the event as a banner in the Calendar for the date of the event.

To edit an event, you can double-click the event banner.

How do I edit a reminder?

To change the details about a reminder that you add to any appointment or event, reopen the Appointment window for the appointment or event, click the **Reminder** button (🔲), and change the setting. To remove the reminder entirely, click the **Reminder** button and click **None**. To change the sound associated with the reminder, click the **Reminder** button, and then click **Sound** to open the Reminder Sound dialog box. Use the **Browse** button to assign another sound file.

How do I add a holiday to my calendar?

By default, holidays do not appear in Outlook. You can add a holiday by clicking **Tools**, clicking **Options**, and then clicking the **Calendar Options** button in the Preferences tab. This opens the Calendar Options dialog box. Click the **Add Holidays** button and then click the country whose holidays you want to add to the calendar.

Plan a Meeting

If you use Outlook on a Microsoft Exchange Server network, you can use the Plan a Meeting feature to schedule meetings with other users. You can send e-mail messages inviting attendees, track responses, and designate resources, such as conference rooms or equipment.

Plan a Meeting

① Click **Actions**.

② Click **Plan a Meeting**.

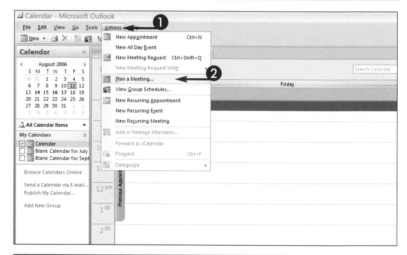

Outlook displays the Plan a Meeting window.

③ Click ☑ and set the start date and time for the meeting.

● You can also click the time in the Meeting pane.

④ Click ☑ and set a meeting end time.

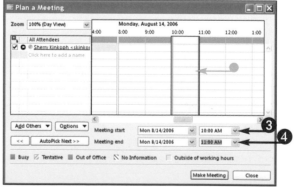

5 Type the names of the attendees.

When you press `Tab` after typing the first attendee name, Outlook automatically checks for the person's name in your Contacts list.

● You can also click **Add Others** and select attendee names.

6 Click **Make Meeting**.

7 Type a subject for the event.

Outlook adds the subject to the window's title.

8 Type a location for the event, if applicable.

● You can type a message to the attendees here.

9 Click the **Send** button.

Outlook e-mails an invitation to each attendee.

Note: See Chapter 23 to learn more about e-mailing with Outlook.

10 Click **Close** to close the Plan a Meeting window.

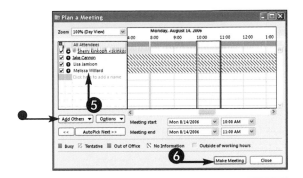

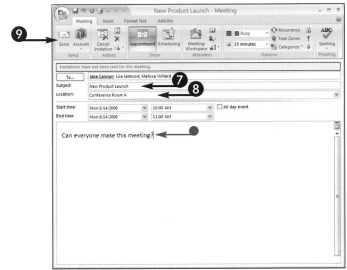

How do I know if people respond to my meeting invitation?

To see who is attending the meeting, you must open the Plan a Meeting window and click the **Scheduling** tab. Outlook keeps track of replies to your invitation. To open the window, double-click the meeting appointment in your calendar. To respond to an invitation yourself, simply click the appropriate button at the top of the e-mail message in Outlook's Mail component.

How do I publish my calendar so that others can see it on the network?

To publish your calendar, click **Tools**, click **Options**, and then click **Calendar Options** on the **Preferences** tab of the Options dialog box. Click **Free/Busy Options** to open the Free/Busy Options dialog box, and turn on any publishing features that you want to set.

Create a
New Contact

You can use the Contacts component to keep a list of people that you contact most often, such as family, coworkers, or clients. You can keep track of information such as addresses, e-mail addresses, phone numbers, and more.

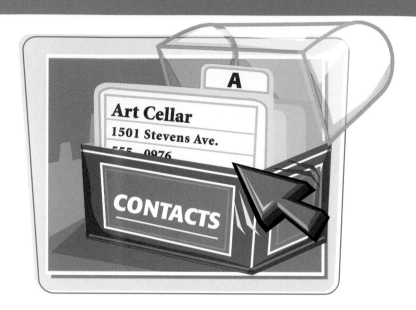

① Open the Contacts component.

Note: See the "View Outlook Components" task, earlier in this chapter, to learn how to open a component.

② Click the **New** button.

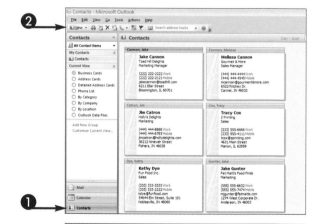

Outlook opens the Contact window, and displays the General page.

③ Fill in the contact's information on the General page.

You can press Tab to move from field to field.

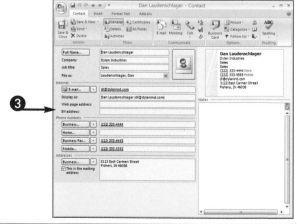

④ Click the **Details** button.

⑤ Fill in additional information about the contact, as needed.

⑥ Click the **Save & Close** button.

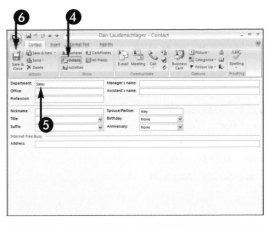

● Outlook saves the information and displays the contact in the Contacts list.

To edit contact details, you can double-click the contact to reopen the Contact window.

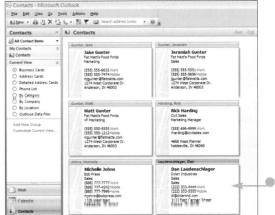

 TIPS

Can I import a list of contacts from another program?

Yes. Click the **File** menu and then click **Import and Export** to open the Import and Export Wizard. The wizard guides you through the steps for importing a list of contacts from other sources, including Outlook Express.

How do I send an e-mail to a contact?

You can right-click the contact name, click **Create**, and then click **New Message to Contact**. This opens the Message window, where you can type a message to the contact. To learn more about e-mailing with Outlook, see Chapter 23.

Create a New Task

You can use Outlook's Task component to keep track of things that you need to do, such as a daily list of activities or project steps that you need to complete.

Create a New Task

① Open the Tasks component.

Note: See the "View Outlook Components" task, earlier in this chapter, to learn how to open a component.

② Click the **New** button.

Outlook displays the Task window.

③ Type a subject for the task.

● Outlook adds the subject to the window's title.

④ Type a due date for the task.

⑤ Click the **Status** 🔽 and click a progress option.

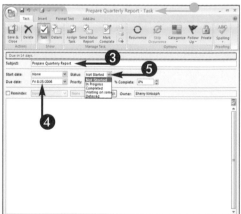

⑥ Type a note or details about the task here.

● You can set a priority level for the task using the **Priority** ⌄.

● To set a completion amount, you can click the **% Complete** ⬍.

⑦ Click the **Save & Close** button.

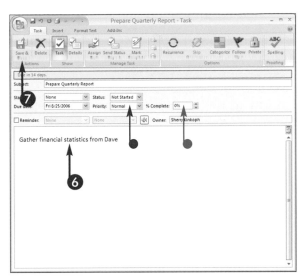

● Outlook displays the task in the Tasks list.

To view the task details again or make changes, you can double-click the task to reopen the Task window.

● To change your view of tasks in the Tasks list, you can click a view option (◯ changes to ◉).

How do I mark a task as completed?

You can click the check box next to the task name to mark the task as complete. Completed tasks appear with a strikethrough on the Tasks list. To remove a task completely from the list, right-click the task and click **Delete**.

Can I turn a task into an e-mail?

Yes. You can assign a task to another user by turning the task into an e-mail message. Right-click the task and then click **Assign Task** to open the Task window. You can add an e-mail address and a message concerning the task, and then send the message. To learn more about e-mailing in Outlook, see Chapter 23.

You can use the Notes component to create notes for yourself. Much like an electronic version of yellow sticky notes, Outlook's Notes allow you to write down ideas and thoughts, or any note text that you want to remind yourself of later. You can attach Outlook Notes to other items in Outlook as well as drag them onto the Windows desktop for easy viewing.

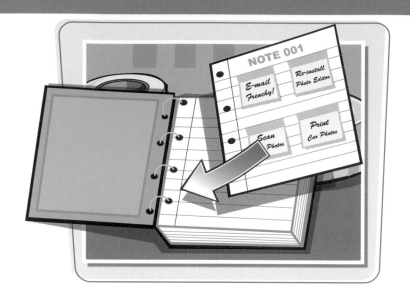

Add a Note

❶ Open the Notes component.

Note: See the "View Outlook Components" task, earlier in this chapter, to learn how to open a component.

❷ Click the **New** button.

● Outlook displays a yellow note.

❸ Type your note text.

❹ When you finish, click the **Close** button (⊠).

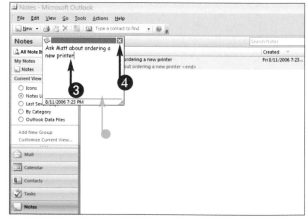

● Outlook adds the note to the Notes list.

To view the note again or to make changes, you can double-click the note to reopen the note window.

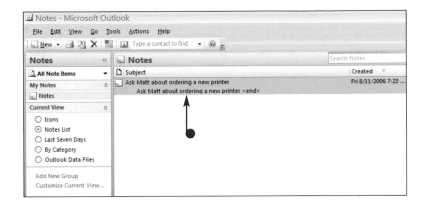

● To change your view of notes in the Notes list, you can click a view option (○ changes to ◉).

● This example displays the Icons view.

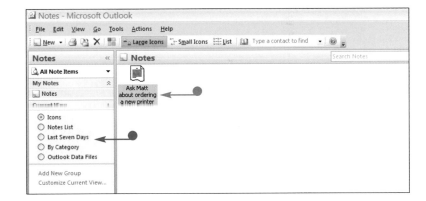

Can I forward the note to another user?

Yes. You can turn any note into an instant e-mail attachment. Simply right-click the note in the Notes list, and then click **Forward** to open an e-mail Message window. You can address the note and add any additional message text. To learn more about e-mailing with Outlook, see Chapter 23.

How do I delete notes that I no longer want?

Right-click the note in the Notes list and then click **Delete** or press Delete. Outlook immediately deletes the note. To delete multiple notes at the same time, press and hold Ctrl while clicking the notes and then press Delete.

Organize
Outlook Items

You can store your Outlook items, whether they are messages, tasks, or notes, in folders. By default, Outlook creates a set of folders for you to use when you install the program, including e-mail folders for managing incoming, outgoing, and deleted messages. You can use the Folders list to move items from one folder to another and create new folders in which to store Outlook items.

Organize Outlook Items

VIEW THE FOLDER LIST

① Click **Go**.

② Click **Folder List**.

● You can also click the **Folder List** icon
(□) on the Navigation pane.

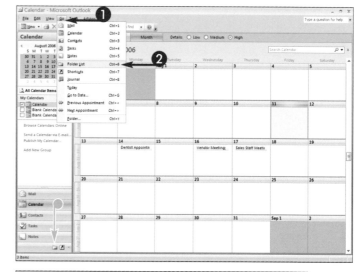

● Outlook displays the Folder List pane.

③ Click the folder whose contents you
want to view.

● Outlook displays the folder's contents.

To move an item to another folder,
you can click and drag the item and
drop it on the folder's name.

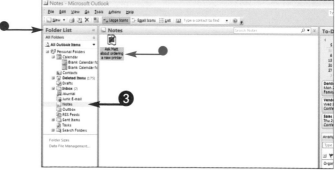

CREATE A NEW FOLDER

① Click **File**.

② Click **New**.

③ Click **Folder**.

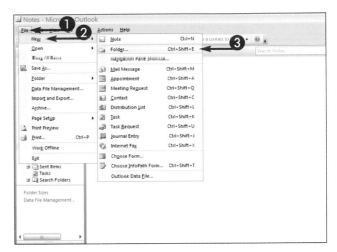

The Create New Folder dialog box appears.

④ Type a name for the new folder.

⑤ Click the **Folder contains** ⊡ and choose an item type.

⑥ Click the parent folder in which you want to store the new folder.

⑦ Click **OK**.

● Outlook creates the new folder.

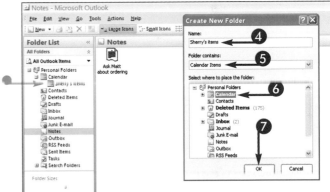

How do I delete an item from a folder?

Select the item that you want to delete, and then click the **Delete** button or press `Delete`. The deleted items are immediately placed in the Deleted Items folder. To empty the folder, click **Tools** and then click **Empty "Deleted Items" Folder**. To delete an entire folder and all of its items, click the folder name in the Folder list and then press `Delete`.

Can I create subfolders for my work items and home items?

Yes. You can create as many folders as you need for each type of Outlook item or for a variety of items. For example, you might create a subfolder in your Inbox folder to place all of the corporate correspondence that you send and receive, or create a folder in the Tasks folder for a special project.

You can use Outlook's new search tool to quickly find an item in your Outlook components. Each component includes an Instant Search box that you can use to quickly look for a keyword or phrase within the component's items.

① Click the component that you want to search.

② Click inside the **Search Inbox** and type a keyword or phrase.

● You can also click the **Tools** menu, click **Instant Search**, and then click **Instant Search** again.

The Instant Search command on the Tools menu offers access to advance search options.

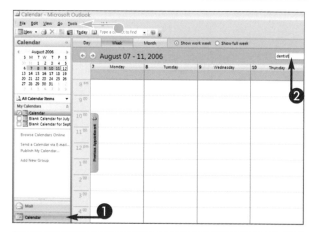

● Outlook immediately conducts a search and displays any matching results.

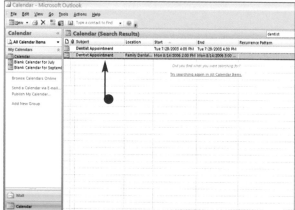

You can use Outlook's new To-Do Bar to quickly view the Date Navigator and the current day's appointments and tasks. The To-Do Bar appears by default when you open the Inbox, Contacts, or Notes components. You can customize the To-Do Bar to change which items appear in the list.

Customize the To-Do Bar

① Click **View**.

② Click **To-Do Bar**.

③ Click **Options**.

● You can click here (⧉) to minimize the bar.

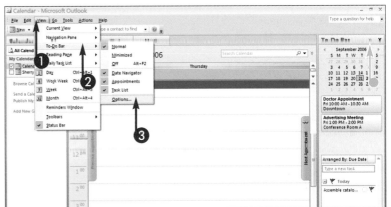

The To-Do Bar Options dialog box appears.

④ Click a check box to deselect a feature on the To-Do Bar view (☑ changes to ☐).

● You can control the number of months or appointments that appear on the bar.

⑤ Click **OK**.

● Outlook applies the changes.

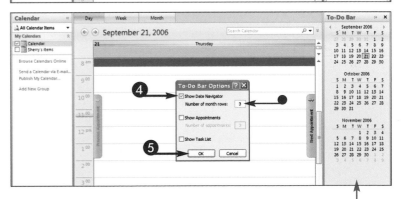

Compose and Send a Message

You can use Outlook to create and send e-mail messages. When you compose a message, you can designate the e-mail address of the person or persons to whom you are sending it, and type your message text. You can also give the message a subject title to help the recipients know what the message is about.

You need to log on to your Internet connection in order to send a message. If you compose a message while offline, the message is stored in Outlook's Outbox folder until you send it.

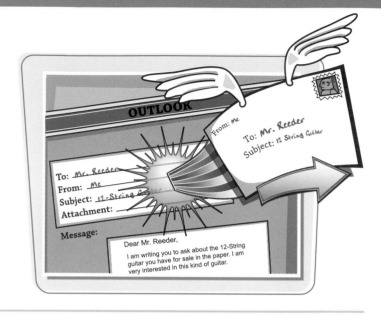

Compose and Send a Message

① Open the Mail component in Outlook.

Note: See Chapter 22 to learn how to view components using the Navigation pane.

② Click the **New** button.

Outlook opens an untitled message window.

③ Type the recipient's e-mail address.

● If the e-mail address is already in your Address Book, you can click **To** and select the recipient's name.

If you enter more than one e-mail address, you must separate each address with a semicolon (;) and a space.

④ Type a subject title for the message.

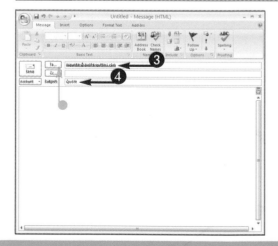

5 Type the message text.

● You can use Outlook's formatting buttons to change the appearance of your message text.

● To set a priority level for the message, you can click **Importance: High** (⚠️) or **Importance: Low** (⬇️).

Note: By default, the message priority level is considered Normal.

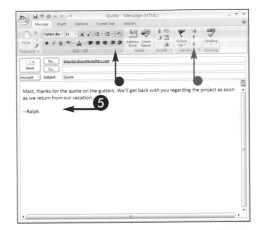

● If you have several e-mail accounts, you can click **Account** and specify your user ID.

6 Click **Send**.

Outlook sends the e-mail message.

Note: You must be logged on to your Internet account in order to send the message.

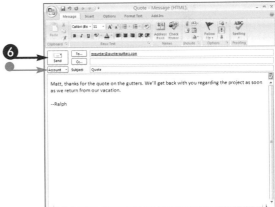

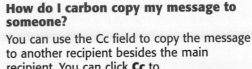

Where can I find messages that I have previously sent?

You can click the **Sent Items** folder to view a list of e-mail messages that you have previously sent. The Sent Items folder is one of the main Mail folders in Outlook. To view a message from the Sent Items list, simply double-click the message to open it in a new window.

How do I carbon copy my message to someone?

You can use the Cc field to copy the message to another recipient besides the main recipient. You can click **Cc** to open the Address Book and select the person's name. To send a copy of the message without revealing the Cc recipient's name, use the blind carbon copy, or Bcc, feature. Click **Cc**, click the person's name, and then click **Bcc**.

Read an Incoming Message

When you open Outlook's Mail feature, you can retrieve and view incoming e-mail messages. You can view a message in a separate message window or in the Reading pane.

You need to log on to your Internet connection in order to receive e-mail messages.

Read an Incoming Message

1 Open the Mail component in Outlook.

Note: *See Chapter 22 to learn how to view components using the Navigation pane.*

2 Click the **Send/Receive** button.

● Outlook accesses your e-mail account and downloads any waiting messages.

Note: *You must be connected to your Internet account to download messages.*

● If the Inbox is not displayed, you can click the **Inbox** folder.

3 Double-click the message that you want to view.

● The message appears in a message window.

You can now read and respond to the message.

Note: *You can also view a message in the Reading pane as soon as you click the message. See the next task to learn how to turn the pane on or off.*

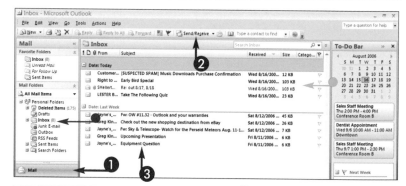

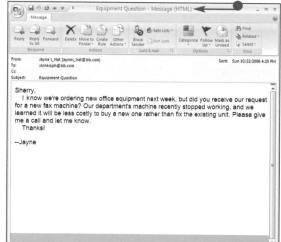

Control the Reading Pane

Outlook features a Reading pane that you can use to view your messages. You can turn the pane on or off, and control its placement. In today's world of spam e-mails, you may prefer to leave the Outlook Reading pane off when working with incoming and outgoing messages. You can also turn off Outlook's Reading pane to prevent viewing of unsolicited e-mails and to free up on-screen workspace to view more of your message lists.

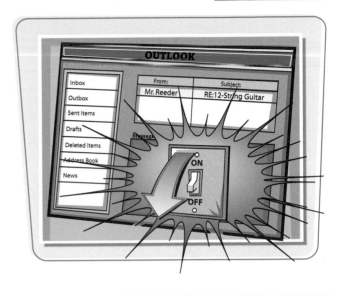

Control the Reading Pane

① Open the Mail component in Outlook.

Note: See Chapter 22 to learn how to view components using the Navigation pane.

② Click **View**.

③ Click **Reading Pane**.

④ Click **Right** or **Bottom**.

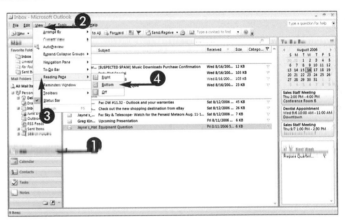

Outlook displays the Reading pane.

● In this example, the pane appears at the bottom of the Outlook window.

To turn the pane off again, you can simply repeat these steps and select the **Off** option instead.

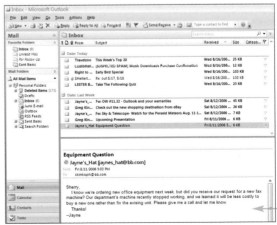

Reply to or Forward a Message

You can reply to an e-mail message by sending a return message to the original sender. You can also forward the message to another recipient.

You need to log on to your Internet connection in order to send e-mail messages.

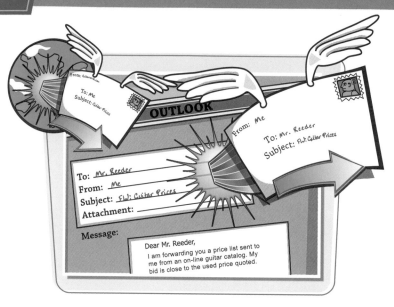

Reply to or Forward a Message

REPLY TO A MESSAGE

① Open the message that you want to answer.

Note: *See the "Read an Incoming Message" task, earlier in this chapter, to learn how to view an e-mail message.*

② Click the **Reply** button to reply to the original sender.

● To reply to everyone who received the original message, you can click the **Reply to All** button.

③ Type any return message that you want to add to the e-mail.

④ Click **Send**.

Outlook sends the e-mail message.

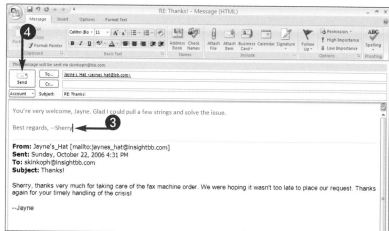

FORWARD A MESSAGE

1 Open the message that you want to forward.

Note: See the "Read an Incoming Message" task, earlier in this chapter, to learn how to view an e-mail message.

2 Click the **Forward** button on the Message tab.

3 Type the recipient's e-mail address.

4 Type any message that you want to add to the e-mail.

5 Click **Send**.

Outlook forwards the e-mail message.

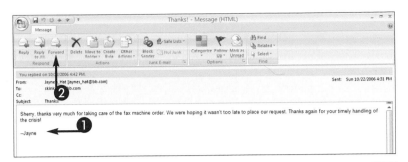

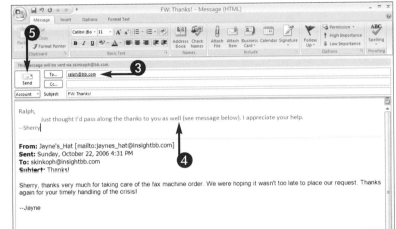

How do I get rid of the original message in my reply?

By default, Outlook retains the original message when you click the Reply or Reply to All buttons. To turn off the feature, follow these steps:

1 Click **Tools**.

2 Click **Options**.

3 In the Options dialog box, click the **E-mail Options** button on the Preferences tab.

4 In the E-mail Options dialog box, click the **When replying to a message** ☑ and click **Do not include original message**.

5 Click **OK** to exit each dialog box.

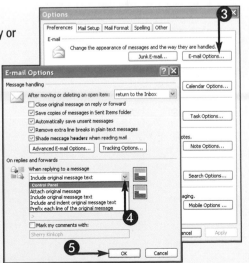

Add a Sender to Your Address Book

You can add the e-mail address of any message that you receive to your Outlook Address Book. This makes it easy to send e-mails to the person at a later time.

Add a Sender to Your Address Book

① Open the e-mail message of the sender that you want to save.

Note: See the "Read an Incoming Message" task, earlier in this chapter, to learn how to view an e-mail message.

② Right-click the sender's name.

③ Click **Add to Outlook Contacts**.

● The Contact window opens with the sender's name and e-mail address already filled in.

● You can add additional information as needed.

④ Click **Save & Close**.

Outlook saves the e-mail address.

Note: The next time you want to send a message to the person, you can click **To** in the message window and choose the name from the Address Book.

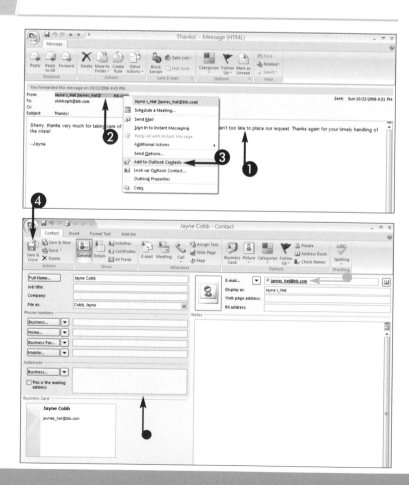

Delete a Message

You can remove messages from your Inbox to eliminate clutter and keep your folder manageable. When you delete a message, Outlook moves it to the Deleted Items folder. You can remove all of the deleted Outlook items at your leisure.

To maximize your computer's storage capacity, remember to purge the Deleted Items folder regularly.

Delete a Message

① Open the Mail component in Outlook.

Note: See Chapter 22 to learn how to view components using the Navigation pane.

● If the Inbox is not displayed, you can click the **Inbox** folder.

② Click the message that you want to remove from the Inbox.

③ Press Delete or click the **Delete** button (☒) on the toolbar.

Outlook deletes the message from the Inbox and adds it to the Deleted Items folder.

● You can click the **Deleted Items** folder to view the message that you deleted.

● To empty the Deleted Items folder, click the **Tools** menu and click **Empty "Deleted Items" Folder**.

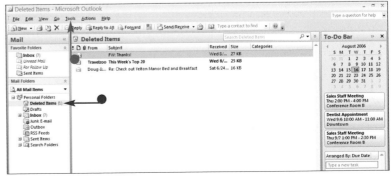

Attach a File to a Message

You can send files stored on your computer to other e-mail recipients. For example, you might send an Excel file to a work colleague, or send a digital photo of your child's birthday to a relative.

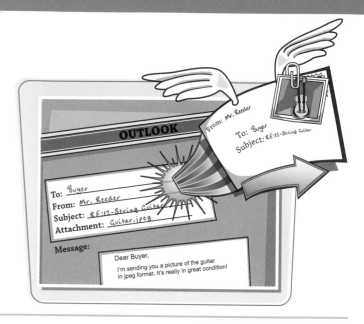

Attach a File to a Message

1 Open and address the message that you want to send.

Note: See the "Compose and Send a Message" task, earlier in this chapter, to learn how to create an e-mail message.

2 Click the **Attach File** button on the Message tab.

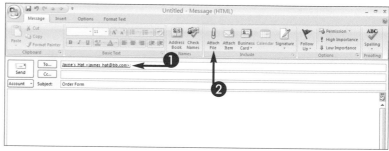

The Insert File dialog box appears.

3 Navigate to the folder or drive containing the file that you want to send.

4 Click the filename.

5 Click **Insert**.

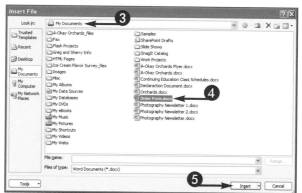

● Outlook adds the file attachment to the message and displays the filename and the file size.

⑥ Type any message text that you want to send.

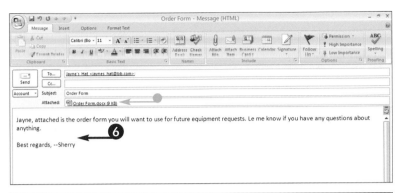

⑦ Click **Send**.

Outlook sends the e-mail message and attachment.

Note: Some Internet providers and e-mail systems are not set up to handle large file attachments. Check with the recipient to see if his system can receive the attachment size that you want to send.

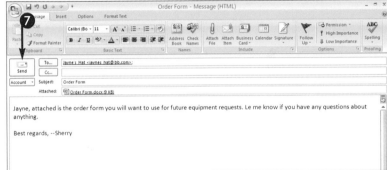

How do I open an attachment that someone sends me?

You can double-click the attachment filename to open the item. When you do, a prompt box appears, warning you about opening attachments and presenting options to open or save the file. If you click **Open**, the associated program opens and displays the file. Never open a file unless you trust the person who sent it. If you click **Save**, you can save the attachment to a folder or drive on your computer.

Why does Outlook block some file attachments?

Some attachments, such as those ending with the extensions .bat, .exe, .vbs, and .js, are associated with viruses, and Outlook automatically blocks the files. Always use a good virus protection program, such as McAfee, Norton Antivirus, or another reputable program, to help keep your computer safe from unwanted viruses.

Clean Up the Mailbox

You can use the Mailbox Cleanup feature to tidy up your Outlook mailbox, delete old e-mail messages, archive messages, and more.

Clean Up the Mailbox

1 Click **Tools**.

2 Click **Mailbox Cleanup**.

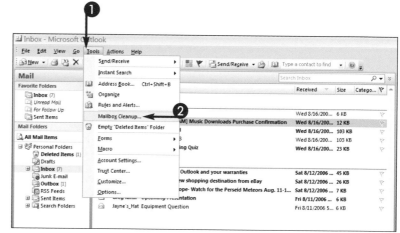

The Mailbox Cleanup dialog box appears.

3 Click the type of items that you want to locate (○ changes to ⊙).

● To find old messages, you can click ⬍ and specify an age.

● To find large message files, you can click ⬍ and specify a size.

4 Click **Find**.

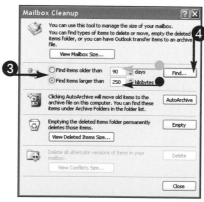

● Outlook searches for the items that you
specified and displays the results.

5 Click **Edit**.

6 Click **Select All**.

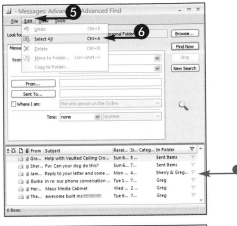

● Outlook selects all of the old messages
that it found.

7 Click **Edit**.

8 Click **Delete**.

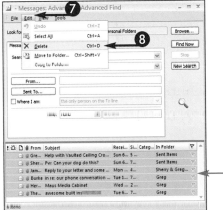

How do I archive old messages instead of deleting them?

To archive old e-mails, click the **AutoArchive**
button in the Mailbox Cleanup dialog box. The
AutoArchive feature helps you to
store Outlook items that you
do not use frequently, yet
still want to keep. By
default, AutoArchive is
turned on, archiving
older items and
placing them in an
Archive.pst file.

How do I check on my overall mailbox size?

To view the size of your entire mailbox
folder in Outlook, click the **View Mailbox
Size** button in the Mailbox Cleanup dialog
box. The Folder Size dialog box
appears, detailing the total
file size of each of the
main Outlook folders.
Viewing the folder
sizes can help you to
determine which folders
to archive or delete
items from.

continued

Clean Up the Mailbox *(continued)*

After you locate and delete old or space-consuming e-mail messages, you can delete them permanently from Outlook by emptying the Deleted Files folder.

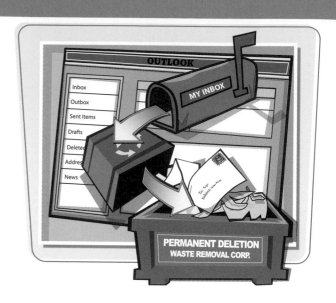

Clean Up the Mailbox *(continued)*

● A prompt box appears, warning you about the deletion.

⑨ Click **Yes**.

● Outlook deletes the items from the Inbox and moves them to the Deleted Items folder.

⑩ Click the **Close** button (🗵) to exit the dialog box.

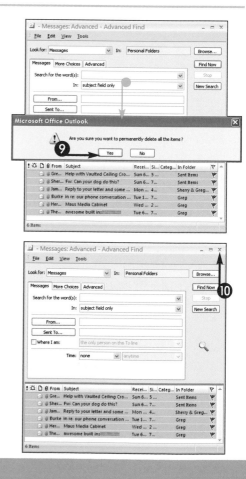

⑪ Click **Tools**.

⑫ Click **Empty "Deleted Items" Folder**

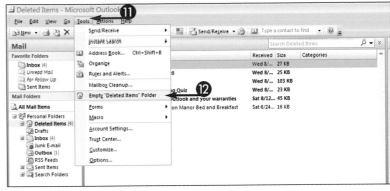

A prompt box appears, warning you about the deletions.

⑬ Click **Yes**.

Outlook permanently deletes the items.

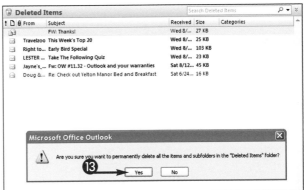

Can I tell Outlook to automatically empty the Deleted Items folder for me?

Yes. Among the General preferences, you can set up Outlook to empty the folder whenever you exit the program. Follow these steps:

❶ Click **Tools**.

❷ Click **Options**.

❸ Click the **Other** tab.

❹ Click the **Empty the Deleted Items folder upon exiting** option (☐ changes to ☑).

❺ Click **OK** to apply the new setting.

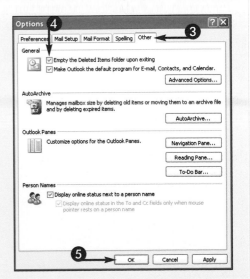

Screen
Junk E-mail

Junk e-mail, also called spam, is overabundant on the Internet and often finds its way onto your computer. You can safeguard against wasting time viewing unsolicited messages by setting up Outlook's Junk E-mail feature. You can target e-mail from specific Web domains and make sure that it is deposited into the Outlook Junk E-mail folder.

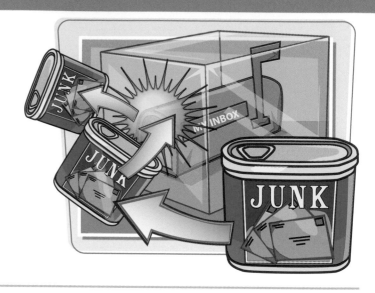

Screen Junk E-mail

VIEW JUNK E-MAIL OPTIONS

1 Click **Actions**.

2 Click **Junk E-mail**.

3 Click **Junk E-mail Options**.

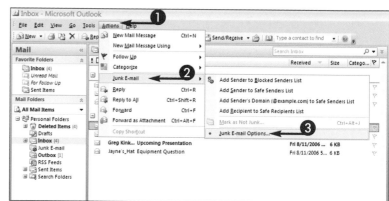

The Junk E-mail Options dialog box appears.

You can use the various tabs to view junk e-mail settings, blocked domains, and safe senders.

● You can click one of these options to control the level of junk e-mail filtering that Outlook applies (○ changes to ◉).

● You can click this option to permanently remove any junk e-mail that you receive (☐ changes to ☑).

4 Click **OK**.

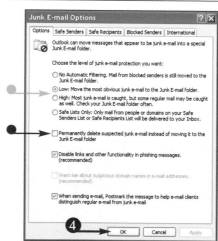

DESIGNATE A MESSAGE AS JUNK

1 Right-click the message.

2 Click **Junk E-mail**.

3 Click **Add Sender to Blocked Senders List**.

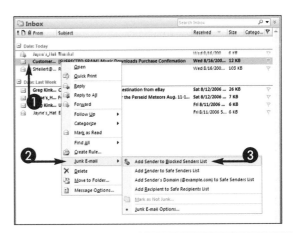

● A prompt box appears.

4 Click **OK**.

● Outlook adds the sender's e-mail address to the list of filtered domain names and moves the message to the Junk E-mail folder.

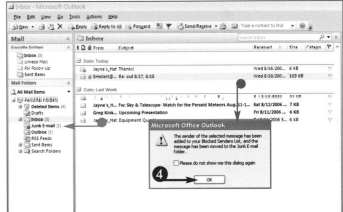

How can I restore a junk e-mail to my safe list?

If you accidentally send a message to the Junk E-mail folder, you can correct the action and remove it from the filter. First, click the Junk E-mail folder. Right-click the message that you want to restore. From the menu that appears, click **Junk E-mail** and then click **Mark as Not Junk**. Outlook restores the message and removes it from the filter list.

Does Outlook empty the Junk E-mail folder?

No. To empty the folder, right-click over the Junk E-mail folder name in the Navigation pane and click **Empty "Junk E-mail" Folder**. Outlook moves all of the items to the Deleted Items folder. You can permanently remove the items by emptying the Deleted Items folder. Right-click the Deleted Items folder name in the Navigation pane and click **Empty "Deleted Items" Folder**. See the "Clean Up the Mailbox" task, earlier in this chapter, to learn more about the Deleted Items folder.

Create a Message Rule

You can use rules to help control messages that meet a specific set of conditions, such as placing messages from a certain sender or domain directly into a folder of your choosing as soon as the message arrives in the Inbox. Rules are also useful in filtering out unwanted spam messages.

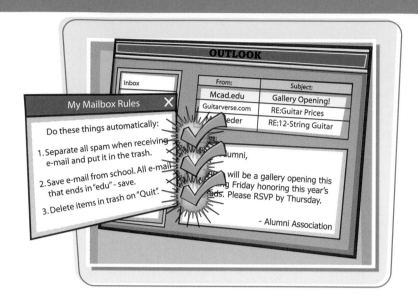

Create a Message Rule

① Right-click the message on which you want to base a rule.

② Click **Create Rule**.

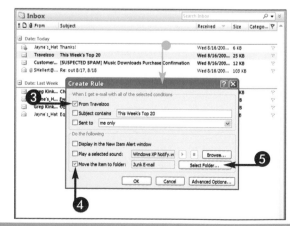

● The Create Rule dialog box appears.

③ Click the conditions that you want to apply (☐ changes to ☑).

④ Click the **Move the item to folder** option (☐ changes to ☑).

⑤ Click the **Select Folder** button.

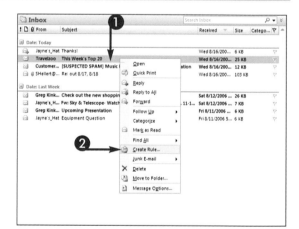

● The Rules and Alerts dialog box appears.

6 Click the folder where you want Outlook to store the messages.

7 Click **OK**.

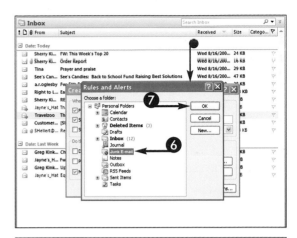

● Outlook prompts you to run the rule now.

8 Click **OK**.

9 Click **OK**.

The next time you receive a message matching the criteria that you specified, Outlook places the message directly into the folder that you selected.

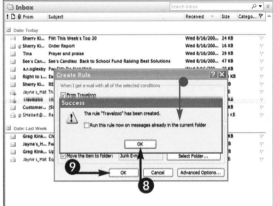

 TIPS

How can I add more criteria to a message rule?

You can click **Advanced Options** in the Create Rule dialog box to display the Rules Wizard and view additional options that you can set concerning the message. The Rules Wizard includes several sets of criteria that you can specify, such as exceptions to the rule, actions, and even a dialog box for naming the rule. Click the **Next** and **Back** buttons to view all of the available criteria that you can specify.

How do I remove a rule that I no longer want?

To delete a rule from Outlook's list, click the **Tools** menu and then click **Rules and Alerts** to open the Rules and Alerts dialog box. Click the rule that you want to delete and click **Delete**. If you have more than one e-mail account, you must first select the correct Inbox for the account that contains the rule.

PART VII

Part VII: Publisher

Publisher is a desktop publishing program you can use to design and produce a variety of publications. You can create anything from a simple business card to a complex brochure. Publisher installs with a large selection of pre-designed publications that you can use as templates to build your own desktop publishing projects. In this part, you learn how to build and fine-tune all kinds of publications, and tap into Publisher's formatting features to make each document suit your own design and needs.

Create a Publication

You can use Publisher to create all kinds of publications, such as brochures, flyers, newsletters, and letterheads. Publisher installs with a wide variety of publication types, including preset designs that control the layout and formatting of the publication. To start a new publication, simply select a design from Publisher's varied list of publication types.

Create a Publication

1 Launch Publisher.

The Welcome screen appears by default.

2 Click a publication category from the Publication Types list.

● You can use the scroll bar to scroll through the available publications.

● Click **Newer Designs** to view the newest designs installed with Publisher 2007.

● Click **Classic Designs** to view classic designs.

● Click **Blank Sizes** to view blank design templates that you can use.

● You can drag the Zoom slider to enlarge or reduce the size of the sample display.

3 Click a publication design.

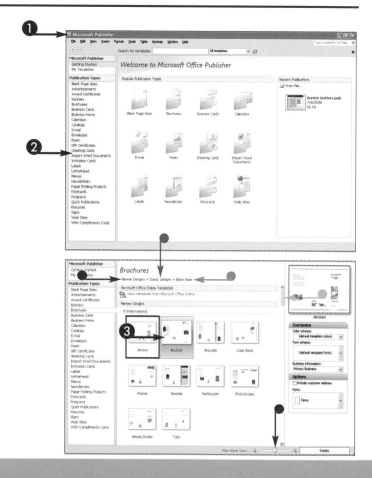

● Publisher displays the selected design here.

● You can customize a design's color scheme or fonts using these options.

④ Click Create.

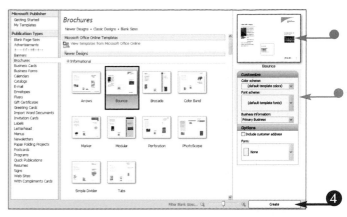

● Publisher creates the publication.

● The Format Publication pane displays options for changing the page elements, color scheme, and fonts.

● If the publication has more than one page, you can click a page number to view a page.

Note: After creating a publication, you can save it to reuse later. To learn how to open and save Office files, see Chapter 2.

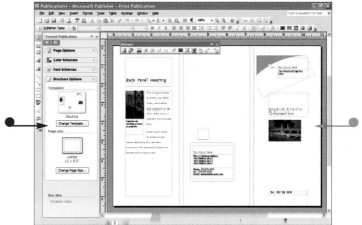

TIPS

How do I change the design of my publication?

You can click the **Change Template** button in the Format Publication pane to view other templates that you can apply to the publication. To change the color scheme, click the **Color Schemes** tab and select from a range of preset color schemes for the publication. If the task pane is not displayed, click the **View** menu and then click **Task Pane**.

What design options can I control in a publication?

Two of the most important design options that you can change to customize a publication are the color scheme and font scheme of the design. The color scheme controls the colors used throughout the design. You can select from a wide variety of preset color schemes to create just the look you want. You can use the font scheme to control the font sets used for all of the various text elements in a design template.

Create a Blank Publication

You can create a blank publication, populate it with your own text boxes, and design a layout to suit your project. For example, you might want to create your own brochure or invitation and customize it by adding your own text boxes and art objects.

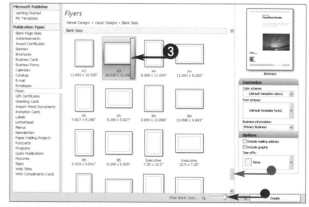

Create a Blank Publication

1 Launch Publisher and click a publication category from the Publication Types list.

● If Publisher is already open, you can click **File**, and then click **New** to display the Welcome screen.

2 Click **Blank Sizes**.

● You can drag the Zoom slider to enlarge or reduce the size of the sample display.

● You can use the scroll bar to scroll through the available page sizes.

3 Click a page size.

● Publisher displays the selected size here.

● You can customize the color scheme or fonts using these options.

④ Click **Create**.

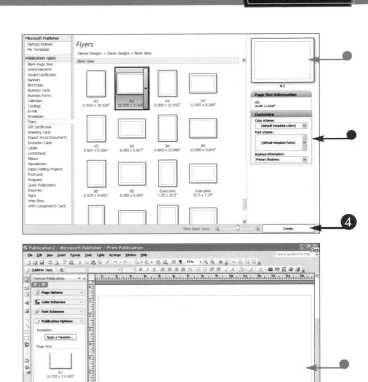

● Publisher opens the blank publication.

You can now add your own text boxes and pictures to the document.

Note: *See the "Add a New Text Box" task, later in this chapter, to learn more about adding text to a blank publication.*

TIPS

Can I create my own templates in Publisher?

To turn any publication that you create into a template that you can reuse again, simply click **File**, and then click **Save As**. The Save As dialog box appears. Click the **Save as type** ⋁ and then click **Publisher template (*.pub)**. Give the file a unique name and save it to the folder or drive where you keep your template files. The next time you want to use the file, open the template and reuse the information to create a new publication.

How do I select another publication to create?

You can start a new Publisher publication at any time, even if you are currently working on an existing publication. To do so, click **File**, and then click **New** to return to Publisher's Welcome screen, where you can select a publication type and design. See the "Create a Publication" task to learn more.

Zoom In and Out

You can use the Zoom feature to control the magnification of your publication. By default, Publisher displays your document in a zoomed-out view so that you can see all of the elements on a page. When you begin working with the publication and add text and formatting, you can zoom in to better see what you are doing.

ZOOM IN   ZOOM OUT

Zoom In and Out

SPECIFY A MAGNIFICATION

① Click the area of the publication where you want to change the zoom magnification.

● When you click an object on the page, Publisher surrounds it with selection handles.

② Click the **Zoom** ▼.

③ Click a percentage.

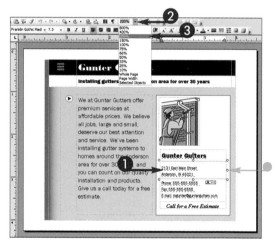

Publisher changes the magnification setting for your publication.

● In this example, the publication is magnified to 200 percent.

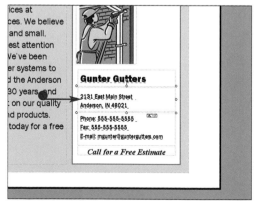

USE ZOOM BUTTONS

1 Click the area of the publication where you want to change the zoom.

2 Click the **Zoom Out** (🔍) or **Zoom In** (🔍) button.

You can click the Zoom buttons multiple times to change the level of magnification.

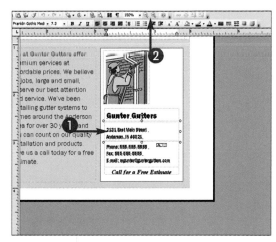

Publisher changes the magnification setting for your publication.

● In this example, the publication is zoomed out.

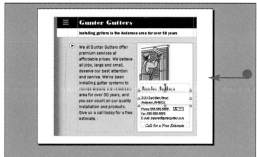

TIPS

How can I free up more workspace on-screen?

You can close the task pane to quickly free up on-screen workspace. Click the pane's **Close** button (✕), or click **View** and then click **Task Pane**. A check mark appears next to the Task Pane command name on the View menu when the pane is displayed. No check mark indicates that the pane is hidden. To view the pane again, click **View** and then click **Task Pane**.

Is there a quicker way to zoom my publication?

Yes. You can press F9 on the keyboard to quickly zoom in and out of a publication. To quickly view the entire page in the work area, press Ctrl + Shift + L.

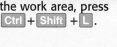

When you create a new publication based on a design, Publisher inserts a layout for the text and displays placeholder text in the text boxes, also called *objects* or *frames*. The placeholder text gives you an idea of the text formatting that is applied by the design, and what sort of text you might place in the text box. You can replace the placeholder text with your own text.

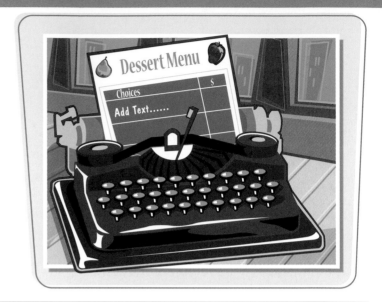

Add Text

① Click the text object that you want to edit.

● You may need to zoom in first to see the text object.

Note: *See the previous task, "Zoom In and Out," to learn how to magnify your view.*

● Publisher surrounds the selected object with handles, and highlights the placeholder text within.

② Type your own text.

Publisher replaces any placeholder text with the new text that you type.

● You can click anywhere outside of the text object to deselect the text box.

Note: *To learn how to apply formatting to objects, see Chapter 25.*

You can continue entering text to build your publication.

To edit the text at any time, you can click the text box and make your changes.

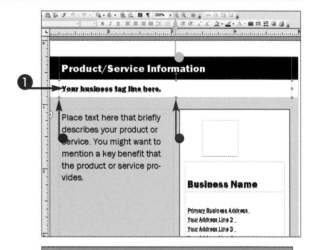

You can add new text boxes to a publication and type your own text. For example, you may need to add a new text box to an empty area in your layout to include additional information, or you may need to add new text boxes to a blank publication.

Add a New Text Box

1 Click the **Text Box** button (▣) on the Objects toolbar.

● If the Objects toolbar is not displayed, click **View**, click **Toolbars**, and then click **Objects**.

The ▷ changes to +.

2 Click and drag the text box to the size that you want to insert.

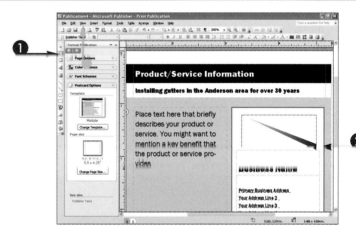

3 Type the text that you want to insert into the text box.

● You can apply formatting to the text.

Click anywhere outside of the text object to deselect the text box.

Note: *To apply formatting to objects and to move and resize text box objects, see Chapter 25.*

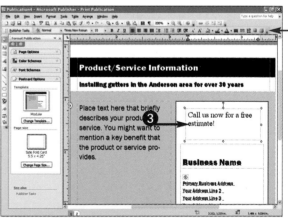

Add a Picture to a Publication

You can add digital photographs or other picture files to your Publisher creations. For example, you might add a photo of your company's latest product to a new brochure, or include a snapshot of the new baby on a family e-mail newsletter.

① Click the **Picture Frame** button (🖼) on the Objects toolbar.

● If the Objects toolbar is not displayed, click **View**, click **Toolbars**, and then click **Objects**.

② Click **Picture from File**.

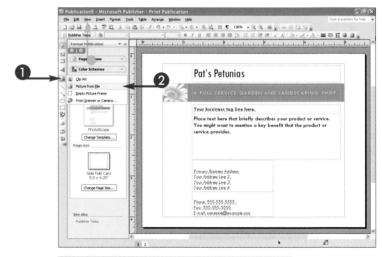

The ⌖ changes to +.

③ Click and drag the frame to the size that you want to insert.

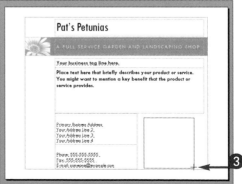

The Insert Picture dialog box appears.

④ Navigate to the folder containing the picture file that you want to use.

⑤ Click the filename.

⑥ Click **Insert**.

Note: *You can also double-click the filename to insert the image directly.*

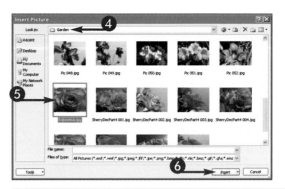

● Publisher inserts the picture file.

● The Picture toolbar appears.

You can move and resize the picture.

Note: *To learn how to resize objects in Publisher, see Chapter 25.*

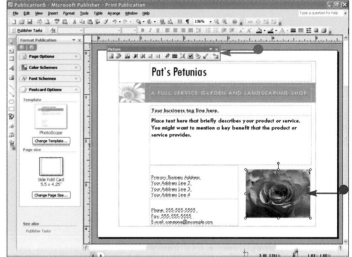

TIPS

How do I fill in an existing picture object?

If the publication design that you select already has a picture object in the layout, then you can replace the placeholder image with another picture file on your computer. Double-click the placeholder picture to display the Picture toolbar, and then click the **Insert Picture** button (🖼). The Insert Picture dialog box appears, where you can select a file from your own computer to use in the publication.

How do I delete a picture object that I no longer need?

To remove an object from a publication, whether it is a picture, a text box, or any other object, click the object to select it and press Delete. Publisher immediately removes the object from the page. You can select more than one object to delete by pressing and holding Ctrl while clicking each object.

Add Clip Art to a Publication

You can illustrate a publication with artwork from Publisher's Clip Art collection. You can search for a specific type of clip art to suit your project needs. The Clip Art collection includes a wide variety of clip art images.

① Click the **Picture Frame** button (🖼) on the Objects toolbar.

● If the Objects toolbar is not displayed, click **View**, click **Toolbars**, and then click **Objects**.

② Click **Clip Art**.

Note: You can also draw your own shapes to use as art. See Chapter 3 to learn how to use the Office drawing tools.

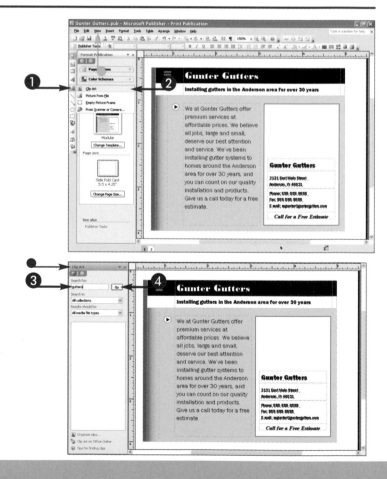

● The Clip Art task pane opens.

③ Type a keyword describing the type of clip art that you want to insert.

④ Click **Go**.

Note: To learn more about inserting clip art into Office projects, see Chapter 3.

● The Clip Art task pane displays any possible matches.

● You can move the mouse pointer over an image to view the image properties.

If the search does not produce any results, you can try another keyword.

5 Click the clip art that you want to insert.

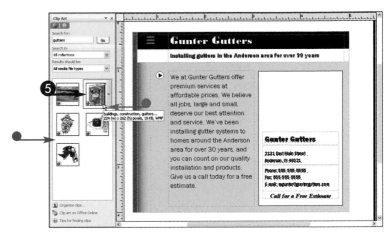

● Publisher inserts the clip art.

● The Picture toolbar appears.

You can move and resize the clip art.

Note: To learn how to resize objects in Publisher, see Chapter 25

TIPS

I cannot find a clip art image to use. Is there another place I can look for clip art?

You can look for more clip art images on the Web. For example, you can click the **Clip art on Office Online** link at the bottom of the Clip Art pane to search the Microsoft Web site for clip art to suit your project. You can also find free clip art images on the Internet. Simply conduct a Web search for free clip art to find out what is available for downloading.

How can I add a border to my clip art?

To add a border to your clip art, select the clip art object, click the **Line/Border Style** button (▤) on the Picture toolbar, and then click a style. As soon as you make a selection, Publisher adds the border to the selected clip art image. If the Picture toolbar is not displayed, click **View**, click **Toolbars**, and then click **Picture** to open the toolbar.

Change the Text Font and Size

You can control the font and size of your publication text. By default, when you assign a publication design, Publisher uses a predefined set of formatting for the text, including a specific font and size. You may need to change the font or increase the size to suit your own publication's needs.

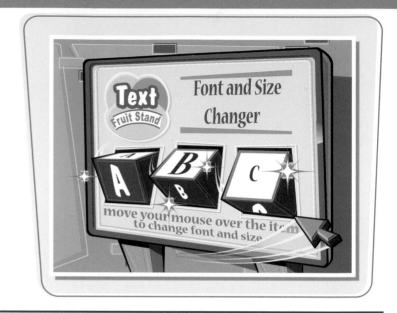

Change the Text Font and Size

① Click the text object or select the text that you want to format.

② Click the **Font** ▾ on the Formatting toolbar.

③ Click a font.

● You can also use the Font dialog box to assign a font and size. Click **Format** and then click **Font** to open the dialog box.

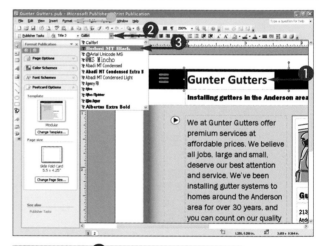

● Publisher applies the new font.

④ Click the **Font Size** ▾.

⑤ Click a size.

Publisher applies the new size.

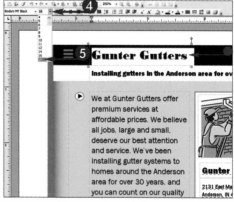

Change the Text Style

You can change the style of your publication text by applying bold, italic, or underline formatting. For example, you might need to make a paragraph bold to stand out in a newsletter article, or change a flyer heading to italics for emphasis.

Change the Text Style

① Click the text object or select the text that you want to format.

② Click a formatting button on the Formatting toolbar.

Click **Bold** (B) to make text bold.

Click **Italic** (I) to italicize text.

Click **Underline** (U) to add an underline to the text.

● You can also use the Font dialog box to assign text styles. Click **Format** and then click **Font** to open the dialog box.

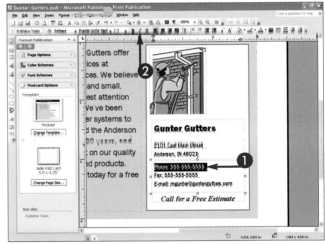

Publisher applies the new style.

● This example applies bold and italic styles to the phone number text.

Change Text Alignment

You can use Publisher's alignment commands to change the way in which text is positioned horizontally in a text object box. Depending on the publication design that you select, alignment is preset to best suit the publication type. You can change the alignment to suit your own needs.

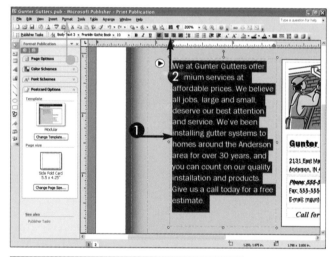

① Click the text object or select the text that you want to format.

② Click an alignment button on the Formatting toolbar.

Click the **Align Left** button (▤) to left-align text.

Click the **Center** button (▤) to center text.

Click the **Align Right** button (▤) to right-align text.

Click the **Justify** button (▣) to justify text between the left and right margins of the text object.

● You can also use the Paragraph dialog box to change the alignment. Click **Format** and then click **Paragraph** to open the dialog box.

Publisher applies the new alignment.

● In this example, the postcard body text is now centered in the text object.

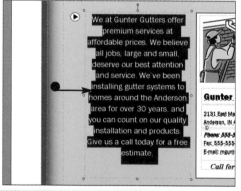

You can add color to your text to enhance the appearance of a publication or add emphasis to your text. You can also use the new Sample Font Color feature to duplicate colors in your publication. When selecting text colors, be careful not to choose a color that makes your text difficult to read.

Change Text Color

① Click the text object or select the text that you want to format.

② Click the **Font Color** button (🔺) on the Formatting toolbar.

● You can also use the Font dialog box to assign a font and color. Click **Format** and then click **Font** to open the dialog box.

③ Click a color.

By default, Publisher displays colors that are associated with the design.

● To choose another color, you can click **More Colors**.

● You can assign the same color as another element in the publication by clicking **Sample Font Color** and then clicking the color that you want to duplicate.

Publisher immediately applies the color to the text.

● This example applies purple to the text.

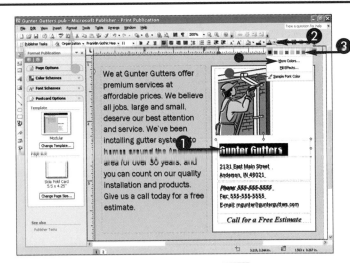

Control Text Wrap

You can control the way in which a text object wraps text around a picture object or any other object in a publication. For example, you may want a column of text to wrap tightly around a clip art object.

① Click the picture object or other object that you want to edit.

② Click the **Text Wrapping** button (▣) on the Picture toolbar.

● If the Picture toolbar is not displayed, click **View**, click **Toolbars**, and then click **Picture** to open the toolbar.

③ Click a text wrapping option.

● You can also click **Arrange** and then click **Text Wrapping** for text wrapping options.

Publisher immediately applies the text wrapping.

● This example applies tight text wrapping.

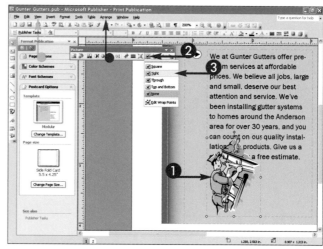

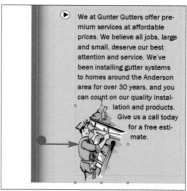

You can add a border to any object in a publication, including text boxes, clip art, and pictures. You can also control the line thickness of the border.

Add a Border

① Click the object that you want to edit.

② Click the **Line/Border Style** button (▤) on the Formatting or Picture toolbar.

③ Click a line style.

● To remove a border, click **No Line**.

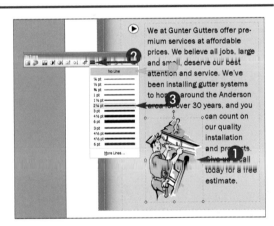

Publisher immediately applies the border to the object.

● This example adds a border to a clip art object.

● You can also change the color of any border or line using the **Line Color** button (▨).

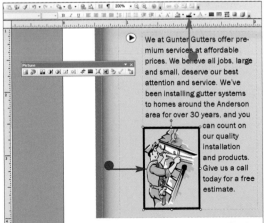

Move a Publication Object

You can move a publication object to better suit your layout. For example, when building a publication from a blank document, you may need to move text objects or picture objects around to create a better layout.

① Click the object that you want to move.

● Publisher surrounds the selected object with handles.

② Move the mouse ⌖ over the edge of the object until ⌖ changes to ✛.

③ Drag the object to a new location.

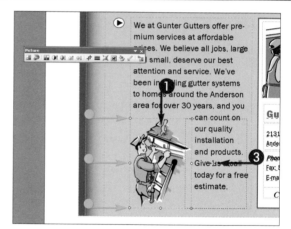

Publisher moves the object.

● This example moves a clip art object.

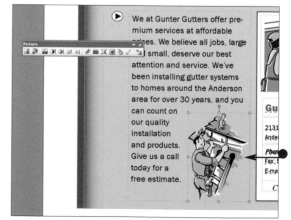

Resize a Publication Object

You can resize a publication object to improve the appearance of the object or the layout. For example, you may need to resize a clip art object to make it bigger, or resize a text object to fit more text into the box.

Resize a Publication Object

1 Click the object that you want to resize.

● Publisher surrounds the selected object with handles.

2 Move the mouse ⬉ over the edge of the object until ⬉ changes to ＋.

3 Click and drag a handle to resize the object.

● You can also rotate an object by clicking and dragging the green rotation handle at the top of the selected object.

When you release the mouse button, Publisher resizes the object.

● This example resizes a clip art object.

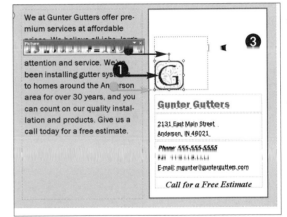

Connect Text Boxes

You can link text boxes to create a relationship between the text in each box. For example, you may want to connect two text boxes so that the text flows from one to the other, such as two columns in a newsletter. You can also break a text box connection to turn a grouped text box into two separate boxes. You can use the Connect Text Boxes toolbar to navigate and connect text boxes in a publication.

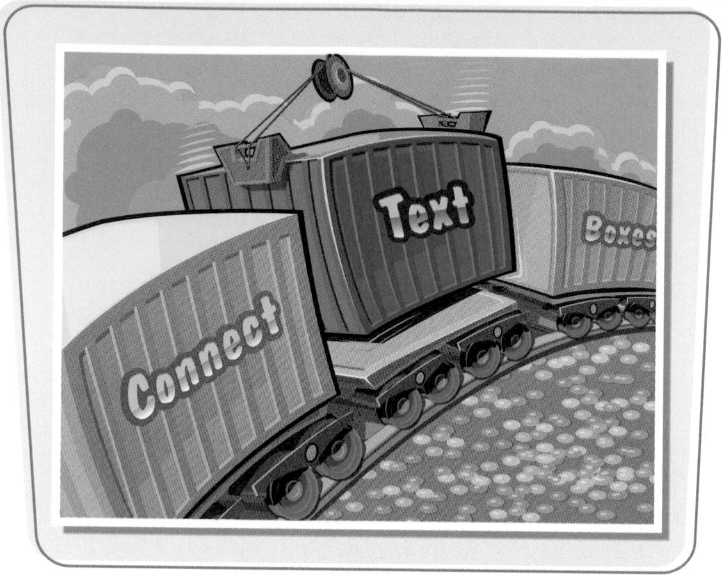

Connect Text Boxes

LINK TEXT BOXES

1. Click the first text box that you want to connect.
2. Click the **Create Text Box Link** button ( ) on the Connect Text Boxes toolbar.

- If the toolbar is not displayed, you can click **View**, click **Toolbars**, and then click **Connect Text Boxes** to open the toolbar.

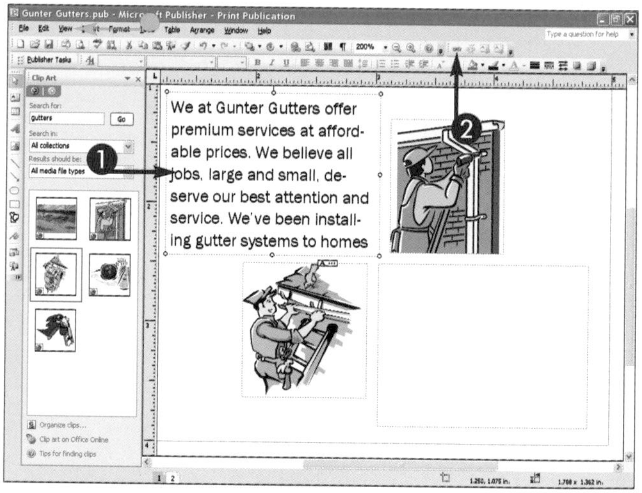

3. Click the text box to which you want to link (the changes to).

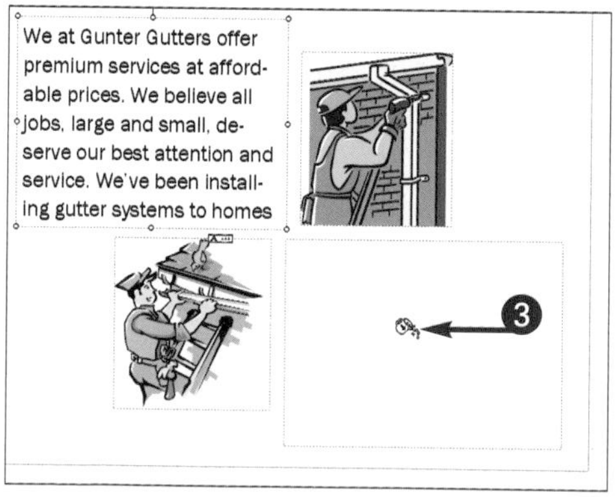

● Publisher links the two boxes, and moves any extra text from the first box into the second text box.

● You can click the **Previous Text Box** button () to return to the previous text box.

● You can click the **Next Text Box** button (📄) to go to the next text box.

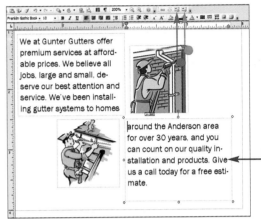

BREAK A LINK

① Click the first text box that you want to disconnect.

② Click the **Break Link** button (🖼) on the Connect Text Boxes toolbar.

Publisher breaks the link.

TIPS

What happens if my text exceeds the size of my text box?

When you add too much text to a text object, it is called *overflow*. You can correct overflow text by connecting the text box to an adjacent text box and flowing the text into it using the Connect Text Boxes toolbar. Another option is to click the **Format** menu and then click **AutoFit Text**, which allows you to choose from three text-fitting options. You can also enlarge the size of the current text box or reduce the font size of the text to make it fit.

Why does Publisher reduce my font size to fit my text in a box?

With some publication designs, AutoFitting is turned on by default, and Publisher tries to fit your text into the space provided. To turn this feature off, right-click the text box and click **Format Text Box** to open the Format Text Box dialog box. Click the **Text Box** tab and click the **Do not fit** option (○ changes to ◉) to turn the feature off.

Edit the Background Page

You can change the background of your publication page by assigning a new background color, gradient effect, or texture. You can apply a background to the current page, or to all of the pages in your publication.

Edit the Background Page

1 Click **Format**.

2 Click **Background**.

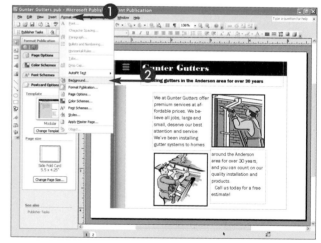

● The Background pane opens.

3 Click a background tint.

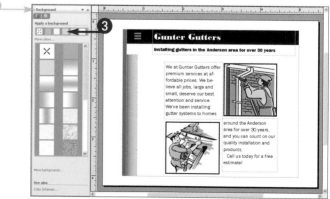

Publisher displays a list of backgrounds in the list box.

● You can use the scroll bar to scroll through the list of background selections.

④ Click the background that you want to apply.

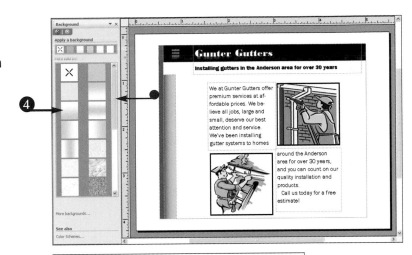

Publisher assigns the background to the publication.

● This example adds a gradient background to the page.

How do I remove a background that I no longer want?

To remove a background, reopen the Background pane and click the **No Color** option — the selection with a large × in the middle. Publisher immediately removes the background and returns the publication to the original background setting.

Can I assign backgrounds other than what is shown in the Background pane?

Yes. You can assign color backgrounds, turn a picture into a background, and more. To add a color background, click the **More colors** link in the Background pane and choose a color. Click the **More backgrounds** link to open the Fill Effects dialog box, where you can assign a different gradient effect or background texture, or turn a picture into a background.

Add a Design
Gallery Object

You can use Publisher's Design Gallery to add all kinds of extra touches to your publication projects. For example, you can add a calendar to a newsletter, or a graphical marquee to a letterhead. The Design Gallery features a wide variety of design objects, such as mastheads, borders, boxes, and even coupons and logos.

Add a Design Gallery Object

INSERT A DESIGN GALLERY OBJECT

① Click the **Design Gallery Object** button (🗐) on the Objects toolbar.

● You can also click **Insert**, and then click **Design Gallery Object**.

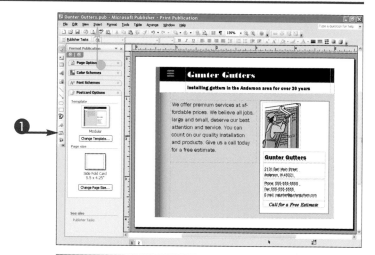

The Design Gallery dialog box appears.

② Click a category.

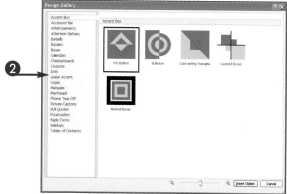

3 Click a style.

4 Click **Insert Object**.

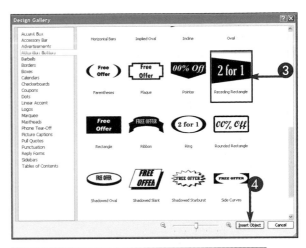

● Publisher adds the object to your publication, applying the color scheme that is assigned to the publication design.

You can move and resize the object to suit your layout.

Note: See the "Move a Publication Object" and "Resize a Publication Object" tasks to learn more.

 TIPS

Can I customize a Design Gallery Object?

Yes. Many of the Design Gallery objects are made up of simple lines and shapes. You can customize the appearance of an element by selecting individual parts of the object and making changes to the element's formatting. For example, you might change the border of an object or change the fill color. To learn more about formatting drawn objects in Microsoft Office, see Chapter 3.

I want to customize an object. How do I select an individual line or fill color to edit?

You may need to ungroup an object in order to edit individual elements, such as lines, fills, and shapes. To apply the Ungroup command, click the object, click the **Arrange** menu, and then click **Ungroup**. Depending on the complexity of the object, you may need to activate the command more than once to free all of the individual elements that comprise the object. Once you finish making your edits, you can apply the Group command to turn them back into a single object.

Use the Content Library

If you find yourself using the same elements in each publication that you create, you can save the elements in Publisher's Content Library. Anything placed in the Content Library is accessible from any other Publisher files that you open. For example, if you use the same pull quote or headline in every publication that you create, you can save the element in the Content Library and insert it any time that you need it.

Use the Content Library

ADD AN ITEM TO THE CONTENT LIBRARY

① Click the element that you want to save.

② Click **Insert**.

③ Click **Add to Content Library**.

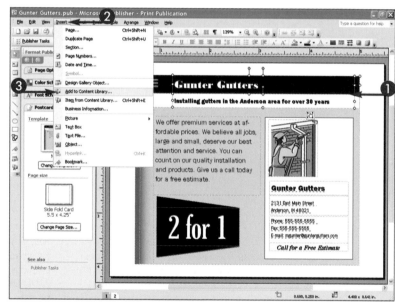

The Add Item to Content Library dialog box appears.

④ Type a name for the item.

⑤ Click a category to which you want to assign the item (☐ changes to ☑).

⑥ Click **OK**.

Publisher adds the item to the Content Library.

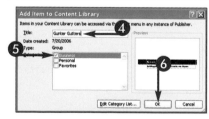

PLACE AN ITEM FROM THE CONTENT LIBRARY

① Click the **Item from Content Library** button (⊞) on the Objects toolbar.

● You can also click **Insert**, and then click **Item from Content Library**.

● Publisher displays the Content Library task pane.

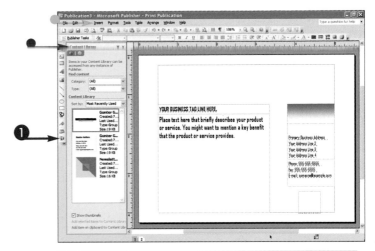

② Double-click the item that you want to add.

● Publisher places the item in the document.

You can move and resize the item to best fit the publication.

Note: *See the tasks "Move a Publication Object" and "Resize a Publication Object" to learn more.*

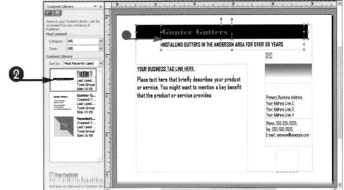

TIPS

How do I remove an item that I no longer want to keep in the Content Library?

To remove an item, display the Content Library task pane by clicking the **Insert** menu and then clicking **Item from Content Library**, or by clicking the **Item from Content Library** button (⊞) on the Objects toolbar. Once the library displays, move the mouse pointer over the item that you want to remove, click the arrow next to the item, and then click **Delete**. Publisher asks you to confirm the deletion. Click **OK** to delete the item.

Can I create new categories for the Content Library?

Yes. The Content Library installs with three default categories: Business, Personal, and Favorites. You can create new categories or edit existing categories. To do so from the Content Library pane, move the mouse pointer over an item in the library, and then click **Edit Category List**. The Edit Category List dialog box appears, where you can add new categories, move categories in the list, and edit existing categories.

Index

Index

Index

Index